22·99

120003

KT-546-552

Underachievemer

What is underachievement?

The underachievement of particular groups of pupils has been a persistent problem facing educators and policy makers alike for many years. In addition, schools face greater pressure today to raise the educational standards of their pupils than ever before.

This timely book provides an in-depth examination of the many facets of underachievement and explores the reasons why it may occur. The authors highlight ways in which schools and policy makers might increase achievement through changes in policy and practice. Some of the topics considered are:

- What is underachievement?
- Social background and achievement
- School structures and achievement
- Raising attainment – case studies of successful schools.

Underachievement in Schools will be a valuable resource for anyone involved in educational policy, teachers and those training to teach.

Anne West is Professor of Education Policy in the Department of Social Policy at the London School of Economics and is also Director of the Centre for Educational Research.

Hazel Pennell is a Research Fellow based in the Centre for Educational Research at the London School of Economics.

School Concerns Series
Edited by Peter Blatchford
Institute of Education, University of London

This topical new series addresses key issues that are causing concern in schools. Each book is based around a case-study school, which is used to illustrate and contextualise best practice whilst showing the real implications of current research on the everyday classroom.

The books provide an innovative and accessible approach to dealing with the inclusive classroom and are written by leading names in their respective fields. They will be essential reading for teachers, heads of department, headteachers and policy makers determined to address the key concerns in education today.

Supporting Inclusive Education
Jenny Corbett

Educating Children with Emotional and Behavioural Difficulties
John Thacker, Dave Strudwick and Elly Babbedge

Bullying
David Thompson, Sonia Sharp and Tiny Arora

Enhancing Personal, Social and Health Education
Sally Inman, Martin Buck and Miles Tandy

Underachievement in Schools
Anne West and Hazel Pennell

Underachievement in Schools

Anne West and Hazel Pennell

RoutledgeFalmer
Taylor & Francis Group

LONDON AND NEW YORK

ST. HELENS
COLLEGE

371.926
WES

Sept 07

120003

LIBRARY

First published 2003 by RoutledgeFalmer
11 New Fetter Lane, London EC4P 4EE

Simultaneously published in the USA and Canada
by RoutledgeFalmer
29 West 35th Street, New York, NY 10001

RoutledgeFalmer is an imprint of the Taylor & Francis Group

© 2003 Anne West and Hazel Pennell

Typeset in Sabon by Wearset Ltd, Boldon, Tyne and Wear
Printed and bound in Great Britain by TJ International Ltd,
Padstow, Cornwall.

All rights reserved. No part of this book may be reprinted or
reproduced or utilised in any form or by any electronic, mechanical,
or other means, now known or hereafter invented, including
photocopying and recording, or in any information storage or
retrieval system, without permission in writing from the publishers.

British Library Cataloguing in Publication Data
A catalogue record for this book is available from the British Library

Library of Congress Cataloging in Publication Data
West, Anne, 1956–
    Underachievement in schools / Anne West and Hazel Pennell.
        p. cm. – (School concerns series)
    Includes bibliographical references and index.
    1. Underachievers–Great Britain. 2. Academic
achievement–Great Britain. 3. Children with social
disabilities–Education–Great Britain. I. Pennell, Hazel, 1948–
II. Title. III. Series.

    LC4696.G7W47 2003
    371.92'6–dc21

                                              2002045482

ISBN 0-415-24131-6 (HB)
ISBN 0-415-24132-4 (PB)

Contents

APPENDICES 199

Figures

Tables

Preface

This book is concerned with one of the most important issues facing schools and society today, namely the underachievement of the UK's future citizens: pupils in schools. It is a subject that has – and should have – a high profile for policy makers in central and local government, for teachers, academics and all those with an interest in education and equity.

The book is designed to provide students (both undergraduate and postgraduate), teachers and policy makers with an understanding of the current state of knowledge on this topic, an analysis of what might be done in terms of policy and practice and an exploration of some of the ways that schools might try to raise levels of achievement – notwithstanding the enormous difficulties that some schools, particularly in very disadvantaged areas, face.

The book is divided into two parts. Part 1 examines what we mean by the term 'underachievement' before exploring the differences in achievement between different groups of pupils – those from different social classes, those from low-income families, girls and boys, children from different ethnic groups, and so on.

Each chapter examines what we know about the achievement levels of different groups of pupils and, where possible, what might account for the differences observed. Where guidance exists on how the achievement of particular groups of pupils might be raised, this is given. At the end of each chapter, the key points that have emerged are presented.

Part 2 has a somewhat different focus. Here we concentrate on three specific areas that we consider have a bearing on underachievement in schools. First, we look at school structures that might act as barriers to achievement; second, we look at what school effectiveness research has to offer in both understanding the level of underachievement and what schools can do to combat it; and third, we turn our attention to government policies and consider a range of initiatives related to raising attainment. In our penultimate chapter we present two case studies of schools that have succeeded in raising achievement levels. The final chapter reviews the evidence presented on underachievement and the implications for policy and practice.

Part 1 of the book consists of the following chapters:

- Chapter 1 examines the concept of underachievement and how it is used in this book;
- Chapter 2 focuses on the relationship between achievement and social class, low-income levels and parents' educational levels;
- Chapter 3 examines differences between girls and boys in terms of achievement;
- Chapter 4 is concerned with differences in achievement between pupils from different ethnic groups;
- Chapter 5 focuses on a range of other factors that are associated with achievement, such as pupils' age at starting school, pupil mobility, truancy and school exclusion, together with area effects, divorce, diet, drug abuse and teenage pregnancy.

Part 2 consists of the following chapters:

- Chapter 6 examines school structures;
- Chapter 7 is concerned with school effectiveness research, attainment and disadvantage;
- Chapter 8 examines government policy in relation to raising educational achievement;
- Chapter 9 presents two case studies of schools;
- Chapter 10 discusses the findings and examines the policy implications of the research and other evidence reviewed.

It is important to stress at this stage that although schools and government policy can 'make a difference', levels of achievement may be completely out of the control of the school. And just as no one expects hospitals to make people 'healthy', it is not reasonable to expect schools to compensate for disadvantage that is related to the structure of society. This is not to say that schools cannot make a difference – but it is important to stress that raising achievement levels cannot be seen in isolation from the environment in which children live, their families, homes and peer groups.

Acknowledgements

We would like to thank all those who have helped with the preparation of this book. Robert West, Philip Noden, Peter Blatchford and Alex Bellamy have all provided invaluable advice, comments and suggestions. Many other academics and researchers, from universities, local education authorities and elsewhere, have kindly provided material. We would like to thank all those concerned, in particular Colin Alston, Gavan Conlon, Karen Elliott, Jannette Elwood, David Gillborn, Stephen Gorard, Terry Haydn, Julian Le Grand, Pam Sammons and Steve Strand.

Thanks are also due to the headteachers of the two case study schools who have willingly agreed to share their experiences. We have also appreciated the help received from the Department for Education and Skills on the many occasions we requested clarification of data and policies.

We would like to thank John Wilkes for his assistance whilst we have been researching and writing this book, and for his support with its preparation. Finally, we would like to thank Daniel West and Anna Wexler for their help in the final stages of editing and Matthew West for his help with the graphics.

The benefits of the world wide web and the valuable websites of government departments and research bodies have been brought home to us in the preparation of this book.

Anne West
Hazel Pennell

Abbreviations

CTC	City technology college
DENI	Department of Education Northern Ireland
DES	Department of Education and Science
DETR	Department of the Environment, Transport and the Regions
DfE	Department for Education
DfEE	Department for Education and Employment
DfES	Department for Education and Skills
DTLR	Department of Transport, Local Government and the Regions
EBD	Emotional and behavioural difficulties
GCE A	General Certificate of Education Advanced level
GCE AS	General Certificate of Education Advanced Supplementary Subsidiary level
GCE O	General Certificate of Education Ordinary level
GCSE	General Certificate of Secondary Education
GNVQ	General National Vocational Qualification
HMI	Her Majesty's Inspectorate
ICT	Information and communications technology
ILEA	Inner London Education Authority
IQ	Intelligence quotient
ISCED	International Standard Classification of Education
LARR	Linguistic Awareness in Reading Readiness
LEA	Local education authority
NAEP	National Assessment of Educational Progress
NVQ	National Vocational Qualification
ODPM	Office of the Deputy Prime Minister
OECD	Organisation for Economic Co-operation and Development

PISA	Programme for International Student Assessment
PRU	Pupil referral unit
SEU	Social Exclusion Unit
TAAS	Texas Assessment of Academic Skills
TIMSS	Third International Mathematics and Science Study
TIMSS-R	Third International Mathematics and Science Study – Repeat
UK	United Kingdom
US/USA	United States/United States of America
YCS	Youth Cohort Study

Part I

Facets of underachievement

Chapter 1

What is underachievement?

Introduction

In recent years considerable attention has been devoted to the issue of 'underachievement' in schools. This is reflected in its high political profile and is perhaps not surprising given that governments of both political persuasions have for many years focused their educational policies on improving 'standards' in schools.

The debates on 'underachievement' have changed somewhat over the years, but there is one constant feature, namely that at any given time there is concern that one group of pupils or another is failing to achieve its potential. Sometimes the concern is about the achievement of particular social classes, sometimes about boys, sometimes about those from particular ethnic groups, sometimes about those who are from very disadvantaged backgrounds, and so on. Since the advent of the Labour government in 1997, there has been another concern, namely about those who are at risk of 'social exclusion' particularly as a result, for example, of poverty. All of these issues are legitimate causes for concern not only for politicians, but also for teachers, government policy makers, academics and indeed all those who seek to understand the causes of underachievement and possible remedies.

Underachievement tends to be talked about very generally or, conversely, in much more specific terms – for example in relation to the achievements of boys or of certain ethnic minority groups. The aim of this book is to examine a wide range of different factors that affect levels of attainment. These are the subjects of the chapters that follow. In addition to providing an up-to-date account of the current state of play in relation to research carried out in the UK, examples of how practitioners might seek to remedy low levels of attainment amongst particular groups of pupils are provided where feasible.

It is important to note at this stage that the findings we report relate to the results of *groups* of pupils and are not necessarily applicable to the individual. This is a very important point to bear in mind – it would be totally incorrect to assume that all pupils who are from a particular background are going to underachieve.

The research and statistical material that we refer to derives, in the main, from that produced since 1988. That year was a landmark in education in England and Wales as it marked the coming into law of the Education Reform Act and signalled a fundamental change in the way in which education was delivered. Not only were market principles introduced into the curriculum (see West and Pennell 1997a) but, for the first time, a national curriculum was introduced for pupils between the ages of 5 and 16 in England and Wales.

However, before reviewing and discussing the research evidence and examples of possible remedies, a discussion of the concept of 'underachievement' is necessary. For whilst there may be some consensus about what is meant by levels of attainment or levels of achievement, the concept of 'underachievement' has different connotations to different individuals. It is thus important to explain how the concept is used in this book and this is what the following section seeks to do.

The concept of underachievement

Unfortunately, the concept of 'underachievement' is not one about which there is much clarity and although the term is often used it is rarely clearly defined. Indeed, Plewis notes that it 'lacks a universally agreed and applied definition' (1991: 377). Given that there is no consensus about the concept, this section examines what we mean by the term 'underachievement' in the school context.

For some psychologists educational achievement is seen in terms of the discrepancy between a child's measured intelligence quotient (IQ) and his or her score on an educational test. One of the implications of this definition is that IQ is seen as the main factor causing underachievement in education (Plewis 1991). A major problem with this view is that IQ tests are designed to be measures of mental aptitude or potential, not as tests of achievement or attainment. However, it has been argued that it is not logically possible to separate potential from actual behaviour (for a discussion see Gross 2001) and, moreover, Bee (1994) argues that all IQ tests are achievement tests to some extent; she argues that the difference between tests we call 'IQ tests' and those we call 'achievement tests' is in essence a matter of degree.

The concept of underachievement may also be used as a characteristic of groups not just individuals. Using this definition, some groups of pupils, for example those from disadvantaged backgrounds or certain ethnic groups, may be said to underachieve regardless of their IQ. This approach towards underachievement has been used by educational sociologists rather than by psychologists, so 'generating some operational confusion, especially as there is no necessary connection between the two definitions' (Plewis 1991: 377).

In his discussion of approaches used, Plewis stresses the problems associated with the statistical approaches used by psychologists, but argues that the approach adopted by educational researchers whereby underachievement is defined by a group's relative position is 'simple and unambiguous' (1991: 383). However, it is important to stress that this approach says nothing about *individuals* as opposed to groups.

In spite of the fact that the concept of underachievement is somewhat problematic, it remains the case that teachers are able to discriminate between pupils in terms of whether their achievement is in line with their ability. Indeed, one major research project carried out in the 1980s (Tizard *et al.* 1988) found that teachers do perceive that some of their pupils are underachievers and that these perceptions do seem to vary systematically by age, sex and ethnic group.

However, as noted by Plewis (1991), a preferable concept may be that of relatively low-attaining groups. This is a clearer concept than that of underachievement and does not have the various connotations and lack of clarity that are associated with the concept of underachievement. In fact this is the definition that was used by Gillborn and Gipps (1996). In their review of the achievements of ethnic-minority pupils they use the concept of 'relative achievements' of pupils of different ethnic groups.

Gorard *et al.* also address the issues of underachievement and low achievement. They note that: 'The terms are used almost synonymously in policy documents as though low achievement is automatically also underachievement, in a way that high achievement presumably never can be' (2001b: 137).

Finally, Gillborn and Mirza (2000) are also critical of the concept. They argue in relation to black pupils that 'underachievement' came into particular prominence in the debates about ethnic diversity in British education through the work of the Rampton and Swann Committee Reports (see Rampton 1981; Swann 1985). The term was used to refer to the differential outcomes among ethnic minority groups. They also note:

> Unfortunately, there has been confusion about the meaning of the term. It is often assumed, for example, that the reason for 'underachievement' must lie with the pupils and/or their families rather than the education system itself. It has been argued that the notion of 'underachievement' undermines ethnic minority efforts to succeed and the desire to do well ... What began life as a useful concept, meant to identify an inequality of opportunity, has sometimes slipped into a pervasive 'discourse of despair' among and about ethnic minorities.
>
> (Gillborn and Mirza 2000: 7)

Since the advent of the Labour government in 1997, there has been a broader approach, namely targeting those groups who are at risk of 'social exclusion' particularly as a result, for example, of poverty. Social exclusion, as opposed to underachievement, is a shorthand term for what can happen when people or areas suffer from a combination of linked problems such as unemployment, poor skills, low incomes, poor housing, high crime environments, bad health and family breakdown. This is an overarching multi-faceted concept. It is useful also for teachers, government policy makers and, last but not least, academics who seek to understand the causes of 'underachievement' as it explicitly acknowledges that problems are commonly associated with each other.

The concept of social exclusion has been criticised as being a 'catch-all' phrase meaning 'all things to all people' (Johnston *et al.* 2000: 3). Under this portmanteau term a complicated array of social issues have been grouped together. Whilst there are linkages between experiences in, for example, the housing market and education, and income, each involves a different set of factors. Such problems cannot be reduced merely to unemployment and income inequality (Jeffs and Smith 2001). However, the debates around social exclusion do highlight the 'diverse and interconnected problems which face young people' and 'the processes whereby some young people become socially included and some do not' (Johnston *et al.* 2000: 3).

Morris *et al.* provide a critical review of the literature relating to disadvantaged young people, one aim of which was to identify the extent of disadvantage among those aged 14 to 19 years, but with a specific focus on those between 16 and 17 years of age. They note that 'there is a disparate collection of definitions of "disadvantage", comprising those which are related to a threshold or a norm (for instance, measures of poverty . . .), as well as ideological definitions' (1999: 7).

The report also highlights problems in identifying and quantifying disadvantage; one key problem noted was that:

> data on different forms of disadvantage are not collected in the same way, nor with a uniform set of characterising variables (i.e. gender; age; ethnic and socio-economic background; ability). It is not possible, therefore, to determine the extent to which young people are multiply disadvantaged.
>
> (1999: 52)

The Department for Education and Skills (DfES) has adopted its own definitions of lower and higher attainment that are of interest in this context. Lower achievement is defined as being 'at least two levels below the standard' (DfES 2002a: 4), where the 'standard' is the 'expected' level in the key stage tests/assessments. So, for example, at Key Stage 2, the expected level is 4, and lower-achieving pupils are those who are at or below level 2 (although this excludes pupils who were absent or disapplied). Higher achievement, on the other hand, is defined as being at least one level above the expected level (at Key Stage 3 there are two expected levels, levels 5 and 6, and high achievers are those who reach level 7 or above). There is clearly some overlap between the concept of underachievement and that of 'disadvantage'. Indeed, poor educational performance at school can be seen as a 'common manifestation of disadvantage' (Morris *et al.* 1999: 52).

Rather than looking at disadvantage solely at the individual level, it can also be considered at the school level or at the local education authority (LEA) area level. The report 'Schools Plus:

Building Learning Communities' (DfEE 1999a) has defined and identified 'disadvantaged schools'. These are schools where entitlement to free school meals exceeds 35 per cent (approximately twice the national average). Following on from the identification of schools, LEAs were themselves defined as 'disadvantaged' if a third or more of their schools were 'disadvantaged schools'. (Most LEAs with high proportions of 'disadvantaged' primary schools also had a high proportion of disadvantaged secondary schools and all were urban.) The use of these two definitions enables areas with concentrations of disadvantage to be identified as well as pockets of disadvantage. The latter may be less visible in areas where overall affluence is high.

The concept of 'multiple disadvantage' is also important in looking at underachievement. Sammons (1995) notes that there is evidence of cumulative disadvantage – that experiencing one factor is less closely associated with low attainment than experiencing more than one factor. Research carried out in the former Inner London Education Authority (ILEA) demonstrated that seven background factors can be used to predict the increased risk of low attainment at the age of 11 years. These factors were:

- eligibility for free school meals (an indicator of poverty);
- large family size;
- one-parent family;
- semi-skilled or unskilled manual parental occupation or being unemployed;
- pupil's behaviour;
- lack of fluency in English;
- ethnic background.

More recently, Payne (2000) explored the progress of low achievers (young people in the bottom third of the national distribution of GCSE results in England and Wales) using data from the Youth Cohort Study (YCS) (see Appendix C). She reported that:

> Young people had a higher risk of low achievement if their parents were in low level occupations, were not in full-time employment, or had poor educational qualifications. They were also more at risk if they lived in social rented accommodation, came from a lone parent family, or had several brothers or sisters. There was a very strong link between low

achievement and truancy. Young black people and those of Pakistani and Bangladeshi origin had an above average risk of low achievement, while those of Indian origin tended to do better than whites.

(Payne 2000: 2–3)

Morris *et al.* (1999) in their review of disadvantaged youth also highlighted a number of associations between poor educational and economic outcomes and a range of dimensions of disadvantage, including: bullying, truancy, exclusion from school, residential care, early motherhood and living in poor and/or non-working households. Crucially, however, they note that there is often ambiguity between what constitutes a symptom and what a cause:

> Arguably, there has been too much emphasis on dealing with symptoms and not enough on identifying and tackling the underlying causes, and on what pushes young people to become de-motivated, be disaffected and disengaged
>
> (Morris *et al.* 1999: 53)

How we understand underachievement

We have seen that underachievement in schools is not a simple issue – the way in which the term is used varies and what is considered to be underachievement also varies. As we shall see in the chapters that follow, neither can underachievement be easily remedied.

We now outline briefly how we might conceptualise underachievement. Sparkes (1999) in her review of schools, education and social exclusion highlighted a number of background variables that are associated with educational attainment. These are:

- pupils' personal characteristics: prior attainment, gender, health;
- socio-economic factors: low income, social class (of father), unemployment, housing;
- educational factors: parents' educational attainment;
- family structure: family size, lone parent status, in public care;
- ethnicity/language: ethnic group, fluency in English;
- other: parental interest/involvement/practice, locally-based factors.

These factors can be further elaborated and extended, in order to provide a broader conceptual framework in which to locate underachievement in schools. We have categorised these as follows:

- individual factors: intelligence, attitudes, motivation, self-esteem, gender, health (well being and risk behaviours);
- family factors: family/household composition, educational level of parents, socio-economic status/income levels, parental involvement;
- community and societal factors: social class, ethnicity/race, gender, housing;
- school characteristics: characteristics of pupils in school, school composition/peer effects, curriculum on offer, school structures.

There are also other factors known to be associated with underachievement that are cross-cutting – these include truancy, school exclusion, drug abuse (tobacco, alcohol and illicit drugs) and involvement in crime. These factors are not mutually exclusive.

Underachievement and the individual

Underachievement might be seen as an issue that is determined principally by the individual. This could be the case if one believes that the ability of an individual is solely determined by his or her innate 'intelligence'. The problem with this approach is that individuals do not grow up in isolation – they are part of families, communities and society more generally. Therefore, it would be naïve to assume that underachievement is solely determined by some innate, intellectual endowment. Notwithstanding this, it would also be naïve to assume that the ability of an individual has no bearing on the educational attainment and outcomes of a given individual.

At this individual level we also need to consider the attitudes of the individuals concerned towards education and learning, their motivation to learn, and so on. These are important psychological factors that should not be ignored. Again, however, it is important to bear in mind that attitudes, motivation and self-esteem do not occur in isolation and develop in individuals on the basis of their experiences with others. This brings us on to the role that other individuals have on the achievement of young people.

Immediate family

Underachievement might be seen as an issue that is primarily determined by the family context in which a child grows up and it might be the case that particular attitudes and values are instilled in young people as a result of this family context. They may grow up with one or two parents, with other carers or in public care. Parents may be highly educated or less highly educated, in professional occupations or in manual occupations. As we shall see, family background is indeed associated with attainment.

School and peer effects on attainment

In addition to the influences of the individual and his or her family, there are also school influences on attainment. The research on school effectiveness indicates that some schools are more effective than others. There are also 'compositional' or 'peer-group' effects, which suggest that the background characteristics of pupils within a school also impact on achievement within that school. For example, with a high proportion of pupils from disadvantaged backgrounds, pupils' results tend to be affected detrimentally (see Chapter 6 for a fuller discussion). Thus, in any analysis of what factors might contribute to pupils failing to achieve their potential, issues relating to the characteristics of pupils attending schools need to be given serious consideration.

Community and societal influences

Underachievement might also be seen as being determined more broadly by the society or community in which the young person grows up. Yet another approach is to focus on the economic context in which an individual lives – as we shall see, this is an important issue as the links between poverty and educational attainment and outcomes are very clear. This brings us on to the issue of capital of various types.

Types of 'capital'

To some commentators an important issue, which can be discerned in the above discussion, is the notion of 'capital', which Bourdieu conceptualises thus:

> capital can present itself in three fundamental guises: as economic capital, which is immediately and directly convertible into money and may be institutionalized in the form of property rights; as cultural capital, which is convertible, on certain conditions, into economic capital and may be institutionalized in the form of educational qualifications; and as social capital, made up of social obligations ('connections'), which is convertible, in certain conditions, into economic capital and may be institutionalized in the form of a title of nobility.
>
> (Bourdieu 1986: 47)

It is particularly notable, in the context of the subject of this book, that Bourdieu reports that the notion of 'cultural capital' was developed in an attempt to explain unequal achievement of children from different social classes:

> The notion of cultural capital initially presented itself to me, in the course of research, as a theoretical hypothesis which made it possible to explain the unequal scholastic achievement of children originating from the different social classes by relating academic success, i.e. the specific profits which children from different classes and class factions can obtain in the academic market, to the distribution of cultural capital between the classes and class factions.
>
> (Bourdieu 1986: 47)

For others, however, this concept alone is not in itself sufficient, as an individual child's intelligence or cognitive ability, parental influences and community or societal influences are all likely to be related to attainment. Ganzach (2000) examined the issue of education, cognitive ability, educational expectations and educational attainment from a psychological perspective. He noted that the education of parents and the cognitive ability of the child are likely to be the most important determinants of educational attainment; parents who are more educated are able to create a social and physical environment that facilitates learning. Ganzach investigated the interactions between the determinants of family environment, and the interactions between family environment and the characteristics of the child. He argues that the concept of cultural capital is not sufficient to explain the processes underlying educational attainment. In his opinion, the view that parents' education affects educational attainment by increasing cultural capital is too simplistic:

> A more accurate description of the process of educational attainment should take into account the sex of the parent, and the cognitive ability of the child. That is for the mother – but not the father – the extent to which the education of the parent increases educational attainment depends on the cognitive ability of the child.
>
> (Ganzach 2000: 438)

Underachievement and school

Another factor that we need to consider when addressing underachievement is the school system itself – both in terms of school structures and more generally in terms of whether schools are as 'effective' as they might be in maximising the educational outcomes of young people.

Whilst we have highlighted a range of factors that, on a priori grounds, are likely to impact on educational outcomes, our prime focus in this book is on underachievement in schools. Thus we need to consider for each of the particular issues that we examine what can be done at the school level to tackle the underachievement that we identify. In the first instance, we need to know which factors are associated with underachievement and, if possible, try to establish whether the links are causal or not. The next stage is to try to tackle the problem. As we shall see in the chapters that follow, whilst we know a fair amount about factors associated with underachievement and poor educational outcomes, we know much less about what actually works in terms of addressing the problems identified; and we know even less about the actual processes involved.

Why is it important to maximise students' attainment?

Whilst it is clear that in any population there will be a distribution in terms of achievement, there are good reasons for policy makers to attempt to maximise attainment levels of the population. In this section, some of these are discussed.

For the individual there are gains – in terms of later earnings, job satisfaction, lifestyle benefits and so on – from higher levels of attainment. There are also societal gains in terms of the economy and social cohesion. Conversely, the costs of underachievement are high. Some of these costs and benefits are explored below.

Why does underachievement matter?

Payne (2000), using data from the Youth Cohort Study (see Appendix C), found that the post-16 routes taken by low achievers differed from those taken by higher achievers. Low achievers who stayed in full-time education were more likely than those with better GCSE results to go to a further education college and the majority took vocational courses. Fewer low achievers who had left school at 16 went into government-supported training than those with higher GCSE results. More worryingly, most low achievers in full-time jobs, and a significant minority of those in government-supported training, appeared to be getting no formal training. Low achievers in jobs and government-supported training were over-represented, compared with middle achievers, in manual and low-skill occupations and under-represented in clerical and secretarial occupations. Low achievers also had lower hourly pay than middle achievers.

Other evidence reveals a connection between poverty in childhood, teenage parenthood, failure to stay on at school, contact with the police and higher risks of low wages and unemployment (DfEE 1999a). These are all costs of underachievement in terms of lost opportunity and costs to the economy and society in general.

The connection between delinquency, crime and failure at school has been identified in many research studies, with pupils who fail at school being more likely to become involved in delinquent activities than those who succeed. The evidence suggests that truancy and disruption are not only related to academic failure (and through this to delinquency) but may also be an important element in the development of delinquent careers (DfEE 1999a).

Other studies have found a link between offending and school exclusion. For example, an Audit Commission study (see DfEE 1999a) found that 42 per cent of young offenders in the courts had been excluded from school while a further 23 per cent were significant truanters; and in another study, Parsons *et al.* (2001) found that there was a significant association between offending and poor attendance at school.

Qualifications and later earnings and employment status

It is not possible to do justice to the vast array of literature by economists that has addressed the rate of return to various qualifications. However, it is important to be aware of some of the key findings that relate to this issue. Much of the recent work in this area in the UK has focused on the return to alternative types of qualification.[1]

For example, using data from the Labour Force Survey, Robinson (1997a) found that holding qualifications yielded significantly higher earnings than holding no qualifications but that academic qualifications yielded more benefits than vocational ones. In fact, possession of an academic qualification yielded earnings at the same level as possession of a vocational qualification that was notionally one level higher.

Earnings are clearly of importance for a given individual. However, from a societal perspective, there are concerns about other factors. One key factor is unemployment. Only half of adults with poor literacy skills have a job compared with four out of five adults with the best literacy skills (DfEE 1999a).

Research by Conlon (2001) examined the relationship between qualifications and the likelihood of being employed. He found a clear relationship between individuals with qualifications and the likelihood of being employed, although he notes that there is not necessarily a strictly increasing relationship between increasing qualifications and the likelihood of being employed. For males of working age, an individual in possession of an academic qualification at NVQ level 1 (equivalent) was on average almost 20 percentage points more likely to be employed than a male possessing no formally recognised qualifications; those with academic NVQ level 2 or level 3 qualifications were just over 20 percentage points more likely to be employed. The comparable figures for those with undergraduate and postgraduate degrees were 28 percentage points and 39 percentage points respectively. The picture for vocational qualifications was very different, with males holding vocational qualifications at NVQ level 1 being 5 percentage points *less* likely to be employed than those holding no qualifications, and those holding vocational qualifications at NVQ levels 2, 3 or 4 only 10–12 percentage points more likely to be employed than those holding no formally recognised qualifications. In general, then, qualifications – particularly academic qualifications – are associated positively with the likelihood of being employed.

The costs of underachievement

While the benefits of higher levels of attainment are important both to the individual and to society as a whole, the costs of underachievement are huge. For the individual the results of lower achievement can be measured in terms of lost opportunity, unfulfilled potential and reduced quality of life. For society as a whole there are the social and financial costs, both direct and indirect, in combating underachievement and disaffection, including crime, as well as the payments of benefits such as income support.

A government report (DfEE 1999a) attempted to calculate some of these financial costs. For example, the average cost of educating a pupil in a mainstream secondary school in England in 1998 was £2,400 and at a primary school was £1,700. In contrast, the cost of a place at a pupil referral unit (PRU) for a disruptive child was around £10,000 and the cost of sending a child with emotional and behavioural difficulties (EBD) to a special school was about £40,000 (for a residential place) and £18,000 (for a day place). The cost of places in PRUs and EBD schools was calculated at £185m per year for about 12,000 pupils.

If pupils move from poor behaviour to disaffection and then eventually enter the criminal justice system, the direct costs continue to rise as shown in Figure 1.1.

These given costs do not include the costs of processing cases and the financial and social costs of crime and vandalism to the business and the wider community, including the reduction in quality of life and the fear of crime. The overall cost of youth crime has been calculated at about £1 billion per year if benefit

Community sentencing:

- Supervision order (10 to 17 year olds) £200 per month. 12,400 orders. Cost per annum £30 million.
- Attendance order (10 to 17 year olds) £181 per order. 8,500 orders. Cost per annum £1.5 million.
- Probation order £1,710. 3,000 orders. Cost per annum £5 million.
- Community service £1,500. 4,000 orders. Cost per annum £6 million.
- Combination order £2,790. 1,800 orders. Cost per annum £5 million.

Criminal justice system:

- Detention in a Young Offenders Institution (15 to 17 year olds) £25,000. 6,500 detained. Cost per annum £169 million.
- Local authority secure accommodation. Cost £32,400 per place per year.
- Secure Training Order (for 12 to 14 year olds) £126,000. 260 orders. Cost per annum £32 million.

Figure 1.1 Costs of community sentencing and the criminal justice system.

Source: DfEE 1999a.

payments and other social service, health costs and lost tax revenue are taken into account (DfEE 1999a).

Qualification levels and lifelong learning

Recent years have seen a major policy shift across the whole of the developed world towards an emphasis in education and training of lifelong learning rather than a more traditional pattern, which finishes for most people in their late adolescence or early twenties. This is seen as being of importance in terms of meeting the needs of technological change, ensuring social cohesion, and so on.

Interestingly, research carried out by various academics (for example, Conlon 2001; West and Hind 2000) has found that those who undertake continuing vocational training are those who are already well qualified. West and Hind (2000), for example, used the European Community Household Panel Survey to examine the extent of employer-funded education and training. They examined whether individuals with different levels of education and training reported the same level of free or subsidised education and training. They found that in every country more individuals with higher than with lower levels of education reported that their employer provided free or subsidised education and training.

More sophisticated analyses were carried out by Conlon, who found that individuals who were enrolled and undertaking formally recognised qualifications were those already in possession of formally recognised qualifications. He also noted that 'If the concept of late or lifelong learning refers to the acquisition of additional skills, education and training throughout the individual's lifetime, then these figures indicate that late or lifelong learning is more associated with the academic route of qualification attainment' (Conlon 2001: 31).

Achievement levels in England

Before examining the changes in achievement over time, it is important to add a 'health warning'. Many data are now available for researchers and policy makers in the United Kingdom. The UK is 'data rich' in terms of its education data, particularly that relating to schools. In England and Wales public examination data, both at the end of compulsory schooling (General Certificate of Secondary Education) and at the end of post-compulsory schooling (General Certificate of Education Advanced levels), have traditionally been available and, since the mid-1990s, national test results have also been available.

It is important to note that these measures are somewhat problematic for making comparisons of certain types. Goldstein comments that policy makers consider these tests to be 'objective' but he notes that in public examinations and Key Stage tests:

> different instruments are used over time, so that in order to make statements about changes in performance over time, it is essential that a common scale can be constructed for the various tests that are used. The difficulty is that, because of a lack of a common 'objective' yardstick, there is no unique way to do this. Whichever way it is done, it is not possible to decide whether any change in test score is really due to a change in performance or a change in the difficulty of the test, or a mixture of the two ... Thus when policy-makers base policy ... upon changes in 'standards' (test scores), they have no way of knowing whether what is observed is real or not.
>
> (Goldstein 2001: 434–5)

The situation is in fact even more complex than this, as there are incentives for performance to be maximised. On the one hand, policy makers, who are ultimately in charge of the national tests, wish to see standards increase; this is not only because they have a desire to see improved achievement levels, but also because they now evaluate their success or failure on the performance of schools. On the other hand, the privately-run examination boards responsible for GCSEs and GCE A levels are in competition with each other for candidates to enter the examinations; schools in turn are keen to raise their own position in published examination-performance tables and so wish to select examination boards that they feel will maximise the performance of their students. Thus, in theory there are incentives for relevant bodies to seek to maximise apparent student performance. However, there may be a counterbalancing pressure on government and in turn on examination boards to ensure that standards are maintained and that high-stakes examinations such as GCSEs and GCE A levels are not devalued by, for example, lenient marking.

Examination and test data are reported in this section and indeed in the rest of this book, but the above caution needs to be borne in mind, particularly in comparing year-on-year changes. It is also important to note that at times absolute changes are reported, and at others proportional changes are reported. These two measures serve different functions. For example, absolute attainment is of significance to an individual in terms of gaining a place to study at university or when entering employment. It is also important for schools in terms of their 'league table' position, and for many school and government targets. Proportional (or proportionate) changes serve a different purpose and in particular can enable policy makers to establish whether policies are indeed having the desired impact. However, in our view they should be used with caution and alongside absolute measures of change.

Turning now to GCSE results we find increases over time. Indeed, between 1974/5 and 1987/8 the percentage of *school leavers* achieving the equivalent of five or more high-grade GCSEs[2] increased from 22.6 to 29.9 per cent. In 1988, the General Certificate of Secondary Education (GCSE) was introduced, replacing GCE O levels and CSEs. Key features of the GCSE examination are the fact that papers in most subjects are differentiated ('tiered'), and that course work is assessed and contributes to the final grade achieved (see Daugherty 1995).[3]

Since the introduction of the GCSE, marked improvements in achievement have been recorded. As shown in Table 1.1, the percentage of young people obtaining five or more GCSE grades at A* to C increased from 29.9 per cent in 1987/8 to 50 per cent in 2000/1. These changes over time are also shown in Figure 1.2. However, it is important to note that the methods of data collection have changed over this period[4] and this means that we need to be cautious when interpreting the data.

As can be seen from Table 1.1, there has been an increase of just over 20 percentage points in absolute terms between 1988 and 2001 in 15 year olds achieving five or more high-grade GCSEs. Whilst this is a marked increase, it must be remembered that half of those leaving compulsory education do not achieve five or more high-grade GCSEs, as shown in Table 1.2.

Table 1.1 Achievement of five or more GCSE grades A* to C[a] for pupils aged 15 at the start of the academic year 1988/9–2000/1

Year[b]	% of 15-year-old pupils
1988/9	32.8
1989/90	34.5
1990/1	36.8
1991/2	38.3
1992/3	41.2
1993/4	43.3
1994/5	43.5
1995/6	44.5
1996/7	45.1
1997/8	46.3
1998/9	47.9
1999/2000	49.2
2000/1	50.0

Source: DfES 2001a, 2002b.

Notes

a GCSE grade A* was introduced in 1993/4.

b Percentages from 1988/9 to 1990/1 are taken from the School Examinations Survey and are based on 15 year olds in all schools except special schools; percentages from 1991/2 to 2000/1 are taken from the database on School Performance Tables and are based on 15 year olds in all schools including special schools; percentages from 1996/7 include GNVQ equivalencies.

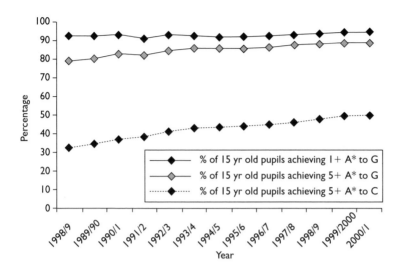

Figure 1.2 Achievement of GCSEs (including GNVQ equivalents) for pupils aged 15 at the start of the academic year 1988/9–2000/1.

Source: DfES 2001a, 2002b.

Note
See Table 1.1.

Table 1.2 Percentage of 15-year-old pupils[a] achieving different numbers of GCSEs[b] by the end of 2000/1

Achievement	% of 15-year-old pupils in schools
5+ GCSEs A*–C	50
1+ GCSE A*–C	74
5+ GCSEs A*–G	89
1+ GCSE A*–G	95

Source: DfES 2002b.

Notes
a Number of pupils on roll aged 15 at the start of the 2000/1 academic year. Includes attempts and achievements by these pupils in previous academic years.
b Includes GNVQ qualifications gained in Year 11.

As shown in Table 1.2, at the end of the academic year 2000/1 (DfES 2002b), 5 per cent of pupils had no qualifications at GCSE (grades A* to G). (Whilst this was the case overall, some schools succeeded in ensuring that all pupils gained some qualifications at this level, as demonstrated in our case-study schools described in

Chapter 9.) Figure 1.2 also shows the changes over time in the percentage of 15-year-old pupils in schools obtaining five or more and one or more GCSEs at grades A* to G.

Another indicator of relevance, perhaps reflecting the increasing priority being given to education by young people (and their parents), is the increase in the proportion of young people now continuing in full-time education after the end of compulsory schooling. Table 1.3 provides details.

As can be seen there has been a large increase, of 23 percentage points in absolute terms, in young people continuing in education post-16. The increase has been from less than 50 per cent of the cohort in 1989 to over 70 per cent in 2000.

Data are also available on the changes in attainment of 15-year-old pupils in school once they have been ranked by their average point scores and divided into equal '20th groups' ('5 per cent groups'). The average point score is calculated by awarding points for each GCSE/GNVQ awarded.[5] An examination of the average point score for all pupils at GCSE (and including GNVQ from 1997) reveals an overall increase of 5.8 points from 33.1 in 1993 to 38.9 in 2000 (see DfEE 1995; DfES 2001a). However, for the bottom 10 per cent of the cohort, the increase was only 1.1 points. This compares with an increase of 8.1 in the top 10 per cent of the cohort, as shown in Table 1.4.

Bellamy (2002) has carried out detailed statistical analyses of the 20th group tables and argues that the overall inequality in achievement at GCSE level fell between 1993 and 2000. By way of example, he analysed the average point scores of the top and bottom quarters and found an overall *increase* in the gap between

Table 1.3 Percentage of young people whose main activity is full-time education: 1989–2000

Year of survey	% of 16 year olds
1989	48
1991	58
1992	66
1994	72
1996	71
1998	69
2000	71

Source: DfES 2001b, Youth Cohort Study.

Table 1.4 Average point score (GCSE/GNVQ) of the top and bottom 10 per cent of pupils in all schools in 1992/3 and 1999/2000

Group	1992/3	1999/2000[a]	Difference 1993–2000
Bottom 10%	0.8	1.9	1.1
Top 10%	63.6	71.7	8.1
Overall	33.1	38.9	5.8

Source: DfEE 1995 and DfES 2001a.

Note

a Includes points for GCSE and General National Vocational Qualification; GCSE grade A* introduced in 1997.

the scores of the top and the bottom quarters of pupils between 1993 and 2000 (a difference of 49.9 points in 1993 compared with 52.9 in 2000). However, his analyses also revealed that the score of the bottom quarter became a greater proportion of that of the top quarter. In 1993 it was 13 per cent of the top quarter's whilst in 2000 it was 17 per cent. This proportional increase, Bellamy argues, can be construed as being a more egalitarian outcome in the context of an increasing absolute gap than, say, the proportional change decreasing or remaining constant.

Clearly both absolute and proportional changes are important but, as Bellamy notes, 'the absolute gap should be the primary measure of inequality of achievement with reference to whether it has increased or not with respect to issues of future educational progress, social welfare, and social exclusion' (2002: 3).

Achievement in the UK – an international perspective

It is perhaps instructive at this stage to provide some context to the debate about achievement in the UK. There are many myths about the achievement levels and a brief review of relevant studies will serve to provide an appropriate context to the debate about underachievement.

England and Scotland have participated in international surveys of mathematics and science performance. England participated, in 1998/9, in the Third International Mathematics and Science Study – Repeat (TIMSS-R). This study focused on the performance of 14-year-old pupils. The study, carried out by the NFER (Ruddock

2000) found that for mathematics, performance in England was similar to the international average for the countries participating in TIMSS-R, and also similar to that in the United States, New Zealand and Italy. However, it was behind that of countries such as Singapore, Japan, Belgium (Flemish Community), the Netherlands, Hungary, Canada and Australia. The performance was significantly higher for boys than for girls in England.

Overall science performance in England was considerably higher than the international average for countries participating in TIMSS-R and was similar to that in Singapore, Hungary, Japan, the Netherlands, Australia, Belgium (Flemish Community) and Canada. It was also ahead of countries such as the United States, New Zealand and Italy.

More recently, a new international testing programme known as the Programme for International Student Assessment (PISA) has been established (OECD 2001). This is a three-yearly survey of the knowledge and skills of 15 year olds in the main industrialised countries co-ordinated by governments of participating countries through the Organisation for Economic Co-operation and Development (OECD). Rather than focus on how well pupils have mastered a specific school curriculum, PISA assesses their capacity to use their knowledge and skills in order to meet real-life challenges. The assessments are designed to measure how well young people can use basic knowledge and concepts learned at school and elsewhere in order to function in their adult lives (see also Appendix B). In PISA 2000, three areas were examined – reading, mathematical and scientific literacy – with the main focus being on reading.

In these tests students in the UK scored significantly above students in OECD countries as a whole. In reading literacy, they were at a similar level of achievement to students in Australia, New Zealand, Japan and Sweden. In only two countries, Finland and Canada, did 15 year olds do better than in the UK.

Students in the UK also did significantly better than the OECD average in both mathematical and scientific literacy; they obtained similar scores to students in Australia, Canada, Finland and New Zealand. Only in Japan and Korea did students obtain significantly higher scores in mathematical literacy and only in Korea did they obtain higher scores in scientific literacy. It is not clear exactly why these differences between subject areas occur – although the curriculum content is one possible explanation – but they do suggest that it is not reasonable to say that overall the education system in England is of a poorer quality than that in other countries given these international comparisons.

Whilst the average score is a useful measure of pupil achievement, it does not shed light on the range and distribution of the scores of individual pupils. This is one area where there was cause for concern in the UK. The range of skills in terms of students' reading-literacy scores was far wider in the UK than in some other countries (such as Korea). Again, while the UK was one of the highest scoring countries for scientific literacy, student scores were more dispersed than in other high-scoring countries (Korea, Japan, Finland and Canada). On the other hand, the variation in the distribution of scores for mathematical literacy was lower and typical of the OECD average (see Office for National Statistics 2001; OECD 2001).

Conclusion

This chapter has examined the concept of underachievement and the problems it poses. It is clearly a multifaceted concept but ultimately one that if defined too narrowly is not of much value in terms of either policy or practice. Given this, unless otherwise indicated, the concept of underachievement will be used in this book to differentiate pupils who are lower attaining than others. Whilst in any population of pupils some will perform less well than others, there are links between achievement and a variety of different forms of disadvantage and other factors. These include gender, ethnic background, poverty, social class and so on.

The following three chapters in this part of the book focus on specific factors that have been shown to be related to differential levels of achievement: social class (and poverty and parents' educational level); gender; and ethnic background (and English as an additional language). The next chapter examines a range of other factors that are associated with attainment – including the age of the child, pupil mobility, truancy and exclusions, special educational needs and a diverse range of non-educational factors (including area effects, divorce and separation, drug abuse, diet and sexual behaviour). The focus in these chapters is frequently on attainment in national tests and in public examinations; whilst standardised testing would be preferable, such test data are not readily available. Although our focus is on academic achievement, we also touch on other outcomes – such as continuing with full-time education post-16 and entering higher education. It is important to stress that although we look at different factors separately, they may well interact with each other. So, for example, there may be interactions between gender, ethnic group or known eligibility for free school meals. Unfortunately, the data available do not enable us to address this issue in a consistent manner, but some individual research studies (Strand 1999a) have sought to do so (see Chapter 4).

The second part of the book focuses on a number of different themes. We explore in the first instance research relating to school structures, before moving on to examine the contribution of school effectiveness research to raising achievement. Government policy is then examined, before case studies of two schools that have successfully raised achievement are presented in Chapter 9. As the evidence reviewed does not provide clear messages about how the achievement gaps for different groups of pupils can be reduced, our case studies focus on 'whole-school' strategies that have been successful in raising achievement levels. The final chapter discusses the key issues that have emerged and provides a number of recommendations for teachers, other practitioners and policy makers.

Chapter 2

Social background and achievement

Introduction

In this chapter we examine three related issues that are associated with achievement in schools, namely social class, poverty and parental educational levels. We focus on a number of studies that have explored these key issues and their relationship to educational achievement. We conclude by examining the factors that may help to explain differences in achievement.

The next section provides an historical context, which is important given the centrality of social class to the development of educational provision. Given that there are distinctive differences in the development of education in the other constituent countries of the UK, we have restricted ourselves for the most part to the situation in England. This is followed by an examination of research and other data relating to social class and achievement; again the focus is on England, although reference is made to international data. An exploration of the relationship between poverty and achievement is then presented. This again focuses in the main on England, although reference is also made to Wales, Northern Ireland and the USA. The penultimate section examines the relationship between parents' educational level and achievement, while the final section provides a summary and conclusions.

Historical background

An understanding of the historical background to educational provision is needed to fully appreciate why social class is such an important issue in England. It is not possible to provide a full account here; all that is given is a very brief résumé.

Our focus in this book is on 'state' (that is, publicly funded) schools, which currently cater for around 93 per cent of the school-age population in England. This section outlines how state-supported education developed. It is none the less important to bear in the mind the 'class divide' in schools in England given that the historical differences between the education of working-class children and of upper-class children goes back many centuries, with the so-called elite 'public' schools for upper-class boys.

Historically, the church was the main provider of education, but the state took on an increasing role in the late nineteenth century. Elementary schooling, which was supported by local ratepayers, was introduced by the Elementary Education Act of 1870 ('The Forster Act'). The aim of the Act was to provide elementary schools throughout the country, to fill the gaps in existing provision (Mackinnon and Statham 1999). Attendance was not compulsory but the Act allowed what were known as 'school boards' to make it compulsory between the ages of 5 and 13. However, schooling was not free and school boards were allowed to prescribe weekly fees.

In 1880, the Mundella Act made education compulsory and the 1891 Education Act in effect made elementary education free (Mackinnon and Statham 1999). By 1900 there were 'elementary schools for the lower working classes, higher grade and technical schools for the more ambitious, endowed grammar schools and public schools for the middle and upper classes' (Batho 1989: 11). In 1902, an Education Act ('The Balfour Act') was passed. This established a system of secondary education. It also replaced the school boards with a system of local education authorities responsible for all forms of education in a geographical area. The Education Act of 1918 abolished exemptions to the compulsory school-leaving age of 14 and also abolished all fees in elementary schools (Mackinnon and Statham 1999).

Over the next twenty years, there was pressure for a larger measure of centralisation in English education and for a move towards equality of educational opportunity for every child (Batho 1989). The 1944 Act set up a unified system of free, compulsory schooling from the age of 5 to 15 (with the recommendation that it should be raised to 16 when practicable – which did not happen until 1972). It also allowed for the implementation of a 'tripartite' system of secondary education – with grammar schools for the most academically able, technical schools for those considered likely to benefit from a more 'technical' education, and secondary modern schools for those who were not selected for either grammar or technical schools. In actual fact, very few technical schools were ever introduced (Gordon *et al.* 1991).

The proponents of this tripartite system aimed to treat children of the same measured ability in the same way and to provide groups of children with an 'equivalent, if different' (Batho 1989: 35) education, according to perceived ability and assumed needs. However, parity of esteem was never created between these different types of school. More fundamentally, there was concern from the mid-1950s about selection from some educationalists and the validity of intelligence testing as the means of selection. In some local education authorities (LEAs) parental choice and reports from headteachers were used in the selection procedures. Confidence in the system was undermined by research that found that the proportion of children from economically deprived homes who went on to grammar school was not markedly greater than it had been a generation before (Batho 1989; see also Gordon *et al.* 1991). The proportion of grammar-school places available varied across England from 10 to over 40 per cent and in parts of Wales reached 60 per cent (the national average in 1956 was just over 20 per cent). However, nine out of ten children in the lowest social stratum did not gain a grammar-school place. In addition, it was estimated that between 10 and 20 per cent of primary children aged 11 were incorrectly allocated to grammar and secondary modern schools (Batho 1989).

The Labour Government, which was elected in 1964, was committed to establishing comprehensive schools for all children, irrespective of their ability, and local authorities were asked to prepare schemes for the introduction of comprehensive systems of education. Although few LEAs did so at this stage, the 1976 Education Act gave the Secretary of State the power to require local authorities to submit proposals for comprehensive reorganisation and by the early 1980s comprehensive education was almost universal (Batho 1989; Gordon *et al.* 1991) – even though by this time there was a Conservative administration.

During the Conservative administrations from 1979 to 1997, policy shifted again. In 1988 the Education Reform Act introduced market forces into the state-school system. Schools were able to 'opt out' of local education authorities and control their own admissions. There were major financial incentives to do so.

Many commentators talked about a new hierarchy of schools developing and concerns have been expressed about the quasi-selection that takes place, via interviews, selection by ability, selection by aptitude etc. The introduction of market forces into the education system is an issue that we will return to in Chapter 6.

We now move on to examine research evidence relating social class, poverty and parents' educational level to educational achievement.

Social class and achievement

Some might argue that social class nowadays is relatively unimportant, given societal changes, social mobility and universal primary and secondary education. However, there is clear evidence that social class is still an important and persistent issue. Indeed, the British educational research literature contains strong evidence of differences in outcomes of pupils from different social backgrounds (for example, Bramley 1989; Sammons 1999). As noted by Bramley: 'The literature has not produced completely consistent results, but it does present a general picture where outcomes are dominated by the socio-economic background of pupils/area' (1989: 55).

As we can see from the previous section, concern has been expressed over the years about social class differences in terms of educational opportunity and thus achievement. In this section we examine some of the research carried out over the past decade or so that has empirically examined the links between social class and attainment.

Social class and cognitive attainment in the early years

At the very earliest stage of education, differences have been found in terms of the relationship between socio-economic background and cognitive development. The Effective Provision of Pre-school Education project (Sammons *et al.* 1999) involved 'in its early stages' an examination of the associations between a range of personal, family and home environment characteristics and cognitive attainment of children aged around 3 years at entry to pre-school. Sammons *et al.* found that socio-economic background was highly significant even at 3 years of age: children whose fathers were in professional or managerial work had higher scores than those whose fathers were in partly or unskilled manual work.

Social class and achievement in the primary school

Pupils' academic attainment and progress

One of the most important studies carried out over the past fifteen years that has explored social class and its effect on attainment was undertaken by Mortimore *et al.* (1988). The 'Junior School Project' was carried out in inner-London schools during the 1980s and involved fifty primary schools. The study found that both mothers' and fathers' occupations were strongly associated with reading and mathematics achievement on entry to junior school (age 7), having taken account of a wide range of other factors, including, amongst others, the child's age, sex, ethnic background, fluency in English, family size and the child's known eligibility for free school meals – all of which had an impact on attainment. For reading, a gap in reading age emerged between children with fathers in non-manual occupations and those with fathers in partly and unskilled manual occupations; the difference between children with fathers in 'professional' or 'intermediate' non-manual occupations and those with fathers in unskilled work was equivalent to nearly ten months in terms of reading age. For mathematics it was also found that pupils whose fathers were in non-manual occupations had significantly higher attainment than those with fathers in unskilled manual work.

As the research study was longitudinal, it was possible to analyse the effects of social class on reading and mathematics *progress* as well as attainment. The results indicated that reading attainment at entry to junior school accounted for most of the variation in test performance three years later. The father's social class was statistically significantly related to progress, although the mother's occupation was not related in this way; this, the researchers suggest, is likely to be because a high proportion of the mothers were not in paid employment. Overall, children whose fathers were in non-manual occupations made significantly more progress than those in other groups. Similar class differences in writing attainment and progress in terms of a judgement both of quality and length were also found. In contrast to reading, *progress* in mathematics was not statistically significantly related to social class when account was taken of the effects of initial attainment and other background factors; in short, although the gap in achievement remained marked it did not increase (Mortimore *et al.* 1988).

Social class and teachers' assessments

Mortimore *et al.* (1988) also examined teachers' assessments of pupils' ability and once again they found clear differences. They found that a higher proportion of children from non-manual backgrounds were rated as being of above average ability whilst a higher proportion of pupils from manual backgrounds were rated as being of below average ability. Even when account was taken of reading, mathematics and writing attainment, social class background was still related to teachers' ratings of pupils' abilities, with teachers tending to have a slightly more favourable view of those from non-manual backgrounds. The researchers concluded that higher teacher expectations may be one factor that contributes to the greater progress in reading and writing made by the non-manual compared with the manual pupils during junior school. The same study also found that socio-economic factors were highly related to teachers' assessments of pupils' behaviour at entry to junior school, with children from semi-skilled and unskilled backgrounds being reported to have a higher incidence of behaviour problems at school.

Social class and pupils' attendance

Mortimore *et al.* (1988) also found that attendance was significantly related to social class. Children with fathers in non-manual occupations were absent from school for the least time, whilst those with fathers who were unemployed, economically inactive or not present were absent the most in the first year of junior school. Interestingly, the mother's occupation was also related to attendance. There was a tendency for children whose mothers were economically inactive or unemployed to be absent for a higher proportion of time than was the case for children whose mothers were employed. Mortimore *et al.* note: 'This may reflect the difficulties working mothers have in obtaining time off work, which could explain why they were less likely than non-working mothers to keep children at home' (1988: 139).

Social class and achievement at the end of compulsory education

Social class and achievement

Whilst the studies described earlier were based on samples of pupils – which may not be nationally representative – national data relating to attainment and destinations post-16 of young people from different socio-economic groups are available from the Youth Cohort Study (YCS) in England and Wales.

Data from the Youth Cohort Study (DfES 2001b) reveal that parents' socio-economic group is related to the number of GCSEs that are achieved at the end of Year 11. In the spring of 2000, the ninth cohort survey of 16 year olds was carried out, around eight months after the young people had completed compulsory secondary education (see Appendix C). Table 2.1 provides details of the number of GCSEs obtained in Year 11 by young people with parents in different socio-economic groups; this information is presented graphically in Figure 2.1.

Table 2.1 Young people's attainment of different numbers of GCSEs[a] at the end of Year 11 by parents' socio-economic group (2000)

Parents' socio-economic group	5 + GCSEs A*–C (%)	1–4 GCSEs A*–C[b] (%)	5 + GCSEs D–G (%)	1–4 GCSEs D–G (%)	None reported (%)
Non-manual	**65**	**21**	**11**	**2**	**3**
Managerial/professional	69	18	9	1	2
Other non-manual	60	23	12	2	3
Manual	**42**	**29**	**21**	**4**	**4**
Skilled manual	45	28	20	3	4
Semi-skilled manual	36	30	25	4	6
Unskilled manual	30	34	23	6	7
Other/not classified[c]	26	28	25	8	12

Source: DfES 2001b, Youth Cohort Study.

Notes
a Includes GNVQ qualifications gained in Year 11.
b Those with 1–4 GCSE grades A* to C and any number of other grades.
c Includes a high percentage of respondents who had neither parent in a full-time job.

In this and subsequent tables percentages do not always add up to 100 because of rounding.

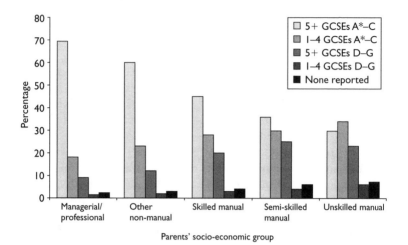

Figure 2.1 Young people's attainment of different numbers of GCSEs (including GNVQ equivalents) at the end of Year 11 by parents' socio-economic group (2000).

Source: DfES 2001b, Youth Cohort Study.

Note
For notes see Table 2.1.

It is clear from Table 2.1 and Figure 2.1 that overall, fewer young people from manual backgrounds reported five or more high-grade GCSEs than those from non-manual backgrounds. This is particularly obvious with young people from unskilled manual backgrounds, more of whom reported no GCSEs or GNVQs. In general, young people from manual socio-economic groups achieved either fewer GCSEs and/or lower grades than those from non-manual backgrounds.

Notwithstanding these differences the YCS shows a rise since the 1989 survey in the proportion of young people gaining five or more GCSEs (or equivalent GNVQs) at grades A* to C amongst all young people of all family backgrounds. Thus, the percentage of 16 year olds with parents in unskilled manual occupations achieving this level more than doubled between 1989 and 2000. However, large differences remained in 2000, with nearly seven out of ten of those with parents in managerial or professional backgrounds gaining five or more GCSEs at grades A* to C in

Table 2.2 Attainment of five or more GCSE grades A* to C 1989–2000 by socio-economic group

Parents' socio-economic group	1989 (%)	1991 (%)	1992 (%)	1994 (%)	1996 (%)	1998[a] (%)	2000[a] (%)
Managerial/professional	52	58	60	66	68	69	69
Other non-manual	42	49	51	58	58	60	60
Skilled manual	21	27	29	36	36	40	45
Semi-skilled manual	16	20	23	26	29	32	36
Unskilled manual	12	15	16	16	24	20	30
Other/not classified[b]	15	18	18	20	22	24	26

Source: DfES 2001b, Youth Cohort Study (year refers to year of survey).

Notes
a Includes GNVQ qualifications gained in Year 11.
b Includes a high percentage of respondents who had neither parent in a full-time job.

Year 11 compared with three out of ten of those with parents in unskilled manual occupations as shown Table 2.2.

Overall, between 1989 and 2000, the increase in terms of the absolute percentage of young people gaining five or more A* to C grades at GCSE was 17 percentage points for those from managerial or professional backgrounds and 18 percentage points for those from unskilled manual backgrounds. Although there was little difference in the percentage change between the two groups over the period, the proportionate increase was much larger for the unskilled manual group compared with the manual/professional group, namely a 150 per cent increase compared with a 33 per cent increase. Nevertheless, despite the high proportionate increase (which can be seen in Figure 2.2), there is still a long way to go before young people from lower socio-economic groups achieve similar absolute levels to those from the higher socio-economic groups.

The YCS also enables us to examine young people's main activity at 16 years. Table 2.3 presents this information by socio-economic background. Young people have been classified as being in full-time education, government-supported training, in employment or out of work.

Table 2.3 reveals that young people from non-manual backgrounds were more likely to be in full-time education post-16 than those from manual backgrounds. Government training was more

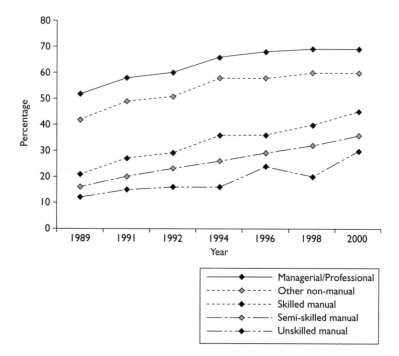

Figure 2.2 Attainment of five or more GCSE grades A* to C (including GNVQ equivalents) 1989–2000 by parents' socio-economic group.

Source: DfES 2001b, Youth Cohort Study.

Note
For notes see Table 2.2.

common amongst those from manual backgrounds. Reflecting at least in part differences in Year 11 attainment, those with parents in manual occupations were more likely to be outside education, training or employment than those with parents in non-manual occupations.

Social class and progress

Some research has also been carried out on social class and progress at the end of compulsory education. Sammons (1995) followed up the children who had been part of the Inner London Education Authority's (ILEA) Junior-School Project. She found

Table 2.3 Young people's main activity at age 16 by parents' socio-economic group (2000)

Parents' socio-economic group	Full-time education (%)	Government-supported training (%)	Full-time/ part-time job (%)	Out of work (%)	Something else/ not stated (%)
Non-manual	**81**	**7**	**8**	**3**	**1**
Managerial/professional	82	7	7	2	2
Other non-manual	79	7	8	4	1
Manual	**66**	**13**	**13**	**6**	**2**
Skilled manual	68	13	12	5	2
Semi-skilled manual	63	14	15	7	2
Unskilled manual	59	15	14	9	4
Other/not classified[a]	63	10	11	9	7

Source: DfES 2001b, Youth Cohort Study.

Note

a Includes a high percentage of respondents who had neither parent in a full-time job.

that the impact of socio-economic factors on attainment at the end of compulsory schooling (age 16) mirrored patterns apparent in junior school. In terms of progress there was evidence of socio-economic effects during secondary education. Taking account of attainment at the age of 11 years, girls and pupils from non-manual backgrounds and those not on low incomes obtained higher GCSE scores than other groups.

Payne (2000) used data from the Youth Cohort Study to examine the progress of low achievers[1] after the age of 16. She found that having parents in higher-level occupations increased the likelihood of staying in full-time education after the age of 16. The pervasive effects of social class are thus apparent even amongst pupils who are not high achievers.

Social class and entry to higher education

Social class is also important when it comes to entry to higher education. Blackburn and Jarman (1993) report that before the Second World War, university education was very much a privilege for a small elite with less than 2 per cent of the relevant age group entering university in 1938 (see also Chapter 3). In the post-war period access to higher education was still very limited and was structured in terms of social class and gender. Social class differences were striking (see Blackburn and Jarman 1993); between 1928 and 1947, an estimated 8.9 per cent of all boys from non-manual backgrounds attended university courses compared with 1.4 per cent of all boys with fathers who were manual workers.

Today university education is open to more students than ever before and participation in terms of the Age Participation Index[2] has increased from 2 per cent in 1940 (House of Commons Education and Employment Committee Eighth Report 1999) to 33 per cent in 2000/1 (DfES and OFSTED 2002). In 1940, 2 per cent of young people from the three lowest social groups (skilled manual, partly skilled and unskilled) experienced university education compared with 8 per cent of those from the highest social groups (professional, intermediate and skilled non-manual) (House of Commons Education and Employment Committee 1999). By 1998 these percentages were 17 per cent and 45 per cent respectively (Connor and Dewson 2001). More recent data (House of Commons 2002) provide a social-class breakdown of the age participation index; this reveals that 76 per cent of those from professional backgrounds participated in higher education in 2000, compared with only 14 per cent of those from unskilled backgrounds. A clear gap still exists in terms of participation in higher education between those from the highest and lowest socio-economic groups (see also Egerton and Halsey 1993).

We can see from our discussion so far that social class is an important factor in predicting young people's achievement in a UK context. We now turn to international data to examine whether the UK findings are replicated elsewhere.

International tests, achievement and socio-economic status

The Programme for International Student Assessment (PISA), first administered in 2000, covered three domains: reading literacy, mathematical literacy and scientific literacy (see Appendix B). An international socio-economic index of occupational status was used, which grouped pupils according to their parents' occupations:

ranked by the direct role that occupation plays in maximising income. In each country, the population is divided into quarters, ranked by the national values on the index. The skills required to perform the requirements of an occupation serve as the primary criterion for distinguishing different levels of occupational status.

(OECD 2001: 140)

The findings from PISA 2000 revealed that differences in the socio-economic index of occupational status were associated with substantial differences in student performance within countries, with students in the top quarters of the index obtaining higher scores on the reading literacy, mathematical and scientific literacy scales than those in the bottom quarters. Interestingly, the countries with the highest differences between students in the top and bottom quarters of the index were Belgium, Germany and Switzerland, followed by the Czech Republic, Hungary, the United Kingdom and the United States. The OECD report notes:

It cannot be assumed, however, that all of these differences are a direct result of the home advantages and higher expectations conferred by parents in higher occupations. Many factors affect students' performance in the three domains. For example, socio-economic status may be related to where students live and the quality of the schools to which they have access ... to the likelihood that they are enrolled in private schools, to the level of parental support and involvement, etc.

(OECD 2001: 140)

Difficulties with the concept of social class

Whilst the concepts of social class and socio-economic status have been used interchangeably and unproblematically in this book, there are a number of difficulties with both as they are determined, in general, on the basis of the occupation of the father.

This is important as an increasing number of children live in lone-parent families. In 2001 (National Statistics 2002) the number of such children was 22 per cent compared with 8 per cent in 1971, and of these, 20 per cent lived with their mother. The occupation of the mother is thus likely to be used more frequently when establishing social class, but importantly the distribution of women in different socio-economic groups varies from that of men.

This was exemplified in a research project examining parents' involvement in their children's education; this found no statistically significant differences between parents' involvement in their children's education in terms of social background as measured using their occupation. The researchers noted:

> several of the families participating in this study included a father in a skilled manual occupation and a mother in a clerical – non-manual – post. The use of a class dichotomy distinguishing non-manual social classes from manual social classes in the situation of parental separation (with the child subsequently staying with his or her mother) results in the child moving from a lower (manual) social class to a higher (non-manual) social class. Thus separation would, paradoxically, be associated with *upward* mobility.
>
> (West *et al*. 1998a: 481)

Another problem arises in relation to parents who are unemployed and are then classified in terms of *employment* status as opposed to *socio-economic* status. An added complication relates to the socio-economic status of parents from minority ethnic backgrounds, particularly those who are newly arrived immigrants or refugees. As a result of problems gaining employment, because of racism or other barriers, such parents may not be able to obtain employment that is of a level that their educational status would merit. Thus the concept of social class, although of value, is problematic, particularly given the changing social context. An added difficulty is that within British society the proportion of individuals now working in manual occupations has declined in recent years (Glennerster 1998), making comparisons over time difficult. It is for these reasons that other measures may be used by researchers. The next section looks at poverty and its association with achievement and this is followed by an examination of the relationship between parents' educational level and achievement.

Poverty and achievement

Research has shown that there is an impact of low income in addition to that of social class (see Sammons 1999). Much recent research has focused on the relationship between poverty and attainment particularly because of the ready availability of such data.

West *et al.* (2001) examined the relationship in England between the proportion of children dependent on an individual claiming a state benefit, income support, and academic attainment at the level of the LEA. They found a very high correlation between the proportion of children dependent on income-support claimants and low attainment. The inclusion of other markers of disadvantage – such as the proportion of children in lone-parent families, the proportion of children from minority ethnic groups, the proportion of children with English as a second language and the proportion of children with and without statements of special educational needs – added little to this prediction. Thus, a single measure of poverty (proportion of children dependent on recipients of income support) can act as a good marker of educational need.

Research at school and individual pupil level has focused on the relationship between levels of achievement and an indicator of poverty, namely known eligibility for free school meals. Children are eligible for free school meals if they are from a family in receipt of the state benefit known as income support or a related benefit known as the job-seeker's allowance. In England as a whole the proportion of children known to be eligible for free school meals was 18 per cent for primary schools and 16 per cent for secondary schools in January 2001 (DfES 2001c). These data are collected annually by the DfES from schools and they provide a readily available measure of deprivation.

At a school level, DfES (2001d) data demonstrate a clear relationship between the concentration of poverty levels in schools and examination results. On average, the greater the level of poverty the lower the aggregate GCSE results. The median percentage of pupils achieving five or more GCSEs (or GNVQ equivalent) at grades A* to C was 67 per cent in non-selective schools (that is, schools that are not grammar schools), with up to and including 5 per cent of pupils known to be eligible for free school meals. The equivalent figures in schools with more than 50 per cent of pupils who were known to be eligible for free school meals was 21 per cent. With other indicators of achievement similar trends are apparent (for example the percentage of pupils obtaining GCSE English, mathematics or science at grades A* to

C and the average GCSE point score). Across England as a whole there are thus clear links between poverty and low attainment levels in schools.

National curriculum assessments (DfES 2002a), which are carried out in England at the ages of 7, 11 and 14 years, also show that known free school meals eligibility at school level is related to achievement levels. At the end of Key Stage 1 (when children are around 7 years old), schools with up to 5 per cent of pupils known to be eligible for free school meals had between 92 and 95 per cent of their pupils reaching the 'expected' level in national tasks/tests in reading, writing and mathematics at the age of 7 years. By contrast, schools with 40 per cent or more pupils eligible for free school meals had between 71 per cent and 82 per cent of pupils reaching this level. In short, as the known eligibility for free school meals increased, the percentage of pupils attaining the 'expected' level fell.

At the end of Key Stage 2 (age 11 years), a similar pattern was found, although the difference in results between the high and low eligibility bands was greater. The percentage of pupils in the lowest free school meals eligibility band reaching the 'expected' level was 13 percentage points *above* the average for all schools in the English test, and 18 percentage points *below* the average in the highest band (DfES 2002a). At the end of Key Stage 3 (age 14 years), the same picture emerged, but a much larger difference was apparent. In the English test the range of achievement in terms of the percentage of pupils reaching the expected level was 84 per cent in schools in the lowest band of free school meals eligibility and 39 per cent for schools with 40 per cent or more of pupils eligible for free school meals; the average for all schools was 65 per cent (DfES 2002a).

Studies on attainment, progress and poverty

Many research studies confirm these strong links between poverty and attainment. For example, Sammons *et al.* (1997a) found that young children from low-income families (who were known to be eligible for free school meals) performed at a lower level than others at Key Stage 1, and Mujtaba and Sammons (1999) also obtained similar results at both Key Stages 1 and 2.

Other research studies have examined progress as well as attainment. Mortimore *et al.* (1988) in their inner London research examined not only the relationship between social class and attainment but also the relationship between eligibility for free school meals and attainment and progress. They found that known eligibility for free school meals had an impact on both reading and mathematics progress. Children who were eligible for free school meals made poorer progress than predicted, given their initial attainment, in both reading and mathematics. They also found that children from low-income families were more likely to have poor attendance than others, with pupils eligible for free school meals being absent for around 10 per cent of the time, and those not eligible being absent for only 8 per cent of the time. These findings, the researchers hypothesised, may reflect a link between ill-health and unemployment or low family income.

More recently, Strand (1999a) examined pupils' progress between the ages of 4 and 7 years. His study of over 5,000 pupils in an inner London LEA analysed educational progress made between 'baseline' assessment[3] at age 4 and national end of Key Stage 1 tasks/tests at age 7. He found that, after controlling for other factors, pupils known to be entitled to free school meals made less progress in all subjects than pupils not entitled to free school meals.

Turning to Wales, there has been a debate about the quality of education provided in schools that teach in the medium of English as opposed to Welsh (Gorard 2000). The view has been expressed that pupils in the former underachieve compared with their peers in Welsh-medium schools. However, Gorard found that once socio-economic factors, in particular eligibility for free school meals, had been taken into account there was no evidence of a difference.

Moving on to Northern Ireland, Shuttleworth (1995) analysed the relationship between personal/family background and attainment at GCSE. His findings also indicate that individual eligibility or ineligibility for free school meals (an indicator of poverty) is a useful measure of social deprivation, over and above parental labour market status, family size and religious background (which is associated with social class in Northern Ireland). At the school level, the percentage of pupils eligible for free meals was associated with pupil examination performance at GCSE level. In addition, there was a strong relationship between the proportion of pupils per school failing GCSEs and the percentage eligible for free school meals.

It is important to note that all studies that use eligibility for free meals as a measure of poverty (or deprivation) at the school level, ignore pupils who are eligible for benefit but have not *applied* (see also Chapter 6). Shuttleworth (1995) notes that indicators using this variable alone are likely to *underestimate* the proportion of pupils who are deprived.

The finding that children from low income families have lower performance, on average, than other children is not unique to the UK. In the USA, an ongoing representative sample survey of student achievement, the National Assessment of Educational Progress (NAEP) is carried out. This covers core subject areas. In 2000, a national assessment of mathematics (Braswell *et al.* 2001) was undertaken involving fourth-, eighth- and twelfth-grade students (typical ages 9, 13 and 17 years). At all three grades, students eligible for the federal free/reduced-price lunch programme, overall, had lower average scores than those who were not eligible. (This programme is intended for children at or near the poverty line and is determined by federal eligibility guidelines.) The same general findings emerged for the fourth-grade reading assessment, which was also carried out in 2000 (Donahue *et al.* 2001). In terms of achievement level, results also showed overall lower performance among students eligible for the programme – 14 per cent of students performed at or above the 'proficient' level compared with 41 per cent of non-eligible students.

Parents' education level

The above discussion has highlighted the links between social class and attainment and poverty and attainment. Related to social class is the level of education obtained by parents. As we have seen, children with parents in higher socio-economic groups are more likely to enter higher education than those in lower socio-economic groups. Research has demonstrated a strong association between social class and educational level for both fathers and mothers (for example West *et al.* 1998a). Thus it should come as no surprise to find that parents' educational level is also strongly related to children's attainment.

Moreover, parents' educational level is an important factor to bear in mind as research indicates that it has an independent impact on attainment. Sammons *et al.* (1999) in their study, the Effective Provision of Pre-school Education, found that children whose mothers had higher qualification levels were at an advantage in terms of overall cognitive attainment at entry to pre-school. The researchers note that this measure, and other measures of social disadvantage/advantage, have independent associations with children's cognitive attainment.

The Youth Cohort Study (DfES 2001b), which covers England and Wales, asked young people about the educational level of their parents. Table 2.4 provides information on young people's qualification levels according to whether one of their parents had a degree, GCE A levels or no A levels. This is shown graphically in Figure 2.3.

As can be seen from Table 2.4, even using somewhat crude measures of parents' educational level – in effect, completion of post-secondary academic education or completion of a higher-education degree – clear differences emerge in the number and grades of GCSEs/GNVQs achieved by young people at the end of compulsory education. In short, more young people with at least one parent who had a degree gained five or more high grade GCSEs than those whose parents had no A levels.

The same measure of parents' educational level is also related to whether young people continue in education full time, as shown in Table 2.5.

As shown in Table 2.5, more young people with at least one parent with a degree continued with full-time education than those whose parents had either at least one GCE A level or no A level. Where neither parent had an A level, more young people were found to be in government-supported training, in employment or out of work.

Table 2.4 Academic attainment[a] in Year 11 by parents' qualifications (2000)

Parents' qualifications	5+ GCSEs A*–C (%)	1–4 GCSEs A*–C[b] (%)	5+ GCSEs D–G (%)	1–4 GCSEs D–G (%)	None reported (%)
At least one parent with degree	72	16	8	2	2
At least one parent with A level	56	24	15	2	2
Neither parent with A level	39	29	22	4	6

Source: DfES 2001b, Youth Cohort Study.

Notes
a Includes GNVQ qualifications gained in Year 11.
b Those with 1–4 GCSE grades A* to C and any number of other grades.

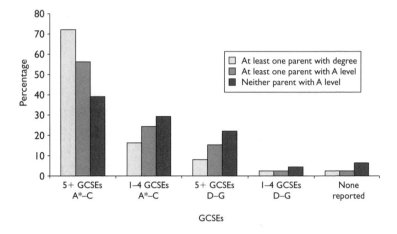

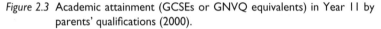

Figure 2.3 Academic attainment (GCSEs or GNVQ equivalents) in Year 11 by parents' qualifications (2000).

Source: DfES 2001b, Youth Cohort Study.

Note
For notes see Table 2.4.

Table 2.5 Main activity by parents' qualifications (2000)

Parents' qualifications	Full-time education (%)	Government-supported training (%)	Full/part-time job (%)	Out of work (%)	Something else/not stated (%)
At least one parent with degree	85	6	5	3	1
At least one parent with A level	75	9	11	3	1
Neither parent with A level	66	12	13	6	3

Source: DfES 2001b, Youth Cohort Study.

International evidence on achievement and mothers' education

As noted earlier, the National Assessment of Educational Progress research carried out in the USA is an ongoing representative sample survey of core subjects (Braswell *et al.* 2001). This shows that parents' educational level is an important indicator of achievement. For example, in mathematics in 2000 it was found that, in general, students in grades 8 and 12 (typical ages 13 and 17 years) with higher scores on the test reported higher levels of parental education.

The Programme for International Student Assessment (PISA) examined the relationship between mothers' level of education and student performance (see Appendix B). The analysis undertaken used the International Standard Classification of Education (ISCED) to group the educational attainment of students' mothers (completion of primary or lower secondary education, completion of upper secondary education and completion of tertiary education). The education of the mother was chosen as the literature often identifies this as a stronger predictor of student achievement than the education of the father (OECD 2001).

Students whose mothers had completed upper secondary education were found to achieve higher levels of performance in reading than other students. This was the case in all countries. In most countries the completion of tertiary education by the mother was found to be associated with a further advantage in terms of performance. On the other hand, students whose mothers had not completed upper secondary education were seen as being 'particularly vulnerable' (OECD 2001: 149).

What accounts for these differences?

Whilst research has consistently demonstrated links between the home environment and attainment, we know less about the processes that might explain this association. However, the Effective Provision of Pre-school Education project (Sammons *et al.* 1999) has examined the associations between a range of personal, family and home environment characteristics and cognitive attainment of children aged around 3 years at entry to pre-school. Sammons *et al.* found that a number of measures of home environment had an independent association with cognitive attainment. The frequency with which parents reported reading to their child was significant, with those who read twice a day showing the most impact, though reading daily or several times a week also showed a positive relationship compared with reading less than once a week. The frequency with which children were taken to the library also showed a significant positive association, with weekly visits showing the strongest relationship. In addition, children whose parents reported that their child frequently played with letters or numbers also showed higher scores, as did those who reported that they taught their child the alphabet, and those who taught a variety of songs to their children. However, what is particularly interesting is that these aspects of the home environment remained significant after having taken account of parents' educational level and occupational status.

It is also possible that the ways in which parents are involved in their children's education are important at a later stage too. West *et al.* (1998a) examined parents' involvement in their children's education and found that differences in terms of educational level emerged even when social class differences did not. Children with more highly qualified mothers were significantly more likely to have used workbooks at home than the children of mothers with lower levels of educational qualifications. And research by Greenhough and Hughes (1998) suggests different types of interaction with children's reading according to parents' educational level. The more nebulous concept of parental 'interest' is also worth mentioning at this stage; Sammons *et al.* (1997a), for example, found that there was a significant impact on attainment at the end of Key Stage 1 of parents' interest in their child's education as reported by headteachers.

Conclusions

The research and data that we have examined in this chapter are clear. On average, students from lower socio-economic groups (particularly those from unskilled manual backgrounds) and who are from low income families achieve less well in a range of tests, examinations and assessments than those who are from higher socio-economic groups and who are not from low income families. The data also indicate that students from families where the parents have higher levels of education tend to gain better results. It is important, however, that policy makers and practitioners do not take a negative stance and assume that improvements cannot be made in disadvantaged schools. One of our case study schools (see Chapter 9) is located in an area where a high proportion of adults have not completed higher education and the school itself has a high proportion of pupils from disadvantaged backgrounds. However, the GCSE results at this school have increased markedly over time – and indeed all pupils gained at least one GCSE pass at grades A* to G in 2001 (in contrast to the situation in England as a whole where 6 per cent of pupils aged 15 obtained no passes).

Neither should it be assumed that children's families are necessarily the reason for the lower performance of children from lower socio-economic groups or from families where the parents are less highly qualified. As we have seen, research indicates that teacher expectations appear to be lower for children from working-class backgrounds and teachers may be more likely to label children from certain social backgrounds as disruptive. In some cases school policies and practices may also be part of the problem. Of course, some schools do have challenging pupils and in these cases behaviour-management schemes can be put in place to help create an ethos where pupils and staff feel secure (see Chapter 9).

In terms of progress made by students from lower socio-economic groups and from low-income families, the evidence suggests that schools have *less* impact in terms of progress in subjects where parental involvement is likely to be greater – such as reading and writing. This implies that parental involvement is an important factor. Whilst we are not able to say that the relationship is indeed causal, it is certainly worth investigating in future research studies. Given that parental involvement is considered by policy makers and practitioners to have a range of benefits, it is important for further policy initiatives in this area to be explored. Chapter 9 provides details of some of the ways in which our case study schools involved parents in their children's education and took cognisance of their concerns.

However, what is less clear, at this stage, is what sort of involvement is important and what kinds of involvement should be further encouraged. Activities such as reading with children and visits to the library have been highlighted in research and it is clear that such findings have important implications for policy makers and schools as they reinforce the notion that parental involvement of a very clearly defined type may have an impact on attainment and progress.

Whilst there is evidence to suggest that young people from lower socio-economic groups have made larger proportionate increases in attainment over the past ten years, absolute achievement levels are still markedly poorer than for higher socio-economic groups. This suggests that further changes are needed to counter the pervasive impact of social class on achievement, which is apparent at the earliest of stages. In later chapters we shall return to this issue and examine relevant policy initiatives that have been implemented in recent years.

Chapter 10 highlights some of the ways in which government, schools and LEAs could respond in order to try to ensure that young people from different social classes and from disadvantaged groups maximise their levels of achievement.

Chapter 3

Gender and achievement

Introduction

This chapter explores the relationship between gender and achievement and includes an examination of the educational performance of boys and girls in the UK. The chapter opens with a brief historical introduction to the area and then the evidence on the performance of girls and boys is presented. Whilst our focus is, in the main, on England, pertinent findings relating to Wales, Scotland and Northern Ireland are presented. Some international findings are then reported, before we analyse reasons for gender differences and possible strategies for addressing them. Recommendations for schools are followed by the conclusions.

Historical background

It seems hard to believe that only forty years ago, the curriculum for girls and boys was far more clearly differentiated than it is now. In the Newsom Report (1963), marked sex-role differentiation was apparent in terms of the curriculum offered – but perhaps more significant are the expectations for boys and girls: 'The use of power-tools ... adds variety in the work, and increases the possibilities of offering "man-sized" jobs, which most boys tackle with zest' (ibid.: 134); and 'Housecraft and needlework easily justify their place in the curriculum to most girls.' In terms of science, the Newsom Report notes: 'A boy is usually excited by the prospect of a science course' and 'The girl may come to the science lesson with a less eager curiosity than the boy' (ibid. 142).

Expectations for the young people's longer-term outcomes also differed in terms of their gender. It was noted that more demanding engineering courses were designed for 'able boys likely to become skilled technicians. But they can be found at more modest levels, for boys hoping to become craftsmen' (ibid. 36). In relation to girls, the report noted that:

> The main groups of occupations most widely taken up by girls – jobs in offices, in shops, in catering, work in the clothing industry and other manufacturing trades – can all provide material for courses at more than one level of ability. For all girls, too, there is a group of interests relating to what many, perhaps most of them, would regard as their most important vocational concern, marriage. It is true that at the age of fourteen and fifteen, this may appear chiefly as a preoccupation with personal appearance and boyfriends, but many girls are ready to respond to work relating to the wider aspects of homemaking and family life and the care and upbringing of children.
>
> (Newsom 1963: 37)

However, a shift in terms of societal attitudes towards the education of girls and boys was beginning to take place. In 1972, the Equal Opportunities Commission was set up, although it did not have the 'powers to deal with many of the unfair practices that were brought before it' (Gordon et al. 1991: 136). This was followed in 1976 by the Ruskin College speech given by the then Labour Prime Minister, James Callaghan (1976), which heralded what became known as the Great Debate. This focused on the school curriculum, the assessment of standards, the training of teachers and the relationship between schools and working life. Specific reference to the education of girls was made in the speech highlighting the problem of girls abandoning science subjects and the need to attract more young people into engineering and science subjects generally.

Concerns about gender differences, largely in relation to the under-representation of females in science and technology, continued during the 1970s and 1980s. The context was the push for equal opportunities between the sexes and 'a growing body of feminist research and literature which critiqued the state and highlighted the disadvantageous position of women' in education and employment (Gaine and George 1999). The response was a range of initiatives to open up the curriculum to girls and, for example, to make subjects such as mathematics and science more 'girl friendly'.

The election of the Conservative Government in 1979 heralded many education reforms. Probably the most important policy change, having an effect on the education of both girls and boys, was the introduction of the national curriculum in England and Wales in 1988, making the study of the core subjects of mathematics, English and science, together with a number of other subjects, compulsory (see Maclure 1992). As we shall see, this had consequences for the subjects studied by girls and in which they took public examinations. In the next section we look more closely at the performance of girls and boys in the UK context.

Performance of girls and boys in the UK

References to the gender gap in educational performance are not new, but there has been an increasing focus in the public debate about the 'underachievement' of boys. However, it appears that until comparatively recently differences in attainment between girls and boys were concealed from public debate. Gallagher (1997) reviewed the apparent underachievement of boys and he provides a valuable historical context to this issue. The review reports on the 'capping' of places for girls who were deemed to have qualified for places in grammar schools as a result of their performance in the 11-plus test.

The policy of establishing quotas of girls and boys on the 11-plus test was used in the past in England and continued in Northern Ireland until the 1980s (Gallagher 1997). Gallagher notes the main justification for this policy was that boys performed less well than girls at 11 years of age because they matured at a slower rate than girls; thus, the argument went, to treat both boys and girls as a single group at the age of 11 could unfairly disadvantage the boys.

Examination results, national test results and individual research studies carried out in England provide information that enables differences in attainment between girls and boys to be measured. In the following sections, we explore the performance of girls and boys at different stages of their education – preschool, primary and secondary – and also examine what happens when they leave compulsory education. We then move on to examine selected research carried out in the rest of the UK.

Gender differences at pre-school stage

A research study by Sammons *et al.* (1999) included an investigation of the contribution to children's early development of individual and family characteristics such as gender, ethnicity, language, parental education and employment. Baseline information relating to over 2,000 children entering over 100 different pre-school centres was collected. The results revealed statistically significant associations between young children's overall cognitive attainment (as measured by the total score on the British Abilities Scale) and a variety of personal, socio-economic and family characteristics. The analyses revealed that girls showed higher cognitive attainments at entry to the study when the impact of other factors had been taken into account. This suggests that differences between the attainment of girls and boys are a function of differential cognitive ability, which reveals itself very early in children's lives.

Gender differences at primary stage

A considerable amount of evidence has accrued over the years about the attainment of girls and boys in primary school. A review by Salisbury *et al.* (1999) highlighted research findings suggesting that on arrival at school, girls are better able to cope with school activities than are boys. The performance gaps were greatest in the areas of social skills, letter identification, writing and drawing. There is also a suggestion that boys are 'potentially more vulnerable than girls to becoming disaffected' (Murphy and Elwood 1998: 98). Other research suggests that girls and boys prefer to learn in different ways and that boys get bored more readily than girls (see Salisbury *et al.* 1999) as their levels of concentration are lower and organisational skills poorer than those of girls.

A number of studies have found that girls achieve higher scores than boys in 'baseline' assessments, which are taken when children enter school. Many of these studies are limited to particular LEAs, where data on attainment and on background factors at an individual pupil level have been collected for a number of years.[1] One such study was carried out by Strand (1999b), who reports on the results of the baseline assessment with over 11,000 pupils carried out in one London LEA. The assessment comprised a checklist completed by teachers to assess children's attainment in English (oral skills, early reading and writing) and early mathematical understanding. In addition, the baseline assessment included a standardised test – the Linguistic Awareness in Reading Readiness (LARR) Test of Emergent Literacy. This focused on early literacy skills. Strand found that girls obtained significantly higher scores on every item of the English checklist and five of the six items of the mathematics checklist. Strand notes: 'The gender difference at 4 does not arise from high performance in one particular area but is general and widespread across all baseline items' (1999b: 19).

Moving on to primary school, national data relating to performance at the end of Key Stages 1 and 2 (ages 7 and 11 years) enable us to examine gender differences in attainment at the completion of junior and primary education. These data (DfES 2002a) reveal that in all Key Stage 1 subjects in 2001, the percentage of girls who achieved the 'expected' level or above (that is, level 2) was higher than the percentage of boys. This was true for both teacher assessments and tests. The largest gaps were for reading and writing, where girls outperformed boys by 8 percentage points (88 per cent versus 80 per cent for the reading task/test and 90 per cent versus 82 per cent for the writing task). For the mathematics test and science teacher assessment the difference was only 2 percentage points. Between 1999 and 2001, the improvement – that is, the change over time – was the same for girls and boys for reading (2 percentage points). For the writing task boys improved more than girls (by 4 percentage points versus 2 percentage points), as they did in the mathematics test (by 5 percentage points versus 2 percentage points).

In a study focusing on one London LEA, Strand examined attainment in the tests at the end of Key Stage 1 at the age of 7 (Strand 1999a). Again girls were found to have higher levels of attainment than boys. Interestingly, this was particularly marked for Caribbean girls compared with Caribbean boys (see also Chapter 4). This study also showed that more progress was made by girls than boys in reading and writing, resulting in an increase in the size of the gender gap. Whilst girls made less progress in mathematics, they still remained slightly ahead of boys in mathematics at the end of Key Stage 1. Of all the groups explored, the progress of girls from English, Scottish, Welsh or Northern Irish backgrounds, who were not known to be eligible for free school meals, was the highest overall; boys in this group were the highest attaining group of boys at the end of Key Stage 1. However, boys and girls with this ethnic background who were known to be eligible for free school meals, made less progress than expected and were amongst the lowest attainers at the end of Key Stage 1. As noted by Arnot *et al.*, 'social class and ethnicity also have powerful effects' (1998: 69).

Turning to the end of Key Stage 2 (age 11), DfES statistics (2002a) reveal that in the English tests in 2001, 80 per cent of girls obtained the expected level (level 4) compared with 70 per cent of boys. In the reading test, girls outperformed boys by 7 percentage points and for the writing test by 15 percentage points. However, in mathematics and science (both tests and teacher assessment) boys and girls performed similarly. The improvement between 1999 and 2001 was similar for boys and for girls in the core subject tests.

Finally, Strand (1997) has noted that particular attention has been paid to the low attainment of boys compared with girls in the secondary sector and more specifically in GCSE examinations. These differences have:

> frequently been attributed to boys 'switching off' during secondary school education. If . . . boys have lower attainment than girls at the start of school at age 4, and have fallen even further behind by age of 7, then research on sex differences in attainment may need to focus on primary schools rather than secondary schools, and on factors in the home in addition to the school. For example, Tizard *et al.* (1988) report some evidence of differential parenting practices with boys and girls of nursery school age. Parents of girls were more likely to have taught them to write other words as well as their names, read to girls more often and provided them with a greater number of books than boys.
>
> (Strand 1997: 484)

Gender differences at secondary stage

National data relating to performance in secondary school at the end of Key Stage 3, when national tests are taken by pupils in state (and some independent) schools in England, reveal interesting differences between the sexes (DfES 2002a). These tests are taken by pupils when they are around 14 years of age in the three core subjects of English, mathematics and science. In the tests and teacher assessments for all three subjects, the percentage of girls achieving the expected level 5 or above was the same as or higher than the percentage of boys.

Overall, in 2001, 65 per cent of pupils reached level 5 or above in the Key Stage 3 English test. The gap between the achievement of girls and boys was marked, with 73 per cent of girls and only 57 per cent of boys achieving this level. This is a notable 16 percentage point difference in absolute terms. Interestingly, there was no difference between girls and boys in the science test and only two percentage points difference (in favour of girls) in the mathematics test.

Whilst the core subjects of English, mathematics and science are tested by means of both teacher assessment and national tests, the non-core subjects are teacher assessed only. Here, again, some differences between girls and boys emerged with girls outperforming boys in all subjects except for physical education; girls outperformed boys by 15 or more percentage points in design and technology, modern foreign languages, art and music. For information and communications technology (ICT), history and geography girls also outperformed boys. However, for physical education, slightly more boys than girls (70 per cent versus 68 per cent) reached level 5, the 'expected' level.

Over the years, a considerable amount of work has been carried out that has explored the attainment of girls and boys in public examinations in England, notably GCSEs and GCE A levels, which are explored in the following sections.

GCSE attainment

As we noted in Chapter 1, attainment levels at the end of compulsory schooling (Year 11) in GCSE examinations have been increasing over the years for both boys and girls. An examination of government statistics (DfES 2001a; DfES 2002b) reveals that girls have outperformed boys every year since 1975; in that year, the difference was not great – 22.2 per cent of male school leavers and 23 per cent of female school leavers (of any age from all schools except special schools) achieved five or more GCE O levels[2] or Certificate of Secondary Education grade 1 (these were the examinations in place prior to 1988, when GCSEs were introduced). By 1987/8, the respective numbers were 28.2 and 31.7 per cent – in absolute terms a difference of 3.5 percentage points. Since then

Table 3.1 Percentage of 15 year old pupils achieving five or more GCSE grades A* to C[a] between 1988/9 and 2000/1

Year[b]	Boys	Girls	Total
1988/9	29.8	35.8	32.8
1989/90	30.8	38.4	34.5
1990/1	33.3	40.3	36.8
1991/2	34.1	42.7	38.3
1992/3	36.8	45.8	41.2
1993/4	39.1	47.8	43.3
1994/5	39.0	48.1	43.5
1995/6	39.9	49.4	44.5
1996/7	40.5	50.0	45.1
1997/8	41.3	51.5	46.3
1998/9	42.8	53.4	47.9
1999/2000	44.0	54.6	49.2
2000/1	44.8	55.4	50.0

Source: DfES 2001a; 2002b.

Notes

a GCSE grade A* was introduced in 1993/4.

b Percentages from 1988/9 to 1990/1 are taken from the School Examinations Survey and are based on 15 year olds in all schools except special schools; percentages from 1991/2 to 2000/1 are taken from the database on School Performance Tables and are based on 15 year olds in all schools including special schools; percentages from 1996/7 include GNVQ equivalencies.

more marked differences have emerged, as shown in Table 3.1 and Figure 3.1.

Table 3.1 shows that the percentage of 15 year old pupils achieving five or more GCSEs at grades A* to C has not increased at the same rate for boys and girls. Indeed, the gap is widening. In absolute terms the change between 1989 and 2001 was 15 percentage points for boys and 20 percentage points for girls. As we discussed in Chapter 1, the methods of data collection have changed over this period so we need to be cautious when interpreting the significance of the differences observed.[3]

Table 3.2 shows in more detail how 15 year old girls and boys performed in their GCSE examinations by the end of 2000/1. It is clear from this table that more girls than boys had achieved five or more or one or more GCSEs at grades A* to C and at grades A* to G.

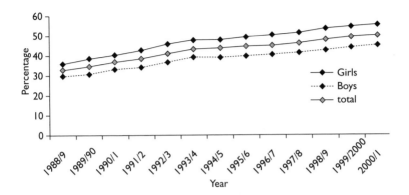

Figure 3.1 Percentage of 15 year old pupils achieving five or more GCSE grades A* to C (including GNVQ equivalents) between 1988/9 and 2000/1.

Source: DfES 2001a; 2002b.

Note
For notes see Table 3.1.

Table 3.2 Percentage of 15 year old pupils[a] achieving different numbers of GCSEs[b] by the end of 2000/1

Achievement	Boys	Girls	Total
5+ GCSEs A* to C	44.8	55.4	50.0
1+ GCSE A* to C	69.1	79.2	74.0
5+ GCSEs A* to G	86.9	91.0	88.9
1+ GCSE A* to G	93.5	95.6	94.5

Source: DfES 2002b.

Notes
a Number of pupils on roll aged 15 at the start of the 2000/1 academic year. Includes attempts and achievements by these pupils in previous academic years.
b Includes GNVQ qualifications gained in Year 11.

Using a different approach, Bellamy (2002) analysed the differences in attainment over time using statistical tables produced by the DfES, which divide pupils into twenty ranked groups of equal sizes based on their GCSE/GNVQ point score (see, for example, DfES 2001a). In 2000, girls outperformed boys in every one of the twenty groups (by 5.4 points overall). However, it is noteworthy that the biggest inequalities between girls and boys were found amongst the lower achievers – peaking at 7.4 points for the fifth and sixth groups from the bottom within the twenty ranked groups. It is also of interest to note that between 1995 and 2000, the greatest increases in achievement – in both absolute and proportionate terms – were amongst the highest 15 per cent of each gender and the lowest 10 per cent.

We now turn to achievements at GCSE in 2000/1. Official statistics also enable us to compare the entries at GCSE of boys and girls and their achievements in different subjects (DfES 2002b). These reveal that very high percentages of 15 year old pupils in schools *attempted* GCSEs in the core national curriculum subjects by the end of 2000/01. Thus, 90 per cent of boys and 94 per cent of girls attempted English; comparable figures for mathematics were 92 per cent and 94 per cent, and for double-award science (the science subject attempted by most pupils) the figures were 75 per cent and 79 per cent.

Indeed, in many subjects more girls than boys attempted GCSE examinations; these included: English literature, French, German, Spanish, art and design, drama, religious education, music, home economics and humanities. However, more boys than girls attempted GCSE examinations in other subjects: geography, information technology, business studies, physical education, physics, and chemistry.[4]

In terms of *achievement*, more girls than boys achieved GCSE grades A* to C in most subject areas: English, English literature, mathematics, double science, design and technology, history, modern languages, art and design and drama. More boys than girls, however, achieved high-grade GCSEs in: information technology, geography, business studies, physical education; physics, chemistry and biological sciences. Figure 3.2 provides information on attempts and achievements in selected subjects for girls and boys.

Young people's involvement in education at age 16

The YCS enables us to examine young people's main activity at 16. In the spring of 2000, the ninth cohort survey of 16 years olds was carried out in England and Wales, around eight months after the young people had completed compulsory secondary education (see Appendix C). Table 3.3 presents young people's main activity by gender. Young people have been classified as being in full-time

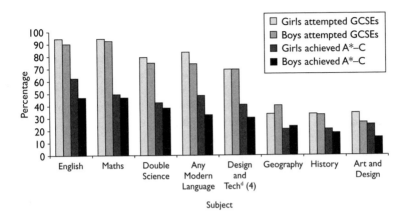

Figure 3.2 GCSE attempts and achievements[a] in selected subjects by 15 year old pupils in schools[b] by the end of 2000/1[c].

Source: DfES 2002b.

Notes
a For each subject only one attempt is counted – that which achieved the highest grade.
b Those in school who were 15 at the start of the academic year 2000/1.
c Including attempts and achievements by these pupils in previous academic years.
d Includes any combined syllabus of which design and technology is the major part.

education, government-supported training, in employment or out of work.

Table 3.3 shows that more girls than boys continued in full-time education (76 per cent versus 67 per cent) post-16, with more boys than girls going into government-supported training (13 per cent versus 8 per cent) or being in work (12 per cent versus 10 per cent). To some extent this is likely to reflect differences in Year 11 attainment.

Table 3.3 Young people's main activity at age 16 by gender (2000)

Gender	Full-time education (%)	Government-supported training (%)	Full-time/ part-time job (%)	Out of work (%)	Something else/not stated (%)
Boys	67	13	12	5	2
Girls	76	8	10	5	3
All	71	10	10	5	3

Source: DfES 2001b, Youth Cohort Study.

GCE A levels

General Certificate of Education Advanced (GCE A) levels are the academic examinations that are taken in England, Wales and Northern Ireland at the end of post-compulsory education. Generally, possession of the equivalent of at least two A levels (see Appendix A for other qualifications) is necessary in order for young people to proceed to higher education (although this is not necessarily the case). Students can choose not only which subjects they study at A level but also how many they study (within school/college constraints).

As noted earlier, more girls than boys continue with their education post-16. Using DfES statistics (DfES 2001c) it can be calculated that in England, in 1999/2000 41 per cent of the 17 year old female population were A/AS/GNVQ candidates compared with 33 per cent of the equivalent male population.

Over time, the pattern of achievement of girls and boys at GCE A level has changed. In 1980/1, 15.4 per cent of 17 year old boys in the population achieved one or more A level pass compared with 14.4 per cent of girls of the same age (Department for Education and Science (DES) 1988). In 1988/9 this situation reversed, with 16.9 per cent of boys and 17.0 per cent of girls in the population reaching this level (DES 1990). Since then, the absolute gap between girls and boys has increased further.

Figure 3.3 provides a graphical representation of GCE A level (or the equivalent) achievements of girls and boys as a percentage of the 17 year old age group from the early 1990s. In 1992/3 (DfEE 1996a), the percentage of 17-year-old boys in England who achieved *one or more GCE A level pass* (or AS equivalent) was 29 per cent whilst the percentage of girls was 34 per cent. By 1999/2000, these figures had increased to 34 per cent and 42 per cent respectively, an increase of 5 percentage points in absolute terms for males and 8 percentage points for females (see DfEE 1996a, 1998, 2001c).

In 1992/3, the percentage of 17 year old boys in the population who achieved *three or more GCE A level passes* (or the equivalent) was 18 per cent and for girls the comparable figure was 20 per cent (DfEE 1996a). By 1999/2000, these figures had increased to 22 per cent and 28 per cent respectively (DfES 2001c). This was an increase of 4 percentage points in absolute terms for males and

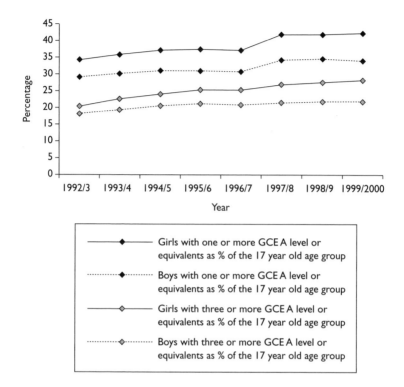

Figure 3.3 GCE A/AS[a] and Advanced GNVQ achievements[b] of students[c] in all schools and FE sector colleges 1992/3–1999/2000.

Sources: DfEE 1996a, 1998; DfES 2002b.

Notes
a Each GCE AS (Advanced supplementary) pass counts as half of a GCE A level.
b Figures for 1998/9 and 1999/2000 include the Advanced GNVQ, equivalent to two GCE A levels.
c Figures are derived from the number of students aged 18 or under who achieved the stated result for the first time, in the relevant years, in all schools and FE sector colleges.

8 percentage points for females (in proportional terms an increase of 22 per cent for males and of 40 per cent for females). Thus in both absolute and proportional terms the achievement gap between girls and boys has increased between the early 1990s and 2000.

We now turn to entries and achievements at GCE A level in 1999/2000. Girls and boys aged 17 in schools and FE sector colleges (including sixth forms and FE colleges) in 1999/2000 entered different subjects at GCE A level (DfES 2001a). More 17 year old female than male candidates *entered*: English, biological science, history, social studies, communication studies (includes, for example, media, film studies), modern languages, music and religious studies (and general studies). More male than female candidates, on the other hand, entered: physics, chemistry, mathematics, computer studies, design and technology, business studies, geography, economics and physical education.

In terms of *achievements*, the percentage of female candidates aged 17 in schools/colleges who gained grades A to C was higher than that for male candidates across all subjects (62 versus 58 per cent); a higher proportion of female than male candidates gained top grades (A to C) for the majority of individual subjects (for example, biological science, chemistry, physics, mathematics, geography, design and technology, physical education) but a higher proportion of males achieved high grades in French, German and Spanish. The proportions of males and females were similar for history, economics and English. Figure 3.4 provides details of entries for selected GCE A levels and achievements in terms of high grade GCE passes (grades A to C) by the end of 1999/2000.

One final point to note is that in 2000/1 (DfES 2002b) the *average point score per entry at GCE A level or equivalent*[5] for students aged 17 to 18 in all schools and FE sector colleges was higher for females than for males (5.7 for females and 5.4 for males). Data are also available on the GCE A/AS examination point scores of 17-year-old male and female *candidates* in all schools and FE-sector colleges for 1999/2000 (DfES 2001a), and here we find that although the *average point score per candidate* was higher for girls then for boys (15.1 versus 13.7), more male than female candidates achieved between 0 to 9 (30.4 versus 26.2 per cent) points and 30 or more points (16.8 versus 16.6 per cent). Fewer male than female candidates achieved 10 to 29 points

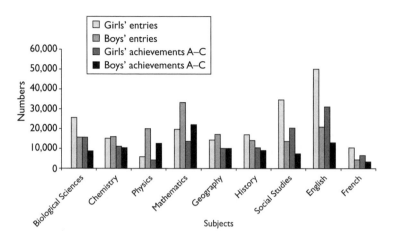

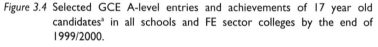

Figure 3.4 Selected GCE A-level entries and achievements of 17 year old candidates[a] in all schools and FE sector colleges by the end of 1999/2000.

Source: DfES 2001a.

Note
a Candidates are those pupils aged 17 at 31 August 1999.

(52.9 versus 57.4 per cent); in short, male candidates obtained more of the lowest point scores and by a small margin of the very highest point scores.

Research on achievement in the rest of the UK

Research has also been carried out in relation to gender differences in attainment in Wales, Scotland and Northern Ireland. Gorard *et al.* (2001b) examined the attainment by gender for all pupils in Wales over a six-year period. They examined attainment from Key Stage 1 to GCE A level. Overall, they found few differences in mathematics and science. However, whilst they found no significant differences in attainment in other subjects at the lowest level of any assessment, for other levels the gap in attainment between boys and girls was found to increase with every grade or level. Proportionately more girls obtained high grades and more boys middle grades than might be expected. Gorard *et al.* note:

Although there are no significant entry gaps, and few achievement gaps at the lowest levels of attainment in *any* subject, there are achievement gaps at higher levels of attainment in English (as well as languages and humanities at GCSE).

(2001b: 137)

Gallagher (1997) reports on two studies carried out in Northern Ireland, one relating to the GCSE attainments of pupils in a sample of grammar schools in 1996, and the other relating to GCE O level attainments of pupils from broadly the same schools, in 1985. The research found that the attainment of the girls had increased at a higher rate than that of the boys over the period in question. Gallagher reported that the most plausible explanation of the findings relating to both these results and later changes in GCE A level choice were:

attributable less to the girls' perception of the academic subjects themselves, and more to their perceptions of the occupational opportunities they believed to be open to them in the future.

(Gallagher 1997: 23)

The role of expectations was also examined in these two research studies. Pupils were asked what they intended to do after they left school. As most grammar school pupils enter higher education it was not surprising to find that this pattern also emerged in the survey. However, there was an interesting difference in the responses over time. In both 1985 and 1995 about 92 per cent of boys indicated that they expected to go to university, whilst for girls in 1985 the figure was 72 per cent and, in 1995, 87 per cent.

Tinklin *et al.* (2001) in a study of gender differences in Scotland, found evidence of these as early as the pre-school stage, with teachers rating girls more highly than boys in a number of areas, including personal, social and emotional development, expressive communication, listening and talking, reading and writing, and mathematics. Girls outperformed boys throughout primary school in reading, with performance in mathematics being less clear cut. Citing evidence from 1999, Tinklin *et al.* note that at the secondary school stage girls on average gain more Scottish Certificate of Education Standard Grade awards (see Appendix A) than boys; the largest differences were found at the highest levels of attainment. A similar pattern was found at Higher Grade.

Tinklin *et al.* report that there were also differences between girls and boys in terms of examination entry. For example, 70 per cent of biology candidates were female compared with 31 per cent of physics candidates; and 80 per cent of candidates for office and information studies were girls compared with 36 per cent for computing studies. Whilst in the past boys tended to attain more highly in areas such as mathematics and physics, data for 1999 revealed that at Standard Grade girls were more likely than boys to obtain awards at the highest level (credit or general/credit level) in almost every subject they entered. The exceptions were for physical education, economics and general science.

The researchers reported similar findings at Scottish Certificate of Education Higher Grade. Although 57 per cent of English candidates and 47 per cent of mathematics candidates were female, gender differences were marked in other subjects. Thus, females formed the majority of Higher Grade candidates in modern languages, history, modern studies, art, drama, music and religious studies. The majority of physical education candidates were male. At Higher Grade, girls were more likely than boys to gain passes at A to C in every subject they entered except for human biology and accounting and finance.

Tinklin *et al.* noted that the attainment of girls was higher than that of boys for all social classes with the exception of those from unskilled backgrounds. The researchers also explored possible reasons for the differences in attainment between girls and boys that have been apparent from the 1970s onwards. They argue that cultural attitudes and expectations have been key factors:

> In the 1950s girls and boys had very different post-school expectations, which affected their attitudes and behaviour within school, whereas our data show that, in the year 2000, both girls and boys hoped for a worthwhile and successful career and saw childcare as a joint responsibility. This marks a change in attitudes and, we would argue, is linked to rising levels of female attainment at school.
>
> (Tinklin *et al.* 2001: 7)

Entry to higher education

Our focus in this book is not on higher education but on schools. Nevertheless, it is important to note that many more girls now enter higher education than previously. In 1938, less than 2 per cent of the relevant age group was entering university – and amongst women it was far lower at less than 0.5 per cent. In the post-war period access to higher education was still more limited for women with men outnumbering women by three to one; indeed, it was not until 1948 that Cambridge University admitted women as full voting members (Blackburn and Jarman 1993).

Over the years there has been a narrowing and then a reversal of this gender gap in access to higher education and in 2000/1 (Higher Education Statistics Agency 2002) the percentage of female students on undergraduate courses in UK higher education institutions exceeded that of males at 58 per cent compared to 42 per cent. In terms of undergraduate degree results for UK-domiciled students, 53 per cent of first-class honours degrees were awarded to females and 47 per cent to males.

The subjects studied by men and women vary. In 2000/1, more women than men were, perhaps not unsurprisingly, studying for nursing (89 per cent of the total); education (73 per cent); and social work (79 per cent). However, more women were also studying for the following subjects/subject areas (amongst others) in 2000/1: medicine and dentistry (54 per cent); biology (58 per cent); and languages (69 per cent).

In the same year, more men than women were studying on courses in the following subjects/subject areas (amongst others): engineering and technology (85 per cent of the total); physics (80 per cent); architecture (72 per cent); computer science (74 per cent); economics (68 per cent); mathematical sciences (62 per cent); and chemistry (60 per cent). It is clear that men and women continue to opt for different subjects at undergraduate level. Many of these choices no doubt reflect earlier achievements and differing vocational interests.

International evidence on gender differences

Gallagher (1997) carried out a review of the research evidence on the apparent underachievement of boys. He found that evidence from Great Britain, Northern Ireland, the European Union and the USA suggested that there was a general pattern of increasing attainment levels of all pupils over time and that within this overall pattern the rate of increase tended to be higher for females than for males (see also West *et al.* 1999). Both trends have developed steadily over time and, Gallagher concludes, appear to be linked to broader processes of social change.

Evidence from the American National Assessment of Educational Progress, an ongoing representative sample survey of student achievement in core areas, revealed that in 2000, fourth-grade girls (typical age 9 years) obtained a higher average score in reading than boys in the same grade (Donahue *et al.* 2001). For mathematics there was no significant gender difference for fourth-grade students but the average score for males was higher than that for females in eighth and twelfth grades (Braswell *et al.* 2001).

There is also evidence relating to gender differences from the Programme for International Student Assessment (PISA) (OECD 2001), which covered the domains of reading literacy, mathematical literacy and scientific literacy (see Appendix B). The results showed a reasonably consistent pattern in terms of gender differences across countries. In every country, it was found that, on average, girls reached higher levels than boys in reading literacy – and the UK was no exception. In mathematical literacy, there were statistically significant differences in around half the countries, in all of which it was found that boys did better; in the UK, there were no statistically significant gender differences. In scientific literacy, there were fewer differences between boys and girls, and the pattern of differences was not consistent; 24 OECD countries (including the UK) showed no statistically significant differences in science performance.

The analysis of these findings pinpoints the gender differences in different subject areas. The OECD report noted that girls expressed greater interest in reading than boys. 'Gender differences in performance in reading and mathematical literacy are thus closely mirrored in student interest in the respective subject areas' (OECD 2001: 129).

Gender differences in favour of females were also found in self-reports of the frequency with which young people read for pleasure, enjoyed talking about books, visited book shops and libraries, and with the importance they attached to reading. The PISA study found that on average across the OECD countries, 46 per cent of boys read only if they had to, compared with 26 per cent of girls. In addition, over half of the boys (58 per cent) compared with a third of girls reported that they only read to get information they needed. In a similar vein, 45 per cent of girls compared with only 25 per cent of boys reported that reading was one of their favourite hobbies. The study also found that, on average across countries, girls were more likely to read fiction whilst boys were more likely to read newspapers, comics, e-mails and web pages than girls (OECD 2001).

Reasons for gender differences

Curriculum and assessment

The introduction of a national curriculum in England, Wales and Northern Ireland and national guidelines in Scotland has meant that girls and boys have had to study the same core subjects. Research (see Murphy and Elwood 1998; Sukhnandan 1999) indicates that girls and boys interact differently with the curriculum content and favour different styles of response, reflecting their reading and writing preferences, and this affects their performance. The evidence suggests that girls' preferred style of response is to write more extensively in a more reflective manner, and boys' preferred style is to write in a more factual manner. Boys and girls also have different tastes in reading, with girls preferring fiction and boys non-fiction (see also OECD 2001). Sukhnandan states: 'Boys generally prefer memorising abstract, unambiguous facts and are often willing to sacrifice deep understanding for correct answers achieved at speed' (1999: 9).

It has been suggested that the introduction in 1988 of the General Certificate of Secondary Education (GCSE) examination, with a written component and a new coursework element (involving extended tasks that are teacher assessed and moderated to ensure comparability of standards), might have had a differential impact on the attainments of girls and boys. Elwood (1995) reported research showing that, in relation to English GCSE, the examinations and coursework emphasised aspects of the subject in which girls have been shown to be more proficient. She commented that large amounts of extended writing 'may be putting boys at a disadvantage but this is compounded by boys' own devaluation of the subject' (1995: 301).

Relations in school

Research reviewed by Sukhnandan (1999) suggests that boys in general feel that they receive less support, encouragement and guidance from teachers; they also feel that teachers have higher expectations of girls. Teachers are also perceived to be more negative towards boys by girls and boys alike, which, it is suggested, can have a negative impact on the attitudes of boys and can contribute to them 'switching off' or 'dropping out'. Research appears to suggest that few teachers acknowledged that they treated girls and boys differently in the classroom (see Sukhnandan 1999).

A number of studies also suggest that amongst boys there is an anti-intellectual, anti-educational and anti-learning culture (see Gallagher 1997; Sukhnandan 1999). On the basis of the research that has been carried out, Sukhnandan puts forward two main explanations for this: first, that boys see few role models of successful men at home and in school; and, second, that 'as part of their gender development, boys tend to take on a desire to be as unfeminine as possible, and an important component of masculinity is the avoidance of what is feminine' (Sukhnandan 1999: 11).

Pupil attitudes and behaviour

A number of research projects have addressed pupils' attitudes and behaviour. Sukhnandan summarises the key findings thus:

> Overall, boys and girls have notably different orientations towards schoolwork and learning which may contribute to gender differences in performance. In general, girls have high aspirations, value presentation and clear expression. They tend to underestimate their own ability and therefore work hard to try and compensate.
>
> (Sukhnandan 1999: 11)

Even among very young children attitudinal differences are apparent. A study by West *et al.* (1997) examined the attitudes of children aged 6 to 7 years (Year 2) towards the national curriculum and their findings provide added support to the view that girls have more positive attitudes towards school. They found that more girls than boys enjoyed reading to themselves, reading to an adult, practising handwriting, working with shapes, and colouring or painting. In relation to school more generally, more girls were positive about 'coming to school'. The authors argued that on a priori grounds it is not unreasonable to suppose that motivation to learn will be higher if overall attitudes towards a particular part of the curriculum are positive. There is also a link between attitudes and academic outcomes: Mortimore *et al.* (1988) found a weak positive relationship between liking a subject and achieving in it.

Gallagher (1997) notes that one common theme to emerge to account for the underperformance of boys was 'a greater likelihood for peer-group pressure among boys to privilege values other than academic ones' (1997: 34). He also noted on the basis of his review of research:

> By contrast, an equally striking theme ... highlights the importance of positive aspirations or perceptions of school as promoting higher educational achievement: this factor operates usually, but not exclusively, to the advantage of girls in that they tend to have more positive attitudes to school than boys.
>
> (Gallagher 1997: 35)

It is also noteworthy that some psychological studies have found gender differences in relation to pupils' psychosocial development. A study by Mantzicopoulos and Oh-Hwang included an exploration of psychosocial maturity. This was conceptualised in terms of the pupil's work orientation, self-reliance and identity; 'work orientation' related to the pupil's 'capacity to experience pleasure in work and in the successful completion of tasks' (1998: 198); 'self-reliance' assessed the pupil's independence in taking decisions, sense of control over life and the ability to take initiative; and 'self-identity' assessed the pupil's self-concept, values and concerns over goals in life. The study found that American girls described themselves as being more mature in terms of 'work orientation' than American boys; this the authors noted was in line with a number of other studies, which reported that psychosocial development is more advanced among girls than boys. The researchers noted that their findings are consistent with the 'supposition that the psychosocial development of females is affected by cultural pressures and expectations' (Mantzicopoulos and Oh-Hwang 1998: 204).

Single-sex and mixed schooling

There has been an ongoing debate about the relative merits of single-sex and mixed schooling. Daly (1996) reports on the relative impact of single-sex and mixed secondary schooling on girls' performance. The study was carried out in Northern Ireland with its many state-supported single-sex schools. This built on earlier research by Steedman (1985), who examined this issue by means of a longitudinal study controlling for prior pupil performance and family background. Her study found little support for the advantageous impact of single-sex schooling on achievement in public examinations at the end of compulsory schooling. Research carried out in the late 1980s by the former Inner London Education Authority (ILEA) found that achievement differences for girls were not significantly related to single-sex/mixed school differences once account had been taken of intake differences (ILEA 1990). Daly (1996) also notes that other studies tended to confirm the view that differences that have been found are largely due to differences in the characteristics of the school intake.

In his own study, Daly (1996) examined differences in the performance of girls in single-sex/mixed schools and his findings were broadly in line with those of Steedman's (1985) study. Other research generally supports this finding (see Sukhnandan *et al.* 2000), although analyses carried out by the DfES (2002c) have found that, on average, during Key Stages 3 and 4, girls in non-selective single-sex schools made more progress than girls in non-selective mixed schools. There was little difference between boys in single-sex and mixed schools.

Non-school factors

It has been argued by commentators that the differences in attainment between girls and boys are related to biological factors, socialisation differences and social change. In relation to biological factors some have suggested that genetic differences can account for the differences in attainment as girls mature more rapidly than boys, and that this makes girls more receptive to learning at a younger age than boys (for a discussion see Sukhnandan 1999). Whatever the merits of this approach in understanding educational achievement, as neither educational policy nor practice can influence biological differences, the issue is not addressed further here.

The socialisation of girls and boys may well be an important factor and this is likely to be reflected in their subsequent and contrasting attitudes towards education. Epstein *et al.* (1998) describe various studies that illustrate the different perspectives of boys and girls. One of these portrays boys as having a fatalistic approach to education, seeing success in particular subjects as being due to natural ability over which they had little or no control; girls, however, tended to give more weight to working hard, so recognising the potential for self-improvement. In another study, school staff felt that boys were concerned to cultivate an image of 'disengagement' with the educational process as it was not seen as being acceptable to appear committed to their studies (Epstein *et al.* 1998).

Social change is also likely to have played an important role in the achievement of girls – including the impact of equal opportunities in the 1980s (Gallagher 1997), the introduction of the national curriculum and the labour market changes.

Strategies for addressing gender differences

A range of strategies has been proposed by commentators to help schools to address gender differences in achievement. Four key strategies have been identified (Sukhnandan *et al.* 2000):

- changing teaching methods and implementing different forms of classroom organisation, for example to engage pupils' interests and work with their strengths;
- improving teacher–pupil relations through raising staff awareness;

- addressing the negative impact of school subcultures and negative attitudes towards school and learning, for example by encouraging a more mature attitude to work;
- introducing mentoring and role modelling to address ideological changes to men's position and role in society.

However, Sukhnandan (1999) noted that there has been little research on what strategies schools are actually adopting, why schools are adopting particular strategies, how different strategies are being implemented and the extent to which different strategies are addressing gender differences in achievement.

She presents findings from a survey of all LEAs in England and Wales (which achieved a response rate of 55 per cent), which found that over eight out of ten LEAs stated that they were aware of strategies to address gender differences in achievement being in place at LEA and/or school level. The strategies were varied, but those that were most commonly reported were staff training (mentioned by 63 per cent), policy development (54 per cent), target setting (49 per cent), role modelling/mentoring (48 per cent), new teaching methods (45 per cent), single-sex classes or grouping (40 per cent), new forms of class organisation (35 per cent) and parental involvement (33 per cent).

Strategies that were most frequently adopted at LEA level focused on whole school initiatives (policy development, staff training, target setting and new teaching methods). On the other hand, strategies most frequently adopted at school level tended, unsurprisingly, to focus on classroom organisation practices and teaching methods; the most popular strategies were single-sex classes/groups, role modelling/mentoring, new forms of class organisation and new teaching methods. Most of the strategies had only been implemented just prior to the survey in 1997/98.

Primary and secondary schools varied in terms of the strategies reported – in primary schools, new teaching methods and parental involvement were most frequently mentioned, whilst in secondary schools role modelling/mentoring, staff training and single-sex grouping were most frequently mentioned. The majority of strategies (55 per cent) were reported to target both boys and girls. Of these, those most frequently in use were reported to be policy development, target setting and staff training.

Sukhnandan et al. (2000) carried out case studies of nineteen schools in order to describe both the implementation and efficacy of strategies that schools had adopted to address gender differences in achievement. Of these schools sixteen were secondary, and these are our focus in this section. Half of these schools had introduced single-sex classes and half mentoring programmes.

Sukhnandan *et al.* (2000) presented detailed information arising from case studies of eight schools that had introduced single-sex grouping and noted that teachers changed their approach to teaching all-male classes by modifying the structure of lessons, teaching methods and curriculum materials. However, few schools had quantitative evidence to support using single-sex classes. Those that did found that single-sex schools were having a positive effect on pupil achievement. The findings from qualitative forms of evaluation appeared to support this finding. Although these preliminary assessments suggested that single-sex classes were having a positive effect on pupil achievement, they also showed that they were not always helping to reduce the gender gap as girls were benefiting as much as boys from single-sex classes. Sukhnandan *et al.* (2000) highlighted factors that staff felt were important for ensuring that single-sex classes were implemented effectively and efficiently. These are given in Figure 3.5.

Sukhnandan *et al.* (2000) also provided case studies of eight schools that had introduced mentoring programmes to address the gender gap:

> Evaluations of the programmes revealed that mentoring appeared to be working in terms of enabling pupils to fulfil their potential, which helped to address gender gaps in performance. However, in roughly half the case study schools, staff did not feel confident about assessing the impact of their mentoring programmes because they had not been in place for a long enough period, had recently been modified, or because of difficulties associated with evaluating them.
>
> (Sukhnandan *et al.* 2000: 65)

Figure 3.6 highlights the main factors that staff and pupils considered essential for the effective implementation of mentoring programmes.

- A school ethos that encourages experimentation with different strategies, enabling staff to modify and expand their approaches.
- Staff who are not only capable of implementing the strategy but who support the theory behind single-sex classes and are therefore willing to modify their teaching approaches accordingly.
- The allocation of members of staff to the all-boy (specifically) and all-girl classes who will be able to build up the rapport needed to ensure that single-sex classes are productive.
- Presenting the strategy positively to pupils.

Figure 3.5 Key factors that make single-sex classes work.

Source: Sukhnandan 2000: 39.

Conclusions

This chapter charts how concern over the performance of girls and boys has shifted over the past thirty years. In the 1970s there was concern about the under-representation of girls in certain subjects that had previously been considered more appropriate to boys. A

- Presenting the strategy positively to the pupils so that they do not feel stigmatised and appreciate its potential benefits.
- Pupils have to want to take part in the programme so that they are both committed and motivated.
- Mentors and pupils must have a strong relationship built on trust and a good rapport.
- Mentors need to be committed, enthusiastic and supportive towards the concept of mentoring for it to work to full effect.
- Mentors are given appropriate training and support so that they can appreciate the aims and objectives of their school's mentoring programme and therefore run the programme effectively.
- Programmes are carefully organised, co-ordinated and resourced, and efforts are made to enable them to become embedded within the culture of the school, in order for mentoring to have maximum impact across all curriculum areas.
- Programmes are carefully monitored and evaluated so they can be modified annually in relation to the differing needs of the pupils being targeted.

Figure 3.6 Key factors that make mentoring programmes work.

Source: Sukhnandan *et al.* 2000: 66.

range of initiatives were introduced to provide more opportunities for girls and to make certain subjects more 'girl friendly'.

More recently, concern has focused on an apparently new phenomenon, the underachievement of boys. However, we have argued that this is not a new phenomenon – but was largely concealed from public debate. The evidence we report indicates that differences in cognitive ability and achievement can be identified before formal schooling.

The research reviewed reveals that girls are generally performing at a higher level than boys throughout the school system. At the primary stage the findings differ somewhat depending on whether the data are national or from individual local authorities. Although the findings are not altogether consistent, it is probably reasonable to say that girls' performance is superior for English. The differences are much less obvious for mathematics and science.

At the end of compulsory education, analyses of GCSE results show superior performance of girls, with the absolute gender gap having increased over time. At GCE A level the absolute and proportional gaps in achievement have increased over time. A range of hypotheses has been put forward for the higher relative achievement of girls than boys, including earlier maturation, different modes of assessment, and so on. Another highly plausible reason is that girls now expect to enter the labour market. Related to this may be a realisation that they are likely to encounter discrimination in the labour market once they leave school and one way of countering this is for them to maximise their achievement levels at school to try to improve their position relative to boys.

A number of proposals have been put forward to address the so-called 'underachievement' of boys. However, the research evidence about successful ways of tackling this issue in schools is limited. Nevertheless, a number of recommendations have been made to address this issue, based on inspection evidence and views of teachers and pupils. Indeed, one of our case-study schools (see Chapter 9), in seeking to improve overall achievement, reported a number of these in order to promote a positive school ethos – these included detailed attainment data on each pupil from Key Stage 2, monitoring, target-setting and celebrating success – together with a range of other strategies including voluntary mentoring by staff of students, a COMPACT scheme using outside mentors from business and two-day residential courses.

In Chapter 10 we return to the issue of the achievement of girls and boys, in particular the need to monitor their attainment regularly and to monitor the impact of any new policies that are introduced, such as single-sex teaching.

Chapter 4

Ethnic background and achievement

Introduction

Over the years, there has been considerable interest in the issue of underachievement of children from different minority ethnic groups and in this chapter we focus specifically on the relationship between achievement and ethnicity and how these differences may be explained. Although in the past lack of data has been a major handicap in examining this area, in recent years more data have become available as a result of a number of research studies and this has shed more light on the possible reasons for these differences. However, there are still limitations in terms of both the quantity and quality of the data available in this important area of study. These issues are discussed in this chapter, together with various proposals that have been made for addressing differences in attainment between different ethnic groups.

The 2001 Census recorded 92.1 per cent of the population of the United Kingdom as being White, with 7.9 per cent belonging to minority ethnic groups (National Statistics 2003). The latter live predominantly in large urban areas of the country; 45 per cent live in the London region and altogether over 80 per cent live in the combined areas of London, the West Midlands, the South East, the North West, Yorkshire and the Humber. The main minority ethnic groups in Great Britain are: Indian, Pakistani, Mixed ethnic groups, Black Caribbean, Black African and Bangladeshi (National Statistics 2003).

In all, ethnic minorities make up 7.9 per cent of the population of the United Kingdom, but they have a younger age structure than the white population; because of the age structure of the ethnic-minority population a far higher percentage of ethnic minority children are in the school-age population (Pathak 2000). Thus, children from ethnic minorities represented around 12 per cent of pupils in state schools in 1999. It is also of interest to note that around 8 per cent of pupils had English as an additional language (DfEE 1999b).

Troyna (1991) noted that 'Of the various issues which have informed the debate about racial matters in education, concern about the "underachievement" of ethnic minority pupils has been pre-eminent' (p. 361). And as Modood notes, one of 'the main stimuli to research on the educational attainment of non-white ethnic minority groups was the concern in the 1970s that children from these groups were "underachieving" in schools' (1998: 24).

The debate about the achievement of ethnic-minority pupils has a long history (see, for example, Modood 1998). In 1979 the Rampton Committee was set up to investigate the education of children from different ethnic minority groups. The Committee commissioned research for its interim report about the achievement of West Indian children, which revealed that they were underachieving compared with White and Asian children. A key reason put forward for this finding was unintentional racism, together with a variety of other reasons such as curricula and teaching materials and the negative effects of discrimination in the labour market, which acted to discourage young people of West Indian origin (Rampton 1981; see also Mackinnon and Statham 1999). In 1985, the Committee, whose chairman had by this time been replaced by Lord Swann, produced its final report, the Swann Report. Research confirmed the earlier findings about the underachievement of West Indian pupils. As noted by Mackinnon and Statham:

> The committee remained convinced that largely unintentional racism was an important factor behind West Indian under-achievement, a claim not undermined by the high achievement of Asians, since stereotyped views of them were generally much less negative, and racism might have different effects on different groups. Of other possible causes of these disparities in achievement, IQ differences were considered at length, but not found to be a significant factor. Differences in socio-economic conditions, however, were found to provide a

partial explanation for the relatively low attainment not only of West Indian but probably also of Bangladeshi children.

(1999: 39)

Pathak made a similar point about socio-economic background, noting:

> Indians in Britain have a higher social profile than the Bangladeshi population (which suffers from severe economic disadvantage . . .) and Indians outperform Bangladeshi pupils.
>
> (2000: 5)

The concept of underachievement in the debate about ethnic minority pupils has thus centred on the allegedly lower performance of certain ethnic groups compared with others.

In the following sections, we examine recent research evidence with a particular focus on the situation in England. At this stage it is important to stress that unlike information on gender, for example, data relating to ethnic background are not readily available at a national level although some data for England and Wales are available. For Scotland the situation is worse, as noted by Powney *et al.*:

> The Scottish research contribution . . . appears to be at best fairly minimal reflecting individual interest in particular themes rather than being systematic and cumulative development of a body of research related to the educational attainment of minority ethnic groups.
>
> (1998: 46)

The following sections examine ethnicity and achievement, drawing on evidence from national statistics and from academic research studies; the relationship between English-language proficiency and achievement, before highlighting some international research findings of particular interest. The next sections examine factors that might account for the differences observed and strategies that might assist in raising the achievement of children from underachieving minority ethnic groups, whilst the final section provides an overall summary and presents conclusions.

It is important to stress that, although some national survey data are available on the achievements of young people from different ethnic groups (for example from the YCS), there are no national data on individual pupils' ethnic background.[1] Much of the research reported here therefore focuses on individual research studies, often restricted to individual LEAs. As we shall see, these data limitations mean we do not know as much as we might about the achievement levels of children and young people from different ethnic groups and how ethnic background interacts with gender and social class.

Ethnicity and achievement

Achievement of pre-school children

Some recent research has examined the achievement of pupils in pre-school and in primary school settings. The initial part of the Effective Provision of Pre-school Education project (Sammons *et al.* 1999) involved an examination of the associations between a range of personal, family and home environment characteristics and the cognitive attainment of children aged around 3 years at entry to pre-school. The sample used was designed to cover the range of pre-school provision in urban, suburban and rural areas, but was not nationally representative. However, it covered a range of different ethnic and social groups. Sammons and her colleagues found that there were differences between children from different ethnic backgrounds in terms of overall cognitive attainments at this stage. Children of White UK heritage had the highest mean score with the lowest being recorded for Pakistani followed by Black African children. However, after controlling for other factors such as child characteristics (for example, age, gender, family size), mother's education and father's employment status and occupation, ethnic differences in attainment were much reduced, although on average children of Black African, Pakistani and Mixed heritage showed significantly lower total baseline scores than White children. The researchers also noted that the ethnic differences in *non-verbal* cognitive attainment were not statistically significant after controlling for other background factors.

A study by Strand (1999a) explored the associations between ethnic group, sex, economic disadvantage and baseline assessment at age 4 for a sample of over 5,000 pupils in an inner London LEA. He found marked differences in pupil attainment associated with ethnic group, having controlled for a variety of other factors also related to attainment (for example, pupils' age, gender, known eligibility for free school meals). In short, he found that the baseline attainment of the African, Caribbean, Black Other,

Indian and Pakistani groups was significantly lower than that of the English, Scottish, Welsh and Northern Irish groups.

Achievement in primary school

In this section, we report in the first instance on the research carried out by Mortimore *et al.* (1988). This was carried out over ten years ago but the findings are particularly important as they address differences between ethnic groups – particularly different Asian groups – during the junior school phase. The research study, with its sample of around 2,000 pupils in fifty inner London junior schools, examined pupils' attainment when they began junior school (at the age of 7 years) and their progress in each of the following three years. The research team examined the effects of a wide range of background factors on pupils' attainment and progress, in addition to ethnic background.

In terms of reading *attainment*, they found that on entry to junior school, and in later years, ethnic background was a highly significant factor in relation to achievement. Even when account had been taken of fluency in English and other background factors, some Asian groups performed differently from other Asian groups. Thus, overall Gujarati speakers obtained above average scores in the reading test and Punjabi speakers below average scores. Children of Caribbean, Greek and Turkish family backgrounds obtained lower reading scores than those from English, Scottish, Welsh or Irish backgrounds. Although the numbers were very small, children from Chinese backgrounds had higher scores than those from other ethnic backgrounds having controlled for other factors. For mathematics attainment at entry to junior school, statistically significant associations with ethnic background were found, with different sub-groups of Asian pupils again performing better than others. It was also found that Bengali speakers tended to gain lower scores than Gujarati speakers. Children from Caribbean and Turkish backgrounds also tended to achieve lower scores.

Turning to *progress*, Mortimore *et al.* (1988) found that the child's ethnic background had a statistically significant association with progress in reading over a three-year period. Children from Caribbean and Asian backgrounds made poorer progress than others after taking account of initial attainment. The gap in attainment in mathematics remained throughout the junior-school years for children of different ethnic backgrounds. However, having controlled for initial attainment, neither Caribbean nor Asian children made significantly poorer *progress* than other children, indicating that differences in performance in this subject area did not increase over the junior school years.

More recent studies also in London have explored the attainment and progress of children from different ethnic groups at the end of Key Stages 1 and 2. Strand (1999a) examined associations between ethnic group, sex, economic disadvantage and pupils' attainment. The research involved over 5,000 pupils in the London Borough of Wandsworth between 'baseline' assessment at age 4 and national end of Key Stage tests at age 7. Strand found marked differences in pupil attainment associated with ethnic group at the end of Key Stage 1, with African, Caribbean and Black Other groups all having lower attainment than the English, Welsh, Scottish and Northern Irish group at this stage. In general, it was found that the differences between ethnic groups tended to increase over time and, in particular, children from Caribbean backgrounds made less progress than those from English, Welsh, Scottish and Northern Irish backgrounds. On the other hand, Indian, Bangladeshi and Chinese pupils were found to start with lower 'baseline' attainment than those from English, Scottish, Welsh and Northern Irish backgrounds, but caught up with the latter by the end of Key Stage 1; Pakistani pupils, however, did not.

Strand (1999a) also examined interactions between ethnic background and disadvantage as measured using known free school meals eligibility. English, Scottish, Welsh and Northern Irish girls who were not eligible for free school meals were the highest attaining group in terms of Key Stage 1 results overall at the age of 7; boys from this group who were not eligible for free school meals were the highest attaining group of boys at this stage. However, English, Scottish, Welsh and Northern Irish boys and girls who were known to be eligible for free school meals were amongst the lowest attaining groups at the end of Key Stage 1 and also made less progress than expected.

The differences found in Wandsworth in relation to pupils from African Caribbean backgrounds have not been found in either Birmingham (see Gillborn and Gipps 1996) or in the London Borough of Southwark (Mujtaba and Sammons 1999). This may be a result of the socio-economic characteristics of different ethnic groups in different parts of the country. These variations between local authorities make it very difficult to generalise to the country as a whole. However, Pathak notes that the evidence suggests that 'on average Black pupils, and Caribbean boys in particular, perform less well than White pupils in early schooling and make least progress through school' (2000: 4). It is noteworthy that low attainment among Bangladeshi and Pakistani pupils has also been identified in local education authority analyses.

Achievement at the end of compulsory school

Most pupils in England, Wales and Northern Ireland sit public examinations, known as the General Certificate of Secondary Education (GCSE), at age 16, the final year of compulsory education (see Appendix A). Data on the achievements of young people of this age in England and Wales are available from the Youth Cohort Study (YCS) (see Appendix C). The data (DfES 2001b) reveal that overall there has been an increase in the percentage of young people gaining five or more high grades (A* to C) in GCSE examinations (including GNVQ equivalents). This rise is apparent for young people from all ethnic groups, as shown in Table 4.1 and Figure 4.1.

Table 4.1 Attainment of five or more GCSE grades A* to C in Year 11 1992–2000 by ethnic background (2000)

Ethnic origin	1992 (%)	1994 (%)	1996 (%)	1998[a] (%)	2000[a] (%)	Difference 1992–2000
Other Asian[b]	46	50	61	61	72	+26
Indian	38	45	48	54	60	+22
Black	23	21	23	29	39	+16
Bangladeshi	14	20	25	33	29	+15
White	37	43	45	47	50	+13
Pakistani	26	24	23	29	29	+3
Other ethnic group	–[c]	37	46	47	43	N/A
Not stated	18	16	29	27	26	N/R
All	37	42	44	46	49	+12

Source: DfES 2001b, Youth Cohort Study (year refers to year of survey).

Notes
a Includes GNVQ qualifications gained in Year 11.
b Not Bangladeshi, Indian or Pakistani.
c Represents a cell size less than 5 or an insufficient base.

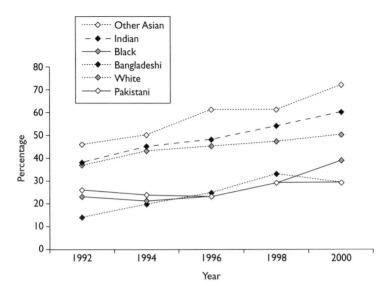

Figure 4.1 Attainment of five or more GCSE grades A* to C in Year 11 1992–2000 by ethnic background (2000).

Source: DfES 2001b, Youth Cohort Study.

Note
For notes see Table 4.1.

As can be seen, there were marked differences between the ethnic groups; the Other Asian group had the highest percentage of young people with five or more high grade GCSEs at the end of Year 11, followed by Indian and White groups. The ethnic groups with the lowest percentages were the Bangladeshi and Pakistani groups.

The increases (and proportionate changes) were greater for all the minority ethnic groups than for the White group, with the exception of the Pakistani group. These differences indicate that achievement levels are not increasing as fast for this group as they are for others – indeed the gap has widened.

If we look at the YCS data in more detail using the 2000 survey data (see Appendix C) we can see that ethnic background was also related to the number of GCSEs achieved at the end of Year 11 (in 1999).

It is clear from Table 4.2 that more students from Other Asian,

Table 4.2 Young people's attainment of different numbers of GCSEs[a] at the end of Year 11 by ethnic background (2000)

Ethnic origin	5+ GCSEs A*–C (%)	1–4 GCSEs A*–C[b] (%)	5+ GCSEs D–G (%)	1–4 GCSEs D–G (%)	None reported (%)
Other Asian[c]	72	15	8	–[d]	4
Indian	60	23	13	–	–
White	50	25	17	3	4
Other ethnic group	43	32	15	–	9
Black	39	30	20	7	5
Pakistani	29	32	31	3	4
Bangladeshi	29	41	19	–	5
Not stated	26	22	21	8	23
All	49	26	18	3	5

Source: DfES 2001b, Youth Cohort Study.

Notes
a Includes GNVQ qualifications gained in Year 11.
b Those with 1–4 GCSE grades A* to C and any number of other grades.
c Not Bangladeshi, Indian or Pakistani.
d Represents a cell size less than 5 or an insufficient base.

Indian, White and the Other ethnic group achieved high-grade GCSEs than those from other ethnic groups, whilst in general more Pakistani, Bangladeshi and Black students gained fewer or lower-grade GCSEs.

Further analyses of YCS data for 2000 (DfES 2002n) reveal that more females than males achieved five or more high grade GCSEs in each ethnic group: 55 per cent of White females versus 45 per cent of White males reached this level; 46 per cent of Black females versus 31 per cent of Black males; 66 per cent of Indian females versus 54 per cent of Indian males; and 34 per cent of Pakistani females versus 25 per cent of Pakistani males.[2]

Not only are there gender differences, there are also differences between socio-economic groups. Analyses (DfES 2002n) reveal that on average young people from non-manual backgrounds achieved higher levels of attainment than other pupils of the same ethnic origin but from manual backgrounds. This held true across ethnic groups – White, Black, Indian, Pakistani/Bangladeshi and Chinese/Other Asian.[3]

Table 4.3 Young people's main activity at age 16 by ethnic background (2000)

Ethnic origin	Full-time education (%)	Government-supported training (%)	Full-time job (%)	Part-time job (%)	Out of work (%)	Something else/ not stated (%)
Asian	86	5	2	1	3	3
Black	84	4	3	—[a]	7	2
White	70	11	9	3	5	2
All	71	10	8	2	5	3

Source: DfES 2001b, Youth Cohort Study.

Note

a Represents a cell size less than 5 or an insufficient base.

Whilst our discussion so far has related to attainment at the end of compulsory schooling, the YCS (DfES 2001b) also enables us to examine young people's main activity at 16. Table 4.3 presents this information by ethnic background. Young people have been classified as being in full-time education, government-supported training, in employment or out of work. The data from the YCS only enable this information to be provided for young people classified as White, Black or Asian but, as can be seen, more young people classified as Black or Asian were in full-time education than those classified as White, with more White young people being in government-supported training or in employment.

Payne (2000) found that this tendency for more young people from a minority ethnic background to remain in full-time education than their White counterparts also held good for low achievers.

Looking solely at those in full-time education (see Table 4.4 and Figure 4.2), we can see that more young people from all minority ethnic backgrounds were in full-time education than those classified as White.

English language and achievement

So far our focus has been on ethnic background and we have seen that this is an important predictor of achievement. Another factor that is related to ethnic background is English fluency. For students to have access to the curriculum it is clear that they need to

Table 4.4 Full-time education by ethnic group at age 16 (2000)

Ethnic group	% in full-time education
Indian	92
Other Asian[a]	90
Black	84
Bangladeshi	81
Pakistani	81
Other ethnic group	81
White	70
Not stated	62
All	71

Source: DfES 2001b, Youth Cohort Study.

Note
a   Not Bangladeshi, Indian or Pakistani.

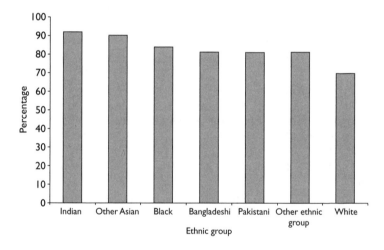

Figure 4.2 Percentage of young people in full-time education at age 16 by ethnic group (2000).

Source: DfES 2001b, Youth Cohort Study.

Note
For notes see Table 4.4.

be fluent in the language of instruction; some students have English as an additional language, and of these, some will be fluent speakers of English whilst others will not be.

In the academic year 1996/7 there were just over half a million pupils with English as an additional language in maintained schools in England. This was approximately 7.5 per cent of all pupils of compulsory school age and above (DfEE 1999c). Over half of the pupils with English as an additional language were located in twenty LEAs – and over one-third of all such pupils were in ten LEAs. Schools in London taught almost half of all pupils in England with English as an additional language. Around one-third of all pupils in inner London and almost one-quarter of pupils in outer London had English as an additional language. In certain LEAs, the concentration of pupils with English as an additional language was very high, with around half of all pupils in schools in Tower Hamlets, Westminster, Brent, Newham and Hackney having English as an additional language. Outside London, between one-quarter and one-third of pupils were recorded as having English as an additional language in Leicester, Birmingham, Bradford and Luton (DfEE 1999c). Whilst there is a heavy concentration of pupils with English as an additional language in some parts of the country, in more than 45 per cent of primary schools and around 20 per cent of secondary schools there were no pupils recorded as having English as an additional language. In terms of achievement, it was found that at school level, the factor showing the highest correlation with attainment at the ages of 7 (Key Stage 1), 11 (Key Stage 2) and 16 (GCSE results) was the percentage of pupils known to be eligible for free school meals; the correlations with the proportions of pupils from different ethnic backgrounds and with English as an additional language were much lower. However, there was a strong association between the percentage of pupils with English as an additional language and the proportion known to be eligible for free school meals. Unsurprisingly, it was also found that there was an association between higher proportions of pupils from ethnic minority backgrounds and higher levels of pupils with English as an additional language.

A number of individual research studies have explored the relationship between English fluency and pupils' attainment and progress. Strand (1999b) reported on the 'baseline' results of a sample of over 11,000 4 year olds collected over a five-year period in one London LEA. He examined the results whilst at the same time controlling for age, gender, the amount of nursery education, known eligibility for free school meals, home language and ethnic background. The results indicated that pupils who spoke English as an additional language scored significantly lower than those who spoke English as their first language. However, this group of pupils made rapid progress and had caught up with their monolingual peers by the end of Key Stage 1.

Mujtaba and Sammons (1999) in their study of attainment in primary schools in an inner London LEA found that at Key Stage 1, children who were not fully fluent in English generally performed less well than pupils who spoke English only. However, children from minority ethnic groups who were fully fluent in English outperformed English-only speakers in each subject.

Turning to the junior school years, Mortimore *et al.* (1988), in their research in inner London junior schools, found that on entry to junior school (and indeed in the following two years), children's fluency in English was a highly significant factor in terms of reading *attainment*. Children whose teachers reported that they were not fully fluent in English obtained lower reading scores than those who were fully fluent. For mathematics attainment at entry to junior school, they also found statistically significant relationships with fluency in English. The gap in attainment in mathematics remained marked throughout the junior school years for children with different levels of English fluency. Similar findings have been reported more recently by Sammons *et al.* (1997a), who found that of the background factors that they analysed, the largest effect on total Key Stage 1 score related to lack of fluency in English. Lack of fluency in English was also a statistically significant predictor of performance in each subject area (English, mathematics and science).

Turning to *progress*, Mortimore *et al.* (1988) found that language fluency had a statistically significant impact on pupils' progress in reading; those who were not fluent in English at entry to junior school made poorer progress in reading although, interestingly, there was no evidence that progress in mathematics was affected.

To sum up, English fluency is an important predictor of attainment. This should come as no surprise given that access to the national curriculum is hindered if children are not fluent speakers of English.

International evidence on ethnic background and language fluency and achievement

Evidence of differential achievement for students from different ethnic backgrounds is not limited to the UK. In the USA, an ongoing representative sample survey of student achievement, the National Assessment of Educational Progress (NAEP) is carried out covering core subject areas. In 2000, a national assessment of mathematics was undertaken involving fourth-, eighth- and twelfth-grade students (typical ages 9, 13 and 17 years) (Braswell et al. 2001). In all three grades, average scores of White students were higher than those of Black, Hispanic and American Indian students. At grade 12, the average score of Asian/Pacific Islander students was higher than the scores of White, Black and Hispanic students. The score gaps between White and Black students, and between White and Hispanic students, were large at every grade. The national assessment found that there was no evidence of any narrowing of the racial/ethnic-group score gaps since 1990.

For reading (Donahue et al. 2001), White and Asian/Pacific Islander students outperformed their Black, Hispanic and American Indian peers. Interestingly, in contrast to the findings for mathematics, the average score of Black students was significantly higher compared with 1994. The percentages of White and Asian/Pacific Islander students at or above the 'proficient' level exceeded that of other racial/ethnic groups.

In terms of language fluency, there is international evidence relating to the language spoken at home and achievement levels from the Programme for International Student Assessment (PISA), which covered the domains of reading literacy, mathematical literacy and scientific literacy (see Appendix B).

Students who participated in the assessment also completed a questionnaire, which asked, amongst other questions, what language they spoke at home 'most of the time'. The study found that in most countries students who spoke the language in which the assessment took place, scored more highly than those who spoke a different language at home from that of the assessment. In the UK, students who did not speak the language of assessment or other national language were nearly twice as likely to be among the 25 per cent lowest performers in reading literacy than those who spoke the language of assessment most of the time (OECD 2001).

What might account for the differences?

The key question that needs to be answered is what might account for the differences in attainment between pupils from different ethnic groups? One factor has already been examined, namely whether or not English is an additional language and/or whether the child is a fluent speaker of English, and this does appear to be significant.

Research has shown (see Pathak 2000) that differences in achievement of pupils from different ethnic groups are likely to be influenced by a *combination* of factors such as his or her cultural background, social class, neighbourhood, peer and teacher influence and school effectiveness. Data limitations mean that it is not possible to draw definitive conclusions about the relative importance of such factors on the attainment of pupils from different ethnic groups and the complexity of the interaction between different factors in any case makes such analysis very difficult. Lack of fluency in English is likely to partly explain the underachievement of at least some ethnic groups such as Bangladeshi and Pakistani pupils. On the other hand, attitudes towards education among pupils and parents from underachieving ethnic groups do not seem to contribute to lower academic performance.

Teachers and pupils from ethnic minority groups

There is considerable evidence that teacher expectations can influence children's academic performance (see Mortimore *et al.* 1988). However, in relation to ethnic background, the research carried out as part of the Junior School Project found no association between teachers' ratings of pupils' ability and children's ethnic background having taken account of other background factors and attainment. The researchers also found that ability ratings were strongly related to attainment and these ratings were lower in reading, writing and mathematics for Caribbean and some Asian pupils than for others:

> This suggests ... that for pupils from all ethnic backgrounds, teacher expectations appear to be tied to specific knowledge of previous attainment and performance in the classroom.
>
> (Mortimore *et al.* 1988: 168)

Gillborn (1998) provides a discussion of qualitative research evidence that sheds light on the achievement of pupils from ethnic-minority groups, particularly those from African-Caribbean backgrounds. As he notes, Black pupils are frequently portrayed as not behaving in the way required by mainstream schools and historically have been more likely to be educated in special schools or units for pupils with special emotional, learning or behavioural problems and to be excluded from school.

He also reports that a number of research studies concerned with the relationship between White teachers and African-Caribbean pupils have been carried out and these highlight the tension and even conflict between White teachers and the students concerned. Gillborn's research revealed that teachers believed that African-Caribbean pupils as a group presented a threat to classroom order and their personal safety:

> They expected trouble from Black students, sometimes perceived a threat where none was intended, and reacted quickly (as they saw it) to prevent further challenges. Consequently, well-intentioned and committed teachers came to recreate familiar patterns of control and conflict with African-Caribbean students.
>
> (Gillborn 1998: 14–15)

Whilst pupils of African-Caribbean heritage are often perceived to be 'loud, aggressive and academically poor' (ibid.: 20), research has demonstrated that boys from a South Asian background are perceived as being of 'high ability and socially conformist' (ibid.).

A number of other factors may result in a greater risk of underachievement, at least in Black Caribbean boys. Two of these are discussed below, namely entry to different examination tiers and permanent exclusion from school.

A further problem is that there are few role models in school for pupils from ethnic minorities due to the lack of ethnic minority teachers. According to the Teacher Training Agency Initial Teacher Training Performance Profiles (reported by Pathak 2000), in 1997/8, only 5 per cent of final year primary teacher trainees were known to be from an ethnic minority, which is much lower than the percentage of ethnic minority pupils in schools.

Examination entry

Gillborn (2002) discusses a hitherto under-researched area, namely that of entry to different tiers of the GCSE examination. Many GCSE examinations have a tiered system with pupils being entered for different papers within the same subject and teachers deciding which examination a pupil will take; these decisions are of utmost importance as they determine the grades that a pupil can obtain as each tier offers only a limited number of grades. The number of tiers is normally two, with pupils being able to gain an A* to D in the higher tier and a C at the most in the lower tier. In mathematics there are three tiers, with the highest attainable grade being a D for the lowest tier. Gillborn and Youdell (2000) showed in their research that Black students are less likely to be entered for the higher tiers compared with White students and suggest that judgements requiring teachers to make decisions about their students' ability and potential, work to the detriment of Black students 'who are generally seen as lacking ability and presenting disciplinary problems' (Gillborn 2002: 12). The policy implications to be drawn that the system of tiering may need to be reviewed are to try and ensure that particular groups of students are not unfairly disadvantaged.

Exclusions and ethnic background

Considerable concern about the exclusion of Black students from school has been expressed over the years and data are now available at a national level that relate to the issue of exclusions and pupils' ethnic background.

Data published by the government (DfES 2001g) reveal marked differences between the exclusion rates for pupils from different ethnic groups. Table 4.5 gives details of the percentage of permanent exclusions of pupils of compulsory school age and above by ethnic group. The exclusion rate for some ethnic groups was much higher than for others. This was the case particularly for pupils classified as Black Caribbean, Black Other and for those in Other (not specified) ethnic groups. The exclusion rate was very low for pupils of Chinese and Indian origin.

Table 4.5 Number of permanent exclusions by ethnic group (1999/2000)

Ethnic group	Number of permanent exclusions	% of permanent exclusions[a]	% of school population[b]
Black Caribbean	455	5.5	0.46
Black Other	218	2.6	0.37
Other ethnic group[c]	289	3.5	0.20
Black African	145	1.7	0.17
White	6,890	82.9	0.12
Bangladeshi	53	0.6	0.08
Pakistani	129	1.6	0.07
Indian	54	0.6	0.03
Chinese	2	0.0	0.01
Ethnicity not known	79	1.0	–
Number	8,314	100.0	0.12

Source: Table derived from DfES 2001g.

Notes

a The number of permanent exclusions of compulsory school age and above expressed as a percentage of the total number of permanent exclusions of compulsory school age and above.

b The number of permanent exclusions of compulsory school age and above expressed as a percentage of the number (headcount) of pupils of compulsory school age and above in each ethnic group, in primary, secondary and special schools (excluding dually registered pupils in special schools) in January 2000.

c Not one of those listed in this table.

What happens after school?

Although this book is concerned with underachievement in schools, it is important to note that young people from minority ethnic groups are more likely to continue with their education post-16 than White young people (see above), as demonstrated by findings from the Youth Cohort Study (DfES 2001b). As Modood notes: 'The knowledge that qualifications are necessary for getting a (desirable) job may well motivate ethnic minorities more than Whites, but it seems to do so positively rather than negatively' (1998: 33).

However, when it comes to entry to higher education, even after taking academic and social class related factors into account, significant ethnic differences in the rates of university admission remain unexplained. In particular, Caribbean and Pakistani applicants have been found to be less likely than other applicants to gain admission to 'old universities' (see Modood 1998). Nevertheless, Modood also notes that ethnic minorities are well represented in higher education today:

> The ethnic minority achievement stands out because of at least three factors. Firstly, it has at least in part bucked the determinants of class: despite their worse parental occupation profile, most minority groups are producing greater proportions of applications and admissions to higher education than the rest of the population. Secondly, most minority groups have had to struggle over the learning of the English language, the acquisition of new cultural reference points and the travails of cultural adaptation and settlement in a new country. Thirdly, all this has had to be achieved in the face of societal racism and, in particular, negative stereotyping, lower expectations and sometimes racial harassment in schools.
>
> (Modood 1998: 37)

Research by Allen (1998) complements the analysis made by Modood. She carried out a research study of full-time ethnic minority students and a sample of White students for comparative purposes. Key findings to emerge are listed below.

- More ethnic minority students than White students said that higher education was highly valued by their family (84 per cent versus 55 per cent).
- More ethnic minority respondents than White respondents (71 per cent versus 36 per cent) reported that their parents/ guardians wanted all their children to go to university.
- More White than ethnic minority respondents rated the influence of parents as important in their decision to enter higher education than the influence of other individuals (relatives, careers advisers, school teachers or friends). However, a higher proportion of ethnic minority than White respondents rated the influence of each of these other individuals as 'very important' or 'important'.
- In terms of why they had decided to take a higher education course, ethnic minority respondents were more likely to say that they had done so because of family pressure or to fulfil family aspirations.

Raising the attainment of pupils from different ethnic groups

Pathak examined the evidence of 'what works' in raising the achievement of pupils from different ethnic groups and noted that research suggests that 'a good school, with strong leadership and tracking systems will benefit all pupils, regardless of ethnic origin' (2000: 5). However, as noted by OFSTED (1999a), few schools were using ethnic monitoring to track attainment and raise standards. It was also noted that targeted approaches under the National Numeracy and Literacy Projects had shown progress among pupils from all ethnic groups – interestingly, though, there were no significant differences in progress between ethnic groups. Indeed, in the case of the National Literacy Project, the greatest progress was made by pupils with very little experience of English (see Pathak 2000).

There is some evidence that mentoring has a positive impact on ethnic minority pupils, but this is anecdotal and cannot be considered to be firm evidence. And while research has shown that study support schemes can benefit pupils from disadvantaged backgrounds, the evidence is not conclusive as the pupils selected to take part may not be representative of the whole school population (see also Chapter 8). Further, summer school literacy programmes have failed to show significant differences in average scores or progress between ethnic groups (see Pathak 2000).

Strategies for improvement

One noteworthy research project has examined the teaching and learning strategies in successful multi-ethnic schools (Blair and Bourne 1998). This study focused on a small sample of schools with over 10 per cent of students from at least one of the following minority ethnic group backgrounds: Bangladeshi, Black Caribbean and Pakistani (additional schools were included to focus on the provision for gypsy traveller and refugee students). The final research report drew on material from a total of nine primary schools and twelve secondary schools, but altogether a total of twenty-nine schools were visited.

Interviews with parents and with students highlighted the range and breadth of concerns held:

There were concerns about racism, about low expectations of minority group children, about stereotyping and lack of respect for parents and for students. African-Caribbean parents and students in particular raised issues about unfair practices of teachers. There were problems of poor communication, lack of understanding and missed opportunities for effective partnership between parents and schools.

(Blair and Bourne 1998: 3)

Effective schools in the study were reported to overcome these problems in a number of ways, as shown in Figure 4.3.

Gillborn and Mirza in their review 'Educational inequality: Mapping race, class and gender' reported that a number of recent studies have attempted to identify school and LEA-based strategies for raising the achievement of pupils from ethnic minority groups. They note that 'certain factors repeatedly emerge as significant' (2000: 27). These are presented in Figure 4.4.

A report produced by OFSTED focused specifically on good practice in secondary schools in relation to the achievement of Black Caribbean pupils. Six schools were visited by inspectors (Her Majesty's Inspectorate or HMI); these schools were identified

---

- A strong and determined lead on equal opportunities was given by the headteacher.
- The schools listened to and learned from students and their parents and tried to see things from the students' point of view.
- They created careful links with local communities.
- They tried to understand and work with the 'whole child'.
- They had clear procedures for responding to racist bullying and racist harassment.
- They worked on strategies for preventing exclusion.
- There were high expectations of both teachers and students and clear systems for targeting, tracking and monitoring of individual student progress.
- Monitoring by ethnicity enabled schools to see whether all groups were achieving equally; to identify unexpected shortcomings in provision and to target specific areas for attention. It also raises wider questions about setting, banding and exclusion processes.

Figure 4.3 Key findings in relation to successful multi-ethnic schools.

Source: Based on Blair and Bourne 1998.

- Strong leadership on equal opportunities and social justice (from the LEA and headteacher in particular).
- Seeking and using pupil and parent perspectives.
- Designing and enacting clear procedures for recording and acting on racist incidents.
- Generating and sustaining an ethos that is open and vigilant, which enables pupils to discuss 'race' issues and share concerns.
- Developing and communicating high expectations accompanied by a clear view that underperformance by any group is unacceptable.
- Reviewing curricular and pastoral approaches to ensure their sensitivity and appropriateness.
- Using ethnic monitoring as a routine and rigorous part of the school's/LEA's self-evaluation and management.

Figure 4.4 Significant factors in raising ethnic minority achievement.

Source: Gillborn and Mirza 2000: 27.

mainly on the basis of relatively good progress being made by Black Caribbean pupils between Key Stage 3 and Key Stage 4. Four of the schools were voluntary-aided.[4] HMI examined how well Black Caribbean pupils were achieving and focused on the curriculum; the quality of teaching and learning; the ways in which the schools monitored pupil performance; support and guidance provided to pupils; and the school's links with parents and the wider community. The report commented on the schools:

> These are popular schools with strong leadership and strong systems. They have a culture of achievement. Central to their work are high expectations and the provision of intensive support so that pupils meet them ... A particular strength of the schools is their communication with parents.
>
> (OFSTED 2002: 29)

The report concludes by presenting a number of recommendations about what schools should do. These are given in Figure 4.5.

- Use data analysed by ethnicity to check the participation and achievement of ethnic groups.
- Gather and debate the views of staff, pupils, parents and the wider community about barriers to achievement and responses to school.
- Focus sharply in response to the Race Relations (Amendment) Act on what can be done through the curriculum, teaching, assessment and guidance to remove barriers to achievement and to reflect ethnic and cultural diversity.
- Set clear objectives and targets for improving participation and achievement based on a comprehensive whole-school plan and use the opportunities represented by mainstream improvement initiatives.
- Provide access for all staff to high-quality training so that the needs of minority pupils can be tackled with confidence.

Figure 4.5 Recommendations made by HMI in relation to the achievement of Black Caribbean pupils.

Source: OFSTED 2002.

Conclusions

The research and data that we have examined in this chapter present a complex picture of the educational performance of different ethnic groups in England. Although the evidence is not clear cut, it is apparent that pupils from certain ethnic groups perform well in tests and examinations, whilst others do not.

A major problem is the limited data that are available on the achievement of young people from different ethnic groups. The key national data set is derived from the Youth Cohort Study surveys. This contrasts with the situation in the United States, where there are ongoing representative surveys, which enable the achievement of pupils of different ages and from different ethnic groups to be compared.

One of the problems we have encountered is having to rely on a wide range of studies, many small scale, which may be specific to the particular populations under investigation. This is particularly likely to be the case with the inner-London studies given the high levels of disadvantage in this part of the country, coupled with the high percentage of children from minority ethnic groups who live in London.

It is not clear what accounts for the differences between different ethnic groups. However, it appears on the basis of available research that there are complex interactions between a range of factors, notably social class, gender, peer and teacher influence, cultural background, neighbourhood and school effectiveness. Among the variety of reasons for the relatively low achievement levels amongst some minority ethnic groups are social deprivation on the one hand and the policies and practices within schools on the other. These are probably the most significant. In addition, lack of fluency in English is likely to explain the underachievement of at least some ethnic groups.

In terms of the strategies that schools can use to raise attainment levels, again the evidence is not at all clear, but there are suggestions that mentoring may be of value. In addition, there appear to be a number of key areas in raising ethnic minority achievement that have been identified by LEAs and OFSTED as important. But clearly more investigation is needed to evaluate the particular approaches that schools have initiated.

More encouragingly there is evidence to suggest that achievement levels of young people from some ethnic groups have improved over time – in terms of both the actual and proportionate increases – but for other groups of pupils there remains considerable cause for concern. In Chapter 8 we shall return to this issue and examine the policy initiatives that have been implemented in recent years and Chapter 10 highlights some of the ways in which government, schools and LEAs could respond in order to try to ensure that young people from different social groups – including those from lower achieving minority groups – maximise their levels of achievement.

Chapter 5

Other factors and achievement

Introduction

Earlier chapters have examined the relationship between educational attainment and three main factors: social class, gender and ethnicity. This chapter considers how a range of other factors may be associated with achievement.

The factors that will be explored include those that can be considered to be pupil-related, such as pupils' age at starting school, pupil mobility and special educational needs. Others, such as truancy and school exclusions, could be characterised as pupil-related or could additionally be related to home or school factors. Finally, a number of other factors are examined that are perhaps more a function of the child's home environment, for example, the area in which the child lives, diet, drug abuse, teenage pregnancy and divorce.

Pupil-related factors

Children's age

A number of research studies have examined the relationship between the age of starting school and educational attainment. The evidence suggests that autumn-born children do better than those born in the summer term. Possible reasons for this include the length of time that the older children have had at school; their age *per se* and the fact that the summer-born children are the youngest in their year group; and 'term of entry' effects – spring and summer entrants may have difficulties as they are part of a small group joining an already established class (West and Varlaam 1990; see also DfES 2001e).

The age difference effect in achievement has been found in the pre-school setting. As part of the Effective Provision of Pre-school Education project, Sammons *et al.* (1999) found that older children had significantly higher cognitive ability scores than others at entry to pre-school; this is perhaps unsurprising given the relationship between cognitive development and maturity.

A larger study by Strand (1999b) of young children on entry to primary school (in one London LEA) is one of the most thorough carried out. It related scores on a baseline assessment with later attainment. The results indicated that age was significantly related to attainment. The amount of early education (nursery school, nursery class or other educational experience – but excluding childminding) was also related to attainment. The study examined the results whilst simultaneously controlling for a range of factors known to be associated with attainment – age, gender, amount of nursery education, eligibility for free school meals, home language and ethnic background.

A further study, which examined the links between children's age and their attainment, was carried out by Mujtaba and Sammons (1999) in one London LEA. They found that at Key Stage 1, older children (born in the autumn term) performed significantly better than children born in either the spring or the summer term. Children born in the summer term had significantly lower results than those born in other terms. At Key Stage 2 they also found that the youngest children in the academic year had poorer attainment levels in all subject areas. The difference in attainment between autumn-born and summer-born children was more marked for science than for other areas. Sammons *et al.* (1997a) found that term of birth was a statistically significant predictor of both overall performance and of each individual subject.

Pupil mobility

The issue of pupil mobility is a relatively new area of interest for researchers and policy makers alike. There is now a greater awareness of the importance of pupil mobility and its impact on pupils' attainment (see Dobson *et al.* 2000).

A number of research studies looking at pupil mobility have been carried out. Mujtaba and Sammons (1999) in their study in an inner London education authority found that the number of full terms that pupils had spent in school was related to attainment in all subject areas at Key Stage 1, suggesting that pupil mobility should be seen as an important factor in contextualising schools' results.

Hackney LEA, which has a high level of pupil mobility, has researched the extent and impact of pupil mobility on pupils' attainment over a number of years. A recent report (London Borough of Hackney 2000) notes that since 1996 clear evidence has been found that 'mobile' pupils tend to attain lower results than 'stable' pupils who have had an uninterrupted education in the same school.

In this research, it was found that the pupil characteristics of newly arrived pupils varied in key ways. In the context of our discussion on achievement, it is notable that these characteristics were eligibility for free school meals, English as an additional language and ethnic background. First, mobile primary school pupils were rather more disadvantaged than pupils on average. Interestingly, in secondary schools, the association between pupil mobility and free school meals eligibility was not consistent. Second, mobile pupils were more likely, in general, to have English as an additional language than pupils who had been at the same school throughout a key stage. And at the GCSE stage, significantly more of the mobile pupils had English as an additional language. Third, when the ethnic background of the mobile pupils was analysed it was found that pupils from certain ethnic groups were more likely to be mobile than others. It was found that African pupils were over-represented amongst new arrivals in Hackney schools. In contrast, pupils from other ethnic groups were less likely to be mobile; this was particularly clear in the case of English/ Scottish/Welsh pupils at all four key stages.

Strand (2002) examined the association between pupil mobility and attainment at the end of Key Stage 1 (when pupils are aged 7 years) in one urban English local education authority. He found that pupil mobility during the early years of schooling was associated with significantly lower levels of attainment in the national Key Stage 1 tests in reading, writing and mathematics. However, mobile pupils were found to be more likely than other pupils to be disadvantaged – they were more likely to be in receipt of free school meals, to have English as an additional language and to require higher levels of support in learning English than pupils who were not mobile. They were also more likely to have more severe special educational needs and to have higher levels of absence. Strand notes that when the relative impact of these factors is taken into account, the effect of mobility, whilst still significant, was reduced considerably. He also reports that when pupils' progress is explored (that is, the progress made since pupils were assessed at entry to school) mobility was only found to have a significant effect on progress in mathematics.

In commenting on his research findings, Strand (2002) notes that there are resource implications in relation to the management of mobility. This is because considerable time needs to be spent on enrolling pupils, assessing them, obtaining past records, organising special educational needs or language support, making links with the child and his or her parents and facilitating the integration of the child with other children. He also reports on examples of good practice identified as a result of a survey of schools with high levels of pupil mobility in the urban local education authority in which the research took place. Examples of 'good practice' are given in Figure 5.1.

Special educational needs and underachievement

National data relating to attainment of young people with a disability or health problem are available from the Youth Cohort Study (YCS) (see Appendix C). The findings of the YCS study carried out in 2000 (DfES 2001b) reveal a far lower percentage of young people with a disability or health problem gaining GCSEs (or equivalent GNVQs) at the end of Year 11. The percentages of

---

- • The active involvement of parents and pupils in producing materials to inform the new teacher of pupil attainments, to identify specific needs and to provide a summary of significant personal and social details.
- • Targeted support for mobile pupils and regular monitoring of their progress after joining the school.
- • Consideration of the implications for effective progression resulting from possible differences in teaching styles, structures, organisation and ethos between past and present school.
- • Avoiding unnecessary repetition of work.

Figure 5.1 Pupil mobility: examples of good practice.

Source: Strand 2002.

young people with and without such problems gaining different numbers of GCSEs are given in Table 5.1.

In short, fewer young people who reported having a disability or health problem achieved five or more GCSEs at grades A* to C compared with those who did not (28 per cent versus 51 per cent). Conversely, more young people with a disability or health problem reported fewer or lower grade GCSEs.

The YCS also enables us to examine young people's main activity at the age of 16. Table 5.2 presents this information for those with and without a disability/health problem. Young people have

Table 5.1 Young people's attainment of different numbers of GCSEs[a] at the end of Year 11 by disability (2000)

Disability	5+ GCSEs A*–C (%)	1–4 GCSEs A*–C[b] (%)	5+ GCSEs D–G (%)	1–4 GCSEs D–G (%)	None reported (%)
Has a disability/health problem	28	32	24	11	5
Does not have a disability/health problem	51	25	17	3	4

Source: DfES 2001b, Youth Cohort Study.

Notes
a Includes GNVQ qualifications gained in Year 11.
b Those with 1–4 GCSE grades A* to C and any number of other grades.

Weighted sample of those with a disability/health problem is 639 and without is 13,763.

Table 5.2 Young people's main activity at age 16 by disability/health problem (2000)

Disability	Full-time education (%)	Government-supported training (%)	Full-time/ part-time job (%)	Out of work (%)	Something else/not stated (%)
Has a disability/health problem	62	15	11	8	4
Does not have a disability/health problem	72	10	10	5	2
All	71	10	10	5	3

Source: DfES 2001b, Youth Cohort Study.

been classified as being in full-time education, government-supported training, in employment or out of work.

This shows that young people reporting a disability or health problem were somewhat less likely to be in full-time education than those without such a problem (62 per cent versus 72 per cent). This may in part be related to the lower achievement levels reported for those with a disability or health problem.

Turning to one specific category in special educational needs, namely deaf children and young people, an interesting review of the literature was commissioned by the DfEE. Its aims were to identify factors that appeared to be associated with differing levels of educational attainment (Powers *et al.* 2000).

The main findings of the review indicated that deaf learners in general lag several years behind their hearing peers in terms of their reading achievement; however, the authors also note that there are reports that some deaf learners reached levels that were commensurate with those of their hearing peers. Interestingly, the research literature suggests that the degree of hearing loss may not be the most important factor in reading achievement. Significantly the report notes:

> Ethnicity, gender and parental support factors appear to be stable predictors of reading achievement. With respect to gender, female deaf learners appear to outperform male deaf learners.
>
> (Powers *et al.* 2000: 3)

Turning to mathematics, the literature review found that deaf learners, in general, fall behind hearing learners in terms of their achievement. The difference, however, appears to be less pronounced for mathematics than for reading. The report notes that:

> School factors including teacher qualifications and effectiveness, in other words 'educationally managed variables', appear to have the greatest effect on mathematics performance.
>
> (Powers *et al.* 2000: 3)

It is significant that socio-economic status, the presence of additional child difficulties and the language used in the home appear to be more stable predictors of examination success than the degree of hearing loss.

Looking at this area more generally it should be noted that

within the education system in England, pupils with a range of difficulties that impact on their learning may be identified and assessed by schools as having special educational needs. A small proportion of these will have 'statements' of special educational needs with additional resources being attached to the statement. In England, 2001, for example, 2.5 per cent of the mainstream secondary-school population had statements of special educational needs compared with 20.7 per cent who had non-statemented special educational needs (DfES 2001c).

West *et al.* (2001) examined the relationship between pupil characteristics and attainment at an LEA level. They found no statistically significant correlation between the proportion of children with or without statements of special educational needs in relation to the proportion reaching the 'expected level' (level 2) at Key Stage 1, the proportion achieving one or more GCSE at grades A* to G, or the proportion achieving five or more GCSEs at grades A* to C. In fact, the proportion of children with statements of special educational need was not related to other indicators of need.

This is likely to be due to differences between local education authorities and schools in terms of the identification and assessment of pupils with special educational needs leading to 'statementing', whereby additional resources are allocated to meet the needs of that pupil. It is of interest to note that the special educational needs indicators do not relate in any consistent way to educational outcomes and it appears likely that success in obtaining a statement may be related to other factors. As stated in a report produced by the Education Standard Spending Assessment Technical Group (consisting of representatives of local authorities and government officials):

> There was no great correlation between 'pure' deprivation factors (unemployment, poor housing etc.,) and children with special educational needs ... [and] there was no correlation between measures of ill-health and special educational needs which might be expected to provide a greater degree of correlation. In some cases, the [special educational needs] indicators were negatively correlated with particular deprivation measures.
>
> (Department of the Environment, Transport and the Regions 1998: 2.1.14)

It was suggested that the willingness or otherwise of parents in different areas to ask schools to identify any special educational needs they may have might be affecting the apparent level of needs in different areas ... A child who might be deemed to have [special educational needs] when compared with other children in a particular school/authority might not always be deemed to have [special educational needs] when compared with other children in a different school/LEA.

(Department of the Environment, Transport and the Regions 1998: 2.1.15)

Children in care

Since the 1980s there has been increasing concern about the educational achievement of many children cared for by local authorities either in foster care or in residential homes. A review of English and Scottish research found that on average 70 per cent of young people leaving care had no qualifications (Borland 1998). More recent data reveal that more than two-thirds of children in England leave care at the age of 16 with no qualifications at all (compared with only 6 per cent of all pupils). In addition, fewer than one in twenty obtained five good GCSE passes; this compared with nearly half of all children (Cabinet Office 2001).

An earlier report by the Social Exclusion Unit (1998a) stated that on the basis of small-scale studies, it has been shown that the permanent exclusion rate for this group of children is ten times higher than the average; and as many as 30 per cent of children in this group could be out of mainstream education through truancy or exclusion. As we shall see in the following section, there are clear associations between both truancy and exclusions and achievement.

Pupil and school-related factors

Truancy

A number of studies have explored truancy. These have tended to focus on different age groups. For example, Mujtaba and Sammons (1999) in their study in an inner London education authority found that poor attendance was related to lower attainment in all subject areas at the end of Key Stage 1.

National data relating to attainment of young people who have truanted from school in Year 11 are available from the Youth Cohort Study (YCS) (see Appendix C). According to the YCS (DfES 2001b), a lower percentage of young people who reported having truanted gained five or more high grade GCSEs (or equivalent GNVQs) at the end of Year 11. The percentages of young people who were classified as 'persistent' truants, 'occasional' truants or not truants and gaining different numbers of GCSEs are given in Table 5.3. Figure 5.2 represents these different levels of achievement graphically.

As can be seen from Table 5.3, far fewer young people who were persistent truants achieved five or more GCSEs at grades A* to C compared to those who did not truant (10 per cent versus 58 per cent). Conversely, far more young people who were persistent truants obtained no GCSEs (21 per cent versus 3 per cent).

The YCS also enables us to examine young people's main activity at age 16. Table 5.4 presents this information classified according to reported truancy. Young people have again been classified as being in full-time education, government-supported training, in employment or out of work.

Table 5.4 shows that far fewer persistent truants remain in full-time education than either occasional truants or those who reported no truancy (26 per cent versus 61 per cent and 79 per

Table 5.3 Young people's attainment of different numbers of GCSEs[a] at the end of Year 11 by truancy from school (2000)

Truancy in Year 11	5+ GCSEs A*–C (%)	1–4 GCSEs A*–C[b] (%)	5+ GCSEs D–G (%)	1–4 GCSEs D–G (%)	None reported (%)
Persistent truancy	10	24	27	18	21
Occasional truancy	38	31	23	4	5
No truancy	58	23	14	2	3

Source: DfES 2001b, Youth Cohort Study.

Notes

a Includes GNVQ qualifications gained in Year 11.

b Those with 1–4 GCSE grades A* to C and any number of other grades.

Weighted sample of persistent truants is 644, occasional truants is 4,751 and non truants is 9,019.

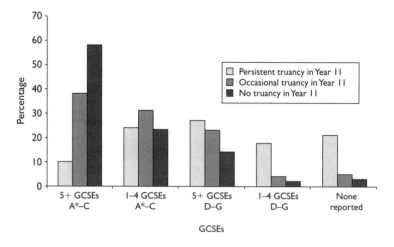

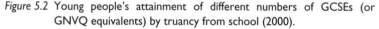

Figure 5.2 Young people's attainment of different numbers of GCSEs (or GNVQ equivalents) by truancy from school (2000).

Source: DfES 2001b, Youth Cohort Study.

Note
For notes see Table 5.3.

Table 5.4 Young people's main activity at age 16 by truancy (2000)

Truancy in Year 11	Full-time education (%)	Government-supported training (%)	Full-time/part-time job (%)	Out of work (%)	Something else/not stated (%)
Persistent truancy	26	13	30	23	7
Occasional truancy	61	12	16	8	3
No truancy	79	9	8	3	2

Source: DfES 2001b, Youth Cohort Study.

cent). Many more persistent truants were in employment (30 per cent versus 16 per cent and 8 per cent). However, nearly a quarter were out of work.

Causes of truancy

In terms of possible reasons for truancy, the research suggests that the rejection of school lessons plays a crucial part in some pupils' decisions to truant from school. A large-scale research project by

O'Keeffe (1994) examined the extent and causes of truancy in English schools in Years 10 and 11. This found that the wish to avoid lessons – as opposed to school rejection more generally – was given by around two-thirds of young people in the sample. Further analyses revealed that there were variations between subjects, with physical education/games and French being notable for their unpopularity (34 per cent and 27 per cent of those truants who studied each subject). This research suggests that there are structural issues that appear to be associated with truancy; to some extent these should be able to be addressed by schools more easily with the increased flexibility of the national curriculum.

The DfES in a recent report also note the possible link between social deprivation, school location and truancy:

> Many schools have groups of pupils who are at risk from circumstances that derive from social deprivation and the locations of schools. This may have an impact on the absence rates at schools.
>
> (DfES 2001f: 5)

Moreover, primary and secondary schools with the highest levels of absence – authorised and unauthorised – were also reported to have the largest percentage known to be eligible for free school meals (an indicator of poverty). These cannot be considered causes of truancy, but the associations are clear, and are reinforced by other research.

In Scotland, Malcolm *et al.* (1996) carried out a study on school attendance and links with attainment in seven secondary schools and seven associated primary schools in two authorities. Information on attendance and attainment in Standard Grade examinations (see Appendix A) was collected. The sample, although small, included both denominational and non-denominational schools and schools of varying sizes in a range of settings and with pupils from different socio-economic backgrounds. Amongst the key findings was that as absence increased, performance at Standard Grade in English and mathematics fell, with mathematics being slightly more affected than English. This finding applied almost equally for boys and girls. The same general pattern applied in all seven secondary schools but, interestingly, the link between attendance and performance varied in strength between schools. It is also noteworthy that 'explained' absence was comparable in its effects on attainment with 'unexplained' absence; if the association between absence and performance is causal – which it is not possible to ascertain on the basis of this research – it would be important for both types of absence to be reduced in order to maximise pupils' examination achievement.

Exclusions

We noted earlier that exclusions are a major risk factor in relation to later problems with a significant minority of young offenders in courts having been excluded from school (DfEE 1999a).

In England in 1999/2000 (DfES 2001g), there were around 1,200 permanent exclusions of pupils from primary schools (a rate of 0.03 per cent), about 6,700 permanent exclusions from secondary schools in England (0.21 per cent) and 384 from special schools (0.4 per cent). The number of exclusions in secondary schools and in special schools has been declining since 1996/7. This is likely to be at least in part due to government policies designed to reduce permanent school exclusions by one-third by 2000/1 from the 1996/7 peak of 12,700 (see also Chapter 8).

Overall, over eight out of ten exclusions (84.5 per cent) were of boys, with girls accounting for only 15.5 per cent. This is likely to be related to the poorer behaviour of boys and their higher levels of disciplinary problems (Gallagher 1997). The permanent exclusion rate for pupils with statements of special educational need was also found to be seven times higher than for pupils without statements (0.61 per cent compared with 0.09 per cent, DfES 2001g).

A study carried out by Parsons et al. (2001) examined the outcomes in secondary education for children excluded from primary school in a sample of pupils in ten LEAs. They found that nearly half of those excluded in primary school received further exclusions in their primary school career and over a third received exclusions in secondary school. Girls excluded at primary school emerged as a distinct group with those excluded being more than three times as likely as boys to be at a special school. Children who had spent time in public care were more likely to have had a *permanent* exclusion as their initial exclusion. Parsons et al. (2001) also noted that there was some evidence of attainment acting as a 'protective' factor in terms of the number of exclusions and an individual's overall outcomes at the secondary stage, with a greater number of fixed-period or indefinite exclusions being associated with a lower level of attainment in English, mathematics and science at Key Stage 3.

As noted in Chapter 4 there are marked differences between the exclusion rates for pupils from different ethnic groups with the rate being higher for some groups than for others. This is the case particularly for pupils classified as Black Caribbean, Black Other and for those in Other (not specified) ethnic groups. The exclusion rate was relatively low for pupils of Chinese, Indian, Pakistani and Bangladeshi origin (DfES 2001g).

Young people who are excluded from school are far less likely than those not excluded to gain any qualifications at the end of Year 11. National data relating to attainment of young people who have been excluded from school either permanently or for a fixed term in Years 10 or 11 are available from the Youth Cohort Study (YCS) (see Appendix C). According to the YCS (DfES 2001b), a far lower percentage of young people who had been excluded from school gained GCSEs (or equivalent GNVQs) at the end of Year 11. The percentages of young people who had been excluded (permanently or for a fixed term) or had not been excluded at all and gaining different numbers of GCSEs are given in Table 5.5 and shown graphically in Figure 5.3.

As can be seen, far fewer young people who reported having been excluded than those who had not achieved five or more GCSEs at grades A* to C (17 per cent versus 52 per cent). Conversely, more young people who had been excluded reported

Table 5.5 Young people's attainment of different numbers of GCSEs[a] at the end of Year 11 by exclusion from school (2000)

Excluded from school in Years 10 or 11	5+ GCSEs A*–C (%)	1–4 GCSEs A*–C[b] (%)	5+ GCSEs D–G (%)	1–4 GCSEs D–G (%)	None reported (%)
Excluded	17	31	31	11	10
Not excluded	52	25	16	3	4

Source: DfES 2001b, Youth Cohort Study.

Notes:
a Includes GNVQ qualifications gained in Year 11.
b Those with 1–4 GCSE grades A* to C and any number of other grades.

Weighted sample of those excluded is 1,059 and not excluded is 12,282.

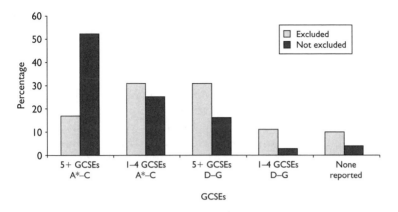

Figure 5.3 Young people's attainment of different numbers of GCSEs (or GNVQ equivalents) by exclusion from school (2000).

Source: DfES 2001b, Youth Cohort Study.

Note
For notes see Table 5.5.

fewer or lower-grade GCSEs. One in ten of those who had been excluded reported no GCSEs or GNVQs.

The YCS (DfES 2001b) also enables us to examine young people's main activity at age 16. Table 5.6 presents this information for those excluded and not excluded in Years 10 or 11. Young people have been classified as being in full-time education, government-supported training, in employment or out of work.

Table 5.6 reveals that far fewer young people who had been excluded permanently or for a fixed term than those who had not been excluded continued in full-time education post-16 (42 per

Table 5.6 Young people's main activity at age 16 for those excluded or not excluded in Years 10 or 11 (2000)

Exclusion in Years 10 or 11	Full-time education (%)	Government-supported training (%)	Full-time/ part-time job (%)	Out of work (%)	Something else/not stated (%)
Excluded	42	15	24	15	4
Not excluded	74	10	10	4	2

Source: DfES 2001b, Youth Cohort Study.

cent versus 74 per cent). More were employed, but over one in ten reported being out of work.

In Northern Ireland, a research study on suspensions (temporary exclusions) and expulsions (permanent exclusions) was commissioned by the Department of Education, Northern Ireland (Kilpatrick *et al.* 1999).

There is a selective education system in Northern Ireland with grammar schools as well as secondary schools that are not academically selective. The study by Kilpatrick *et al.* found that the majority of those suspended were from secondary schools. More boys than girls were suspended – the ratio was five to one. Pupils who had been suspended three or more times during the academic year were identified as having 'multiple' suspensions. The majority of these were boys from secondary schools; they were significantly more likely to be entitled to free school meals, to have lower rates of attendance and to be known to a range of support agencies.

The same study also examined the characteristics of expelled pupils and found that over half of the seventy-six pupils concerned were entitled to free school meals. Around one in ten had a statement of special educational needs or were waiting for one to be completed. A number of school principals 'expressed the view that expelled pupils had special educational needs which required provision to suit these needs' (Kilpatrick *et al.* 1999: x).

Underachievement and non-school factors

Area effects

There are also associations between attainment and areas in which schools are located. Examining the most deprived districts in England, the Social Exclusion Unit (SEU) (1998b) found that one in four children gained no GCSEs; 37 per cent of 16 year olds in these areas left school with no GCSE A* to C grades; more than five times as many secondary schools were on 'special measures' following Office for Standards in Education (OFSTED) inspections; and about a quarter more adults had poor literacy and numeracy skills. A range of other problems tend to be concentrated in poor neighbourhoods and many of these are likely to have an impact on school processes. For example, there are higher teenage pregnancy rates; higher levels of crime and drug use; more health problems; school exclusion rates tend to be higher in areas of social deprivation; truants are more likely to be from poorer backgrounds and truancy appears to be more common in inner-city areas (SEU 1998a).

A recent study (Gore and Smith 2001) examined patterns of educational achievement in two different types of deprived areas – coalfields and socio-economically similar areas that were not coal-fields ('comparison' areas). The study was commissioned by the DfES as below average levels of educational attainment had been identified as a major problem in the regeneration of coalfield areas. The aim of the study was to establish whether children and young people living in coalfield areas in Britain performed similarly, better or worse in terms of their educational attainment when compared with national averages on the one hand and the averages for areas with a similar socio-economic composition on the other.

Key findings to emerge were that up to the age of 16, educational attainment was below the national average in both coalfield and comparison areas. This disparity increased with age, so that the gap compared with the average was much greater for pupils finishing compulsory schooling than for those just starting. Of particular interest was the finding that the most marked differences were found at the higher levels of achievement – that is the proportion obtaining five or more GCSE passes at grades A* to C. It was found that the proportion of pupils achieving this level in both the coalfield and comparison areas was between 7 and 10 per cent below the national average. A similar pattern was found in post-16 education, with the proportion of young people obtaining two or more passes at GCE A level being 3 to 5 per cent below the national average – a point score of 1.0 to 2.3 (half to just over one A level grade) below the average. The authors conclude by noting that the similar patterns of achievement found for comparison areas reveal that lower levels of attainment are 'common to areas that have experienced economic decline and have relatively high levels of deprivation' (Gore and Smith 2001: 4). Whilst these 'area effects' are clearly of interest, it appears likely that they are related to the underlying socio-economic profile of the pupils attending the schools concerned.

Divorce and separation

Rodgers and Pryor (1998) carried out a review of over 200 research reports on the impact of divorce and separation on children. Amongst their findings were that: children of separated families had a higher probability of behavioural problems; performed less well at school; and left school when young. The research also suggests that children from step-families do not fare as well as those from intact families – and in some instances not as well as those from lone-parent families. Rodgers and Pryor note:

> The risk of adverse outcomes for young people in step-families compared with those in lone-parent families appears to be higher for older children, especially in the areas of educational achievement.
>
> (Rodgers and Pryor 1998: 3)

An earlier study, using the National Child Development Study of children born in 1958, and carried out by Kiernan (1997), also found that there was an increased probability that children whose parents divorced would lack formal qualifications, but noted that pre-divorce factors, and in particular financial hardship, were also important in explaining this increased probability. Kiernan cautions that children who grew up with both parents became better qualified and were in better jobs, in large part due to their families being socially and economically advantaged to begin with. As she notes:

> In general, children from divorced families had more negative experiences than children reared by both parents. Nevertheless, for many of the educational and economic outcomes studied there was evidence of powerful influences – notably family hardship – at work before the break-up occurred. Thus, the reason that children who grew up with both parents found themselves better qualified and in better jobs as adults was largely that they were advantaged to begin with – and not necessarily because their parents stayed together.
>
> (Kiernan 1997: 4)

Further evidence about the relationship between family structure and attainment comes from the Programme for International Student Assessment (PISA), which explored, amongst other factors, how family structures impact on performance (OECD 2001). The assessment covered three domains: reading literacy, mathematical literacy and scientific literacy (see Appendix B).

A questionnaire to students was administered, which asked about who they usually lived with at home. Overall, about 15 per cent of students reported living in a lone-parent family. Of the OECD countries, the United Kingdom had one of the highest percentages of students – somewhat over 20 per cent (as did New Zealand and the United States). In the majority of countries (including the UK, the USA and New Zealand), the findings of PISA revealed that students in lone-parent families did less well than those who lived in other family situations (for example, in nuclear families, with a mother and a male guardian). The largest differences were found in the Netherlands, the UK and the USA. However, it was also found that other background factors – such as wealth – often reinforce this relationship. The report states: 'The policy question for education systems and individual schools interacting with parents is what kinds of parental engagement should be encouraged' (OECD 2001: 152).

Health-related behaviours and achievement

A wide variety of behaviours outside the school environment has been shown to be associated with pupil achievement. Some of these behaviours should be seen as 'markers' of other types of disadvantage. For example, a study in the USA by Richardson *et al.* (1993) found an association between unsupervised care after school and a susceptibility to cigarette, alcohol and marijuana use, depressed mood, risk taking and lower academic achievement in the ninth grade (typical age 14); in this case unsupervised care is likely to be associated with socio-economic disadvantage.

Health status and substance abuse may similarly be markers of other forms of disadvantage. The relationship between educational performance and children's health is an area that has been examined to a considerable extent in the USA. Nevertheless, the American findings are pertinent to our discussion. Wolford Symons *et al.* (1997) reviewed the literature relating to student health risk behaviour and education outcomes, education behaviours and student attitudes about education. They examined a range of health risk behaviours, including, amongst others, tobacco, alcohol and other drug use, diet, physical activity and sexual risk behaviours, including pregnancy. They note that the literature points to a strong association between student involvement in specific health risk behaviours and negative outcomes on particular measures of school performance (for example, graduation rates, class grades and performance on standardised tests); education behaviours (for example, school attendance, drop-out rates, behaviour problems at school and homework); and student attitudes (for example, aspirations for post-school education and self-esteem). It was also reported that exposure to violence had lifelong effects on learning.

The research reviewed by Wolford Symons *et al.* revealed that adolescents who used drugs had lower grades, more negative attitudes towards school, and stronger ties to peers. Such students also had increased absenteeism, and showed 'more frequent risk-taking behaviour related to delinquency' (1997: 222). Having controlled for socio-economic background and personality, research has also shown that drug use may directly predict dropping out of school. Drug use has also been linked to truancy and to reduced motivation.

The review also noted that having a child whilst in the adolescent years has consequences for the mother, father, child and community at large; after having had a child, adolescent girls have an increased risk of subsequent disadvantages, including lower-status employment and lower income. Childbirth during the high-school years has also been found to be associated with significantly reduced academic achievement; and adolescents who became pregnant have been found to be less likely to be involved in school activities, with a tendency to obtain lower grades.

Research has also revealed that poor nutrition has a negative impact on learning outcomes (Wolford Symons *et al.* 1997). Children who are hungry or undernourished have been found to show irritability, apathy and physical inactivity, which have a negative impact on learning. 'Hungry children are at increased risk for infection and are more likely to miss school; therefore they fall behind in class work' (ibid.: 223). Interestingly, American research has confirmed that students participating in school-based breakfast and lunch programmes 'demonstrated increased school attendance, greater class participation, improved emotional behavior and increased academic achievement' (ibid.: 224). There is also evidence to suggest that exercise is associated with improved academic outcomes.

Finally, parental health and well-being may also impact on children's achievement. Another American study (McGrath *et al.* 1999) examined whether adolescent children of alcoholics showed poorer academic performance than demographically matched controls. They found that children of alcoholics received lower school grades than did their peers (parents' educational level was controlled for). The results suggest that parental alcoholism is associated with adolescents' lowered academic performance, and that the effects are strongest for adolescents with alcohol-dependent parents (rather than those with alcohol abuse).

Conclusions

The evidence that we have presented here demonstrates that a multitude of factors is associated with low levels of achievement. Many of these are not readily amenable to school policies or practices, although in a number of cases there are ways in which school policy might mitigate the impact of disadvantages. This is the case, for example, with pupil mobility. In other cases, it would appear that government policy might be able to influence practice. This is likely to be the case with the reductions in school exclusions that have taken place in recent years, with a high priority being given to this issue by government. Chapter 9 examines how one of our case-study schools, with a disadvantaged intake, tackled the issue of restoring and maintaining control. As a result of the initiatives introduced, the school has managed to ensure that no pupils are permanently excluded from school.

It is important to note that some of the factors that we have examined here are clearly beyond the control of schools – this is the case with schools that are located in areas where levels of deprivation are high. In these cases, schools are likely to have to cope with a range of difficulties not encountered in more prosperous areas. Some of the health-related behaviours discussed in this chapter will undoubtedly be more common and impact on the teaching and learning provided in such schools.

What is very clear from our discussion is that there is a multitude of factors that are associated with low levels of attainment. Responses to these complex and enduring issues are considered in Chapter 8, which highlights key areas of government policy, and Chapter 10, which focuses on some of the ways in which government, schools and LEAs could respond in order to try to ensure that young people from different socio-economic and from disadvantaged backgrounds maximise their levels of achievement.

Part 2

Policy, practice and solutions?

Chapter 6

School structures and achievement

Introduction

In this chapter we examine what many consider to be among the most politically and socially contentious issues facing education today. First, we outline the market reforms that were first introduced during the 1980s and their impact on school structures. Second, we examine selective schooling and achievement. Third, we examine compositional or peer effects, before turning our attention to ability grouping. Finally, we summarise our findings and present our conclusions on the issues raised in the chapter.

It is important to stress at this stage that our focus is on the situation in England. Although the legislative framework in Wales is similar, there is less diversity in terms of school types – although in both countries parents are able to make choices for a school of their preference (see West and Pennell 1997a). In Scotland there is a completely different legislative framework. In Northern Ireland a selective education system exists, with grammar and non-selective secondary schools (called secondary modern schools in England) (see Appendix A).

Market reforms in education

Policy context

Education reforms introduced during the 1980s and 1990s have had a profound effect on school structures in England, particularly in urban areas. Legislation enacted in 1980 gave a much greater priority to parental choice and the 1988 Education Reform Act introduced open enrolment (see below). School funding was also determined on a predominantly per capita basis. In short, the educational reforms introduced by the Conservative government in 1988 resulted in the introduction of a 'quasi-market' in school-based education (see Le Grand and Bartlett 1993; West and Pennell 1997a; West and Ingram 2001).

One of the Conservative government's main aims was to increase the diversity of schools from which parents could choose. Fifteen city technology colleges (CTCs) were introduced in the late 1980s and early 1990s and the 1988 Act allowed for the creation of grant-maintained schools. Once local education authority schools opted out of local authority control and became grant maintained, they were no longer financed by the local education authority but by central government – at a higher level than previously – and obtained other advantages such as control over admissions to the school (West and Pennell 1997a). Other initiatives to increase the diversity of schools included the Technology and Language Programmes, introduced in 1993, which introduced the concept of specialist schools. These programmes were designed to help maintained secondary schools to 'specialise' in technology, science and mathematics or modern foreign languages. (The specialist schools programme, as it is now known, has been expanded considerably by the Labour government.[1])

The reforms were closely associated with the issue of selection, with schools under the Conservative government being able to select a small proportion of the pupils on the basis of ability or aptitude in music, art, drama and sport or on the basis of general ability without requiring government approval (DfEE 1996b; see West and Pennell 1997a). The reforms were thus also tied to the more general issue of admissions to schools.

Concerns were expressed about admissions policies and practices, particularly those used by grant-maintained schools and voluntary-aided (mostly church) schools (see Audit Commission 1996; Gewirtz et al. 1995; Walford 1993; West et al. 1998b). Inequitable practices allowing pupils to be 'selected in' or 'selected out' of schools were highlighted, including the admissions criteria used in the event of a school being oversubscribed – such as the pupil's interests, character, career ambitions – the use of pre-admission interviews of pupils and/or parents and the use of application forms seeking information unrelated to the school's admissions criteria, such as parents' occupations.

The Labour government sought to tackle some of these concerns following the General Election of 1997 via the 1998 School Standards and Framework Act, which reduced the scope for partial selection by ruling out the introduction of new selection on grounds of ability other than by 'fair banding' (on the basis of pupils' attainment or ability). However, selection on the grounds of aptitude for specific subjects can be introduced for schools with a specialism so long as the proportion of pupils selected does not exceed 10 per cent of the intake (West and Ingram 2001). There is now a code of practice on school admissions and the Act provides a new mechanism – the adjudicator – for resolving local disputes in relation to school admissions. The Act also abolished grant-maintained schools; these became foundation or reverted to voluntary-aided status.

School admissions

The question of school admissions is important given the development of an education quasi-market, with schools' funding being determined predominantly by pupil numbers and schools being placed in competition with one another through the publication of examination performance tables ('league tables'). In such circumstances there are incentives for schools to 'cream skim' in order to maximise their league table position. However, only some schools are in a position to do this – those that are both oversubscribed and in charge of their own admissions – that is, they are their own admission authority.

In the case of community and voluntary-controlled schools the local education authority is the admission authority so it is only voluntary-aided and foundation schools (formerly grant-maintained schools) that are in this position. In these schools the governing body of the school is the admission authority. City technology colleges are officially classified as independent and so are not bound by the same legislation as other state-maintained schools, but they too administer their own admissions. It is important to note that many more schools are now responsible for their own admissions than was the case in the past; in January 1988, the year of the Education Reform Act, 15 per cent of schools were their own admission authority (DfES 2002d) whilst in January 1999, 30 per cent of schools were responsible for their own admissions (DfES 2001c). The introduction of more 'independent' schools, similar to CTCs, known as city academies (see below), will mean that the numbers of such schools will increase further in years to come.

As a result of open enrolment, admission authorities for state schools are required by law to admit children up to the physical capacity of the school (except in the case of selective or religious schools). If a school is oversubscribed (with more applicants than there are places) its published admissions criteria are used to determine who should be offered places. The admissions criteria in LEA (community) comprehensive schools vary, although three main factors are generally used: siblings already attending the school; medical or social need; and distance between home and school or catchment area (see White *et al.* 2001; West and Hind 2003). Voluntary-aided schools (the vast majority of voluntary schools) and foundation schools are responsible for their own admissions (admissions to voluntary-controlled schools are the responsibility of the local education authority). The majority of voluntary-aided schools use religious criteria to select pupils.

Finally, there are fifteen city technology colleges (CTCs) set up by private sponsors, but which receive revenue funding from the government. These schools are required to admit pupils across the full range of ability who are representative of the ethnic and social composition of their (large) catchment area and who are both willing and able to benefit from the type of education offered (Whitty *et al.* 1993). However, research indicates that the tests used to measure aptitude for technology are highly related to later academic achievement, so there is a major concern that pupils are being selected according to their academic ability. New city academies are being set up by the Labour Government. These are modelled on CTCs and they too will be responsible for their own admissions, but subject to the Code of Practice on School Admissions.[3]

The use of various forms of selection by schools that are their own admissions authority has led certain schools in a locality to have more advantaged intakes than others. West and Ingram (2001) in their examination of decisions made by the Office of the Schools Adjudicator, reported the case of a foundation school that was selecting 30 per cent of pupils on the basis of general ability and 5 per cent on the basis of aptitude/ability in music. The adjudicator's ruling was that selection by ability/aptitude in music could be retained, but selection by ability had to be reduced to 10 per cent. The adjudicator noted:

I accept that a comprehensive school may well be more successful if it has a balanced intake but I consider that the measures taken by [the school] have skewed its intake towards the higher end of the ability range ... My judgement therefore, is that taken as a whole, the admissions procedures ... are having an adverse effect upon other comprehensive schools in the area and that they are not, therefore, in the best interests of local children and parents.

(Cited by West and Ingram 2001: 469)

Another concern has been that admissions criteria may allow for social selection. In particular, information obtained during the course of interviews may be used to select particular types of children – for example, the more able, those from higher socio-economic groups or those whose parents will be supportive of the school. Consequently, other schools may be left with intakes with disproportionately high numbers of less able children and pupils with less supportive parents.

The consequence of such admissions policies is that some schools will continue to struggle to raise the achievement levels of their students at the same time as other schools will benefit by having an intake of pupils influenced by selection practices not available to others.

Is there evidence of school stratification?

In the same way that the structure of society has been analysed on the basis of characteristics such as poverty and social class, so attempts have been made to investigate the structure and hierarchy of schools. This research has been somewhat limited by data availability and has been, in the main, restricted to segregation on the basis of low income, using known free meals eligibility as an indicator of poverty. Across England, in 2001, approximately 16 per cent of secondary school pupils were known to be eligible for free school meals (DfES 2001c). To be eligible, children must be dependent on claimants of the state benefits: income support or job-seeker's allowance.

One problem that confronts researchers in this field is that this indicator is not ideal for a variety of reasons. First of all, it is a very crude measure as it only distinguishes between the minority of pupils known to be eligible for free school meals and the majority who are not (16 per cent versus 84 per cent). Second, it may not be an accurate measure of whether a child is dependent on state benefits as parents have to provide evidence that their children are eligible, which they may choose not to do (for example, because of the quality of the meals available or alternatives outside the school). Third, the regulations governing state benefits have changed and this doubtless has an impact on those eligible for free school meals; specifically, a new form of benefit called working families' tax credit has recently been introduced and once parents are in receipt of this benefit, their children are no longer eligible for free school meals.

Research has examined segregation between schools. Gorard *et al.* (2001a) report that there was a decline in segregation in England and Wales between 1989/90 and 1996, before it rose in the period to 1999/2000. One possible explanation of changing levels of social segregation (as measured by free school meals eligibility), noted by Gorard but given greater prominence by others (for example, Gibson and Asthana 2000; Noden 2001, 2002) is that changing social segregation primarily reflects changing levels of poverty. That is, in periods of economic growth, social polarisation tends to increase.

Notwithstanding these national findings, segregation has increased in some LEAs but decreased in others (Gorard and Fitz 2000) and a more recent study (Gorard and Taylor 2001) argues that schools that are selective, or are their own admission authorities, or are designated specialist tend to increase the socioeconomic segregation of school intakes; moreover, when schools have two or more of these characteristics together Gorard and Taylor report that this tendency is much stronger.

Research by Bradley *et al.* (2000) using a different method also examined the extent to which the market-oriented reforms in England resulted in greater divergence between schools in their socio-economic mix of pupils. They examined the change in the proportion of pupils eligible for free school meals between 1993 and 1998 and the initial performance of schools; they found a significant negative relationship, which they suggest indicates that the highest performing schools became more selective during the time period in question. They argue that the educational reforms appear to have 'resulted in some divergence in the socio-economic mix of schools' (2000: 383).

In short, the current quasi-market in schools means that there are incentives for schools that have the opportunity to do so – namely those that are foundation and voluntary-aided and so their own admission authority – to select certain types of pupils. In particular, such schools may select those students who have high levels of prior attainment and who are likely to be high achievers who will aid the school's 'league table' position, so maintaining or enhancing its reputation (in addition, more able children from supportive families are likely to be easier to teach). With limited regulation of admissions, there is not a level playing field in terms of the operation of the quasi-market.

Although the Labour Government introduced a Code of Practice on School Admissions to try to mitigate the effects of the market reforms, the impact has not been as great as it might have been if implementation had been more rigorous and the criteria for admissions more stringent (West and Ingram 2001). It is clear from the above discussion that the market-oriented reforms appear to have exacerbated problems of covert and social selection (see also West and Hind 2003).

Notwithstanding these concerns, it is possible that there are benefits arising from the quasi-market reforms in terms of improved standards as a result of increased competition. The evidence on this issue is not clear-cut. Gorard *et al.*, for example, examined the extent to which the increase in the percentage of students gaining five or more GCSEs at grades A* to C over time can be attributed to the market reforms introduced in 1988. Their overall conclusion – with which we would agree – is that one cannot attribute the raw-score improvement to market forces 'as there were many policy changes all taking place at the same time . . . there are many confounding variables' (2001a: 20).

However, it might also be the case that the most appropriate unit of analysis is not the country, but the local education authority. Using a very different approach, Bradley *et al.* (2000) analysed the performance of schools in England over time. They found that a school's examination results were positively related to the examination performance of schools in the same local education authority. This, they argue, supports the notion that schools are competitive and respond to the performance of other schools in the area.

Whilst acknowledging that there may be some benefits accruing as a result of the quasi-market reforms, there is none the less evidence of increased opportunities for cream skimming and there is evidence of increased segregation in some localities that appears to be associated with school diversity. We therefore move on to try to answer a related question: does the composition of schools – in terms of the concentration either of pupils of particular levels of achievement or of pupils from low income households – matter? We look in the first instance at selective schooling and achievement, and then at compositional effects. We then examine whether selection by ability within schools via streaming or setting matters in terms of attainment.

Selective schooling and achievement

There has been a long-standing debate that has focused on the issue of selection whereby children attend different schools depending on their performance in tests and assessments at the age of 11 years (the 11-plus).

The secondary education system differs in the constituent countries of the UK. In Scotland and in Wales there are no selective (grammar) schools, whilst in Northern Ireland a selective system of grammar and non-selective secondary schools operates. The situation in England is more diverse than in the other countries of the UK. In a number of parts of England, grammar schools still exist but the numbers are small overall. In 2002 there were 164 grammar schools in England accounting for around 5 per cent of secondary schools. They cater in the main for children who are from more advantaged social backgrounds: in 2001, the percentage of pupils known to be eligible for free school meals was 3 per cent in grammar schools compared with 16 per cent for all maintained secondary schools (DfES 2002c).

There is a considerable body of work comparing selective systems (grammar plus secondary modern) with comprehensive systems, but most of the results are equivocal. Research has been conducted on the impact of selective and non-selective school systems on pupil achievement. Reviews of relevant research have been carried out by Crook *et al.* (1999) and Ireson and Hallam (1999). Ireson and Hallam report that some studies have found that there are minimal differences in outcomes when prior ability is controlled for, whilst others have found that pupils' performance becomes increasingly differentiated depending on the kind of school that pupils attend. It is noted that pupils of average ability appear to perform better in high ability schools than in schools where the majority of pupils are of lower ability – this is the so-called 'peer group' or 'school context' effect. However, selective schools, where academically able pupils are 'creamed off', can leave other schools with what Ireson and Hallam call 'an inappropriate balance'; this is similar to the situation with schools that are partially selective, but the consequences are, inevitably, likely to be more extreme. Indeed in Northern Ireland, where there is a selective system, a report based on research commissioned by the Department of Education, Northern Ireland, noted:

> Overall, grammar schools show particularly high levels of academic achievement. However, the corollary of this is that there is a long tail of low achieving secondary schools. This may be an inevitable consequence of a selective system.
>
> (2000: 3)

A research study carried out in Scotland is considered to be one of the most thorough, and reveals interesting findings of system-wide changes to a comprehensive system (McPherson and Willms 1987). The study involved three nationally-representative and comparable cohorts of school leavers. They used a quasi-experimental design for the research, which spanned the later stages of the implementation of comprehensive reform, with repeated observations of schools derived from pupils in the three cohorts.

Their key findings included the following:

- comprehensive reform had an equalising effect on the socio-economic status of pupil catchments; reorganisation reduced socio-economic segregation at both a national level and in the cities, where it was largest;
- pupil attainment suffered in 'creamed' comprehensive schools;
- pupil attainment improved as the severity of creaming declined;
- pupil attainment improved the longer the school had been comprehensive all through;
- the gap between the attainment of middle-class and working-class pupils decreased after comprehensive reorganisation.

More recent English research is also of interest, showing that, on average, progress between Key Stages 2 and 3 is greater for pupils in grammar than non-selective schools with similar levels of free school meals eligibility. However, no such differences were found between Key Stages 3 and 4 (DfES 2002b). The DfES report notes that the sample of pupils was relatively small and so the results need to be treated with some caution.

A further study by Schagen and Schagen (2001) also examined comprehensive and selective *systems* and found little difference between the two. However, they found that selective LEAs achieved better results, in terms of 'value-added', at Key Stage 3. They argue that 'since Key Stage 3 results form the foundation for GCSE work, it is reasonable to hypothesize that selective systems produce somewhat better results overall' (2001: 6). However, on the basis of their analyses, they suggest that the *most able* pupils perform at least as well in comprehensive schools, but that the impact of different school types is most strongly felt amongst those who are of average to above average ability.

Some confirmation of these findings comes from analyses carried out by the DfES (2002c), which also reveal that 'on average' more progress was made by those with higher levels of attainment in selective LEAs between Key Stages 2 and 3. However, between Key Stages 3 and 4 pupils in schools in non-selective LEAs made, on average, *more* progress than those in selective LEAs.

An interesting study relating to progress post-16 is of particular interest as it suggests that the *type* of institution – whether it is selective or comprehensive – is less important than 'compositional' effects. Yang and Woodhouse (2001) examined progress from GCSE to GCE A and AS level. The study focused on the relationship between results obtained in examinations for A and AS levels and those obtained by the same students two years earlier in GCSE examinations. It was found that progress differed between males and females and between students of different ages; in addition, the average GCSE performance of the students in an institution was found to be a significant predictor of individual progress. Once institutions had been matched on this measure and students matched on their own GCSE performance, the effects of most institution types were markedly reduced. Yang and Woodhouse, in relation to state-maintained institutions, note:

> Students in maintained comprehensive schools made similar progress to those in state selective schools ... when these were matched according to the average performance at GCSE of all their candidates. Those in sixth form colleges, similarly

matched for intake, made better progress, amounting to about three-quarters of a grade at A level for males and a full grade for females.

(Yang and Woodhouse 2001: 265)

We now move to examine school composition effects on pupils' achievement and progress.

School composition effects on achievement

UK evidence

Comparatively little research in the field of education has focused directly on peer effects – otherwise known as compositional effects. A report by the former Inner London Education Authority (ILEA) provides an informative description of these effects:

> It has often been suggested that greater *concentrations* of underperforming groups will depress school performance over and above the difference expected as a result of the presence of underperforming individuals (or, conversely, that concentrating high performers raises performance even higher).
>
> (ILEA 1990: 14)

At secondary transfer in the ILEA, pupils were 'banded' into three groups with a view to schools obtaining an academically balanced intake (see West *et al.* 1998b). The analyses carried out by the Research and Statistics Branch of the former ILEA (1990) found that the proportion of pupils in the top 'band' had a significant effect, with a higher proportion enhancing the performance score in the public examinations at the end of compulsory schooling over and above the enhancement expected as a result of the presence of that number of high ability top band students. The reverse of this is that the higher the proportion of students in the second and third ability bands, the lower the level of achievement. Findings such as this suggest that a balanced intake leads to the most equitable results.

The same research also found that the proportion of students known to be eligible for free school meals had an effect of the same order but in the opposite direction – the higher the proportion eligible, the lower the average performance score.

More recent studies have also looked at compositional effects. Strand (1997) found that on average the higher the proportion of pupils known to be eligible for free school meals, the less progress pupils made during Key Stage 1. This was true after controlling for age, amount of pre-school education and whether English was a second language. He also found that a high percentage of pupils entitled to free school meals was negatively associated with progress, over and above the effect of individual pupils' free school meals entitlement. He notes:

> It can be hypothesised that schools with a low proportion of socially disadvantaged pupils may have some benefits associated with their context: they may receive greater help from parents, have fewer disciplinary problems or an atmosphere more conducive to learning.
>
> (Strand 1997: 484–5)

Strand's analysis also revealed that there was a negative association between the percentage of children with English as an additional language and progress, with lower average progress in schools being associated with a high proportion of children with English as a second language. He notes that it is possible that in schools with a high proportion of children with English as a second language 'a larger part of the teacher's effort is directed towards the ESL [English as a second language] pupils, possibly at the expense of stretching other pupils in the class' (ibid.: 485).

However, such compositional effects are not invariably found. Sammons *et al.* (1997a) did not find that the proportion of children eligible for free school meals was significant in their analysis of Key Stage 1 attainment in a sample of inner London schools. They note that this may reflect the greater incidence of disadvantage amongst the inner-city schools in their sample of schools; in their study, over 44 per cent of pupils were from low income families.

Such studies of school effectiveness are valuable in terms of ascertaining the role of schools in facilitating the progress of students. They also confirm that school composition does matter. In short, students attending schools that have more advantaged as opposed to disadvantaged intakes – whether measured in terms of the ability mix or level of poverty – are likely to achieve higher results in part because they are being educated with more-advantaged students. Likewise, students attending schools with more-disadvantaged intakes are likely to achieve poorer results because they are being educated with more-disadvantaged students.

From the point of view of parental choice, it may be considered reasonable for parents to choose to send their child to a school with higher-performing students to maximise their own child's academic performance. However, from the perspective of educational policy, the evidence suggests that there are major negative consequences in terms of those children who attend schools that have been 'creamed'. The benefits for some are thus achieved at the expense of others. We return to this issue in Chapter 10.

International evidence on achievement and school composition

Interesting evidence on compositional effects has been identified by the Programme for International Student Assessment (PISA), which was first administered in 2000. It covered three domains: reading literacy; mathematical literacy; and scientific literacy.

The report of the findings (OECD 2001) provides an analysis of how the social make-up of the school attended reinforces the effects of individual students' backgrounds. It notes that a number of studies have shown that schools with a more advantaged socio-economic make-up tend to have several advantages:

> They are likely to have greater support from parents, fewer disciplinary problems, better teacher–student relations, higher teacher morale, and generally a school climate that is oriented towards higher performance.
>
> (OECD 2001: 198)

The report also notes that some of the contextual effect associated with schools with a high proportion of students from higher socio-economic groups may be as a result of peer interactions – peer pressure and peer competition – or as a result of the nature of the programmes offered.

The analysis undertaken included economic, social and cultural status, gender, ethnicity and family structure at the individual level and mean economic, social and cultural status at the school level. In almost all countries (including the UK) it was found that there appears to be a clear advantage in attending a school whose

students are on average from more advantaged family backgrounds. Indeed, in most OECD countries, the impact of the
average social, economic and cultural status outweighed the
effects of the individual socio-economic background. The report
also notes that as no data on students' earlier achievements were
available, it was not possible to ascertain whether and to what
extent the school background related directly or indirectly to students' performance – for example, by selection or self-selection.

The report notes that in Austria and Germany, the effect on
students' performance of a school's average social, economic and
cultural status was high. It is important to point out that in these
two countries, students are allocated to schools on the basis of
factors that include their ability. Differences in performance
between schools derive mainly from the allocation of students to
different types of school – in Germany to Gymnasium (similar to
grammar schools in England), Realschule (similar to the former
technical schools in England) and Hauptschule (similar to
secondary modern schools in England). Assignment to these different school types is influenced by student performance, which in
turn is closely associated with socio-economic background. So, as
the report stresses, 'the estimated contextual effects ... are
descriptive of the distribution of school performance, and should
not be interpreted as causal' (OECD 2001: 201).

The report also considers that it is important to understand:

> the nature of the formal and informal selection mechanisms
> that contribute to between-school socio-economic segregation,
> and its effect on students' performance. In some countries,
> socio-economic segregation may be firmly entrenched through
> residential segregation in major cities, or by a large urban/
> rural divide. In other countries, structural features of the edu-
> cation system stream or track students into programmes with
> different curricula or teaching practices. To the extent that the
> allocation of students to programmes in such systems is inter-
> linked with students' socio-economic background, those from
> disadvantaged backgrounds may not achieve their full poten-
> tial.
>
> (Ibid.: 201)

The PISA results suggest therefore that whilst social segregation is
beneficial to the advantaged and will enhance performance of

higher ability pupils, segregation is also likely to decrease equality. The report then discusses how evidence from countries with high quality and high equality can assist with policy development and change and identifies the removal of socio-economic segregation or mitigating its effects. The report notes in particular that 'seeking either to remove socio-economic segregation or to mitigate its effects are the policy options. In either case, the central task will be to try to replicate the benefits for quality that social segregation can provide while gaining the benefits for equality that social heterogeneity can provide' (Ibid.: 201).

The PISA study also examined what schools might do to achieve this desired effect. The analyses estimated the separate influences of school factors and family background and their combined influence. For each subject area tested, the impact of school resources, school policies and practice and classroom practice on performance was explored. When OECD countries were analysed together several of the school-resource factors emerged as having a statistically significant impact on student performance – the extent to which students make use of school resources (such as the school library, computers and the Internet), the pupil–teacher ratio, the size of the school and the proportion of teachers with a university-level qualification (see OECD 2001 for a discussion).

School policies and practices having a statistically significant relationship with student performance across OECD countries were: the principal's perceptions of teacher-related factors affecting school climate; teacher morale and commitment; and school autonomy. Aspects of classroom practice having statistically significant positive associations with student performance were: pupils' perceptions of teacher–pupil relations; disciplinary climate of the classroom; and 'achievement press' (this was measured by pupils' perceptions of the extent to which teachers emphasised academic performance and placed high demands on them).

Overall, across the three subject domains examined in the PISA, the combined influence of the above set of school-level variables explained around 31 per cent of variation between schools within countries, and 21 per cent of the variation between countries. Family background and mean socio-economic status of the school explained about 11 per cent of variation between students within schools across the three subjects and over 60 per cent of the between-school variation.

Ability grouping in school

Ability grouping and its possible effect on achievement is another contentious issue. Ireson and Hallam (1999) reviewed the literature on ability grouping and its effects on academic and non-academic outcomes for pupils, noting that grouping in England has, historically, been based on tests measuring general ability or intelligence. In the 1960s and 1970s such tests were frequently used by secondary schools to allocate pupils to streamed classes in which they were taught for all their lessons. Less rigid forms of grouping have since been introduced. From a policy perspective setting is the most significant of these as the Labour government has been promoting its use. This method involves grouping pupils into classes on the basis of their attainment in a particular subject, so a pupil may be in a group with higher attaining pupils for some subjects and lower attaining pupils in others. Ireson and Hallam report that few British studies have examined the effects of streaming or setting on academic performance, and those that have been carried out have provided conflicting results: 'On the basis of the research undertaken in the UK to date it is impossible to draw firm conclusions, although the issue of access to the curriculum is clearly important' (1999: 345). They conclude that:

> we need a clearer picture of the relative effects of grouping both on academic and non-academic outcomes for pupils. We also need a better understanding of the way in which grouping is related to the ethos of the school, to teacher and pupil attitudes and to classroom teaching. Further research is needed on the effectiveness of mixed ability and whole class teaching in relation to different curriculum subject matter.
>
> (Ibid.: 354)

One relevant piece of research was carried out by Boaler (1997), who made a detailed study of two schools; one used setting for mathematics and the other used mixed-ability teaching. She found that in the school that used setting, the setted classes did not achieve better results than the students in the school that had mixed-ability classes. The students who were taught in mixed-ability groups achieved significantly more GCSE A* to G grades than those in set classes, despite the fact that the two cohorts were very similar on entry to their schools.

Boaler also noted that a comparison of the most able students at the two schools revealed that the students achieved more, in terms of the percentage of GCSE A* grades, in the mixed-ability classes than the high sets of the school that used setting. One disconcerting finding was that having controlled for ability, at the school that used setting, students of a low social class were more likely to appear in a low set, whilst at the school that used mixed-ability teaching, there was a tendency for students in the lower social classes to be placed in a higher examination group. Whilst this study was small scale and findings cannot be generalised, students' own perspectives on setting indicated that they felt their achievement had been diminished because of factors related to setting.

Conclusions

This chapter has examined school structures and the associations that exist between school structures and achievement. The market reforms in England have provided opportunities for certain categories of schools to 'select in' some pupils and 'select out' others. At a national level, there have been changes in levels of segregation; these appear to be related to the overall economic situation. However, at a local level, there is evidence of increased segregation in some authorities, which appears to be associated with some of the market-oriented reforms that have been introduced. On the other hand, there is some evidence of competition having had a positive impact on results within a local authority area.

There are a number of policy implications arising from the research we have reported in this chapter. First and foremost, policy makers need to regulate school admissions. At present there is not a level playing field and some schools are in a more advantageous position than others in that they are able, if they so wish, to 'select in' certain pupils and 'select out' others; this in turn will affect their 'league table' position. Creaming of this type is likely to result in some schools having an over-representation of hard-to-teach or low ability pupils compared with other schools in a given locality. Given the peer effects we have discussed in this chapter, this means that the pupils' results in such schools are likely to be lower than they would be with a more balanced ability intake.

Second, and associated with this, selection by ability or aptitude not only enables the schools concerned to cream, it also creates pressure for other schools to do likewise, so that they are not at an unfair advantage. However, some schools are not going to be in a position to cream and in these cases are more likely to have intakes skewed towards lower ability and harder-to-teach pupils. Overall, the evidence suggests that selection benefits the advantaged, is likely to increase segregation and has negative consequences on disadvantaged pupils.

Our case studies demonstrate that schools can improve their results markedly without overt or covert selection. Both of our case study comprehensive schools improved their results more than the national average – in terms of those obtaining five or more high grade GCSEs and in terms of those gaining at least one GCSE at grades A* to G. Indeed, in one of the schools, because of its popularity, pupils can now only obtain a place if they live within a very small radius of the school from the local council estates where households are often overcrowded.

Finally, to conclude, the evidence more generally points in the direction of reducing pupil selection for secondary schools if policy is striving towards increasing equity. This has the potential to create conflict between parental 'choice' and the desire for social cohesion, an issue we return to later.

Chapter 7

School-effectiveness research and achievement

Introduction

No book exploring underachievement in schools would be complete without examining what school effectiveness research has contributed to our knowledge about how schools may affect the progress made by pupils and about the factors that appear to make some schools more effective than others.

In this chapter, then, we examine key findings that have emerged from school effectiveness research, noting the characteristics of effective schools and how research on school effectiveness might be able to assist with raising attainment levels and so reducing underachievement.

These areas are important even though research indicates that non-school factors account for *most* of the variation in terms of educational attainment at school. For example, Thomas and Mortimore (1996) estimated that around 70 to 75 per cent of the variation in attainment at the age of 16 is accounted for by the background characteristics of the pupils. Notwithstanding this finding, there is a broad consensus that schools do have an impact. As Reynolds *et al.* (1997) concluded when reviewing research on school effectiveness, schools appear to have an independent effect on attainment of between 8 to 12 per cent of the total variance.

In the following sections we examine first of all the impact of the school attended on achievement; second, whether it is possible for schools to overcome the effects of disadvantage; third, issues associated with improving disadvantaged schools; and finally, what makes an 'effective' school, with some cautionary words about the importance of structural features of the educational system.

At the outset it is important to note that the concept of 'effective' is not unproblematic. Effectiveness has different meanings for different people. Hargreaves (1997), for example, notes that schools have a range of instrumental functions that are related to task achievement (for example developing students' cognitive achievement) but they also have an expressive function of maintaining social relationships within the school. These two domains, according to Hargreaves, are in potential tension but constitute the core of school cultures. An additional assumption he makes is that in each cultural domain – instrumental-social control and expressive-social cohesion – there is a level that can be considered to be optimal for the effective functioning of the school. Hargreaves argues that:

> The school of a 'balanced' culture achieving some kind of optimum position in both domains might claim to be the most effective, *but only when the criteria of effectiveness assign equal weight to both instrumental and expressive outcomes.* It could be argued of course, that many parents and politicians give more weight to the instrumental.
>
> (Hargreaves 1997: 246)

He goes on to assert that:

> At a time when in Britain, as in other countries, there is a political interest in the detection and improvement of underachieving or 'failing' schools, the relationship between school culture and school effectiveness/improvement needs closer investigation.
>
> (Ibid.: 249)

Notwithstanding the need for this linkage, data availability precludes an investigation of expressive as opposed to instrumental outcomes and, for this reason, the focus in the following sections is specifically on academic attainment.

Impact of the school attended

In their examination of effective junior schools, Mortimore *et al.* (1988) found that the school attended by the child has a significant impact on reading attainment. They reported that 9 per cent of the variation in reading attainment at the end of the child's third year in junior school was accounted for by the school. The size of the school effect was found to be much greater than that of background, once account was taken of initial attainment. However, it is also necessary to underline the point that initial attainment is itself related to background factors. The same research also examined school effects on pupils' attainment in mathematics; again the school accounted for a sizeable proportion of the variation in terms of attainment in children's third year of junior school, once account had been taken of sex, age and background factors. It was found that 11 per cent of the variation was accounted for by the school attended – thus the size of the effect was somewhat larger for mathematics than for reading.

When relative progress was examined, Mortimore *et al.* found that nearly 30 per cent of the variation in children's reading progress was accounted for by school membership and background factors taken together. They reported that the school had a much larger effect on progress than on attainment – accounting for 24 per cent of the variation in progress between the first and the third year of junior school. The finding that background factors had less effect on progress was not surprising given the strong relationship between such characteristics and initial attainment. In terms of progress in mathematics, it was found that 26 per cent of the variation in attainment was accounted for by age, sex, background factors and the school the child attended; the school attended was again responsible for most of the variation (23 per cent) in relative progress.

Can schools overcome the effects of disadvantage?

As we have seen in earlier chapters of this book, there is a range of background factors that can impact on attainment. Mortimore *et al.* examined the extent to which schools were effective with different groups of pupils, noting that in relation to the progress of children from non-manual and manual socio-economic groups:

> Those schools which were effective for one group tended to be effective for the other. Conversely, those which were ineffective for one group were also usually ineffective for the other. Our results show, therefore, that effective schools tend to

'jack up' the progress of all pupils, irrespective of their social class background, while ineffective schools will usually depress the progress of all pupils. This means that in effective schools social class differences in attainment are not likely to be reversed, rather that all pupils will be performing at a higher level.

(Mortimore *et al.* 1998: 208–9)

The research of Mortimore *et al.* thus indicated that schools that are more effective for one group of children tended to be more effective for other groups as well.

The study also investigated whether schools that were very different in terms of their effectiveness in enhancing pupils' reading and mathematics progress could reduce or eliminate social class differences. Social class was chosen as the key variable to examine as differences in attainment associated with social class were particularly marked for junior school aged pupils. The researchers compared school effects on reading progress for children from manual backgrounds with the effects on reading progress for children from non-manual groups in the least effective schools. This was done to establish if, in certain cases, the school attended could reverse the overall pattern of social class differences in attainment. On the basis of their analysis they concluded:

It is clear, therefore, that although there is a general tendency for schools to be effective or ineffective for all groups of children, including those of different social class backgrounds, it is possible for schools to alter the overall patterns of social class differences in attainment. A child whose parents are in manual employment and who attends an effective junior school, is likely to attain more highly in reading and in mathematics than a child who has the advantage of a non-manual background, but who attends an ineffective school.

(Ibid.: 215)

Other studies have also examined differential effectiveness. Sammons *et al.* (1993) re-analysed data for reading and mathematics attainment from the Junior School Project for a range of background factors but again found no evidence of differential school effectiveness for different groups of pupils – classified in terms of gender, ethnic group, social class group and known eligibility for free school meals. Sammons *et al.* note that: 'Overall "good" schools boost the later attainment of students of differing levels of prior attainment, whereas in less effective schools later attainment is lower than predicted for all groups' (1993: 402).

Strand (1999a) found that the particular school a child attends during Key Stage 1 (ages 5 to 7 years) had a significant effect on pupils' educational progress. Some schools were found to be more effective than others in facilitating progress during this period. However, he found no evidence of significant differential school effectiveness. In short, schools that were most effective for one particular ethnic or social group tended to be the most effective for other ethnic or social groups.

Where researchers have looked at the pupil composition of the less effective schools, the findings have been of considerable interest. It has been suggested that Caribbean pupils may be over-represented within less effective schools (see Mortimore *et al.* 1988; Strand 1999a) and Strand noted that this may be a disadvantage that Caribbean pupils share with white working-class pupils.

Although school effectiveness research has found that schools that are effective with one particular group of pupils are also likely to be the most effective for others, it is worth noting that other studies have suggested that there is scope for schools to have differential impacts on different groups of pupils.

In particular, there is evidence to suggest that accountability systems may have a role to play. In the USA such a system has been established in Texas and has been credited with raising the attainment of children of colour and children from low-income homes (Fuller and Johnson 2001). Student performance on the state's Texas Assessment of Academic Skills (TAAS) has improved in recent years, and gaps between pupils from different racial/ethnic/socio-economic groups have decreased over time. The test is a criterion-referenced test designed to measure pupil attainment of the state's academic standards. Interestingly, in terms of the National Assessment of Educational Progress (NAEP) (which is the only nationally representative assessment of pupil knowledge and skills in mathematics), pupils' performance in elementary- and middle-school mathematics has also shown improvements particularly for children of colour and children from low-income backgrounds (Fuller and Johnson 2001). A number of concerns about the TAAS testing system have been expressed (for example, by Klein *et al.* 2000). None the less, Fuller and Johnson argue that the state accountability 'played a central, catalytic role in driving the improvements' (2001: 278). They reported, in particular, on research that revealed school district leaders rethinking what could be done to help children of colour learn. Fuller and Johnson note:

> The reason the accountability system has served as such a catalyst probably has less to do with testing and more to do with the manner in which the test results are used. In Texas, schools are rated as 'low performing,' 'acceptable,' 'recognized,' or 'exemplary.' Whole school districts are given similar ratings. To date, the ratings have been based on three factors: student attendance, drop-out rates, and the percentage of students passing the reading, mathematics, and writing sections of TAAS ... [T]he rates for African American, Hispanic, and White students are disaggregated and examined separately, along with the rates for students who meet the state's 'economically disadvantaged' criteria. A school's rating is based on the performance of the lowest achieving group. Similarly, a district's rating is based on the performance of the lowest achieving group.
>
> (Ibid.: 279)

In many ways the accountability system in Texas is similar to that in England. However, what is of particular interest is that the incentive system is designed to focus attention on the *lowest* achieving groups. Notwithstanding the various concerns expressed about the Texas system, there appears to be some evidence of improvements amongst the most disadvantaged groups and the possibility that incentive-based approaches could assist with reducing achievement gaps between different groups of pupils should not be ignored.

Disadvantaged schools and school improvement

Mortimore and Whitty examined the extent to which school improvement can overcome the effects of disadvantage and their review of the literature showed that schools with disadvantaged pupils can be improved by committed and talented headteachers and teachers. As a word of caution the authors noted that: 'In order to achieve improvement, however, such schools have to exceed what could be termed "normal" efforts. Members of staff have to be more committed and work harder than their peers elsewhere' (2000: 14–15).

Some sociologists of education have been critical of school effectiveness research on the grounds that it focuses too much on schools and not enough on structural inequalities. As Mortimore and Whitty note, regardless of changes in the curriculum and the types of assessment, it is probably inevitable that schools will be affected by their role within a wider society that still has clear social divisions and hierarchies. Mortimore *et al.* (1988) demonstrated that no school reversed the usual pattern within schools, of advantaged pupils performing better than the disadvantaged.

However, some disadvantaged pupils in the most effective schools made more progress than their more advantaged peers in the least effective schools and in absolute terms also did better. But as Mortimore and Whitty note:

> it would appear that, if all primary schools were to improve so that they performed at the level of the most effective, the difference between the overall achievement of the most advantaged social groups and that of the disadvantaged might actually increase.
>
> (2000: 22)

They also stress the importance of resources in overcoming the gap between the achievement of the advantaged and disadvantaged, the need for positive discrimination and the effective targeting of human and material resources to schools with disadvantaged intakes.

Some have claimed that educational measures are unlikely to alleviate the impact of disadvantage (such as Robinson 1997b), and that the real targets should be social and economic disadvantage *per se*. Robinson proposes that attainment and literacy might be boosted more by alleviating child poverty than by intervention in schooling. Mortimore and Whitty argue, however, that schools can make some difference and that schools with disadvantaged intakes can lift attainment levels. 'Within any school, however, the powerful factors associated with a more advantaged home background appear, in general, to be paramount and this is even more evident when we look across the education system as a whole' (2000: 23–4).

What makes an effective school?

It is clear from school effectiveness research that some schools are more effective than others. However, we also need to be clear about what constitutes an 'effective' school. Different researchers have proposed different factors that are associated with effective schools, although similar themes have emerged in British studies (see Reynolds *et al.* 1997). Sammons (1999) provides eleven factors identified in a review carried out for the Office for Standards in Education. These are presented in Table 7.1.

These factors and variants of them are frequently mentioned in school-effectiveness research, but there has been a debate about the extent to which school effects are caused by factors within the school. Coe and Fitz-Gibbon argue that school effectiveness research has still to demonstrate the extent to which differences in schools' effectiveness are 'really caused by identifiable factors within the school and, perhaps more importantly, factors within their control' (1998: 422). In particular, they note: 'Measures of "value added" are generally defined only by default. So-called "effectiveness" usually means that part of pupils' performance which cannot be accounted for by their intake characteristics: in other words, a statistical residual' (1998: 424).

They note that pupil characteristics such as motivation or self-esteem, if measured appropriately, could account for a further part of pupils' performance given that previous research has indicated that such factors are associated with learning gains. This chimes with our earlier discussion about the importance of individual characteristics when exploring issues to do with achievement. To these pupil characteristics we might add factors associated with the child's home and family background – for example, the extent and type of parents' involvement in their children's learning, including, for example, support with homework; the use of private tutors; access to educational resources such as books, computers, and so on. Coe and Fitz-Gibbon make a similar point when they state:

Table 7.1 Factors associated with effective schools

Factor	Characteristics
Professional leadership	Firm and purposeful
	A participative approach
	The leading professional
Shared vision and goals	Unity of purpose
	Consistency of practice
	Collegiality and collaboration
A learning environment	An orderly atmosphere
	An attractive working environment
Concentration on teaching and learning	Maximisation of learning time
	Academic emphasis
	Focus on achievement
Purposeful teaching	Efficient organisation
	Clarity of purpose
	Structured lessons
	Adaptive practice
High expectations	High expectations all round
	Communicating expectations
	Providing intellectual challenge
Positive reinforcement	Clear and fair discipline
	Feedback
Monitoring progress	Monitoring pupil performance
	Evaluating school performance
Pupil rights and responsibilities	Raising pupil self-esteem
	Positions of responsibility
	Control of work
Home–school partnership	Parental involvement in their
	children's learning
A learning organisation	School-based staff development

Source: Sammons 1999.

Perhaps if we had a better understanding of which home background factors were important in influencing achievement, we would not only be able to formulate better value added models, but, more importantly, we might be able to do more to redress the inequality of disadvantage.

(1998: 426)

Another concern is made by Goldstein and Woodhouse, who note that there is a fundamental problem with one of the underlying assumptions of school effectiveness research, namely that schools are bodies that do not interact with the outside world. They comment on some of the problems related to school structures that we discussed in Chapter 6:

> A cursory reflection on the way schools function, especially in England, reveals that the actions and characteristics of any one school are linked to those of other schools. Schools which, in one way or another select students on the basis of their capabilities, influence the capacities of surrounding schools to do so ... Yet there is very little attempt within [school effectiveness] research to take this into account.
>
> (2000: 356)

They note that an important consequence of this is in its impact on school improvement research and practice, with attempts to change school practices being likely to meet with limited success if each school is considered to be a unit that functions independently. This is because:

> Schools function within a social and political system which has its own structures and processes, whether these be ones of inter-school competition or those determined by externally imposed constraints of curriculum or resources ... [T]here seems little in the research itself that seriously attempts to address this problem ... [School effectiveness research] has made almost no attempt to contextualise schools within the wider environment.
>
> (Ibid.: 356)

Observations in a similar vein have been made by Thrupp, who explored school effectiveness research and its limitations, with particular reference to the issue of 'school mix', or the social class composition of the school's pupil intake. He argues that many school processes that have been identified as contributing to pupil attainment may be 'less independent of school mix than researchers have typically allowed' (1999: 5). We return to these issues in our final chapter.

Conclusions

This chapter has examined some of the issues relating to school effectiveness research that have the potential to improve overall achievement levels. This has confirmed that schools do differ in terms of the extent to which they impact on pupils' progress, but the research reviewed highlights the importance of taking into account a range of individual pupil characteristics, such as motivation, family background and other background factors. It is also important for other issues to be addressed – in particular the possible relationship between factors considered to be important in order for schools to be effective and how these might be compromised by the characteristics of pupils within the schools. This is an issue we return to in Chapter 10.

Whilst the concerns raised in this chapter are important, this does not mean that we should ignore the research findings that have emerged over the years. Educational research on school effectiveness uses data that are available and has conceptualised effective schools using an evidence-based approach. Many of the factors identified in research concerned with school improvement are also apparent in our case study schools. There may be other characteristics of effective schools that attention could be focused on – for example, creating a working climate in which teachers can enjoy teaching and pupils who want to learn can do so, and developing a culture of collaboration (Haydn, 2001). These issues are discussed further in our case studies in Chapter 9.

In addition, it may be that by focusing on pupils and their families, as part of a school within a locality with other schools, and in a community with particular characteristics, improved effectiveness models can be produced.

In the meantime, all possible strategies need to be explored in efforts to raise pupils' attainment and the focus on what schools can do to overcome the effects of disadvantage is necessary. In particular, it is important to focus on what can be done at present. The evidence relating to leadership, for example, is likely to be important. Our two case studies demonstrate quite clearly the importance of leadership in motivating pupils and teachers.

This chapter has described and contrasted two distinct avenues aimed at enhancing pupil achievement. School effectiveness research suggests that effective schools 'jack up' the performance of all groups, whilst a different approach has been adopted in Texas, where an accountability system has been introduced. The latter suggests that such systems can result in attention being focused on underachieving groups. Indeed, in England there is evidence that the focus on the 'five or more high grade GCSEs' has concentrated attention on pupils at the C/D borderline at the possible expense of other groups. We would argue that introducing targets that focus specifically on the achievement of *all* pupils would serve to direct attention to lower performing groups of students (see Chapter 10). This is already the case in some schools. Indeed, as noted by one of our case study headteachers (see Chapter 9), 'by getting those from the lower end of the ability range on board there has been an extremely positive effect on the whole school'.

Chapter 8

Government policy and raising achievement

Introduction

Previous chapters have examined underachievement and how it relates to different factors – social class, ethnicity, gender and a range of others. Some of the structural barriers to raising achievement have been explored and the evidence examining the extent to which schools can overcome the effects of disadvantage has been reviewed.

In this chapter we explore government policy and initiatives to raise attainment. We focus in the main on the situation in England. We examine in the first instance how the government targets resources on disadvantage. We then move on to examine a selection of targeted initiatives designed to raise standards, in particular, Sure Start, Excellence in Cities and Study Support. The final section concludes the chapter by summarising the key issues to emerge.

Disadvantage and funding schools

Methods used to compensate for disadvantage

Governments have responded to the deleterious effects of disadvantage on schooling in different ways. In the 1960s and 1970s in England, Education Priority Areas were designated and schools with high proportions of disadvantaged pupils received additional funds in an effort to compensate for the effects of poverty (see Sammons 1999) and although Education Priority Areas no longer exist, current policy also targets funds on areas of disadvantage.

Money reaches schools through various means. Most comes

from central government and is distributed to local authorities via the Office of the Deputy Prime Minister (ODPM). The local element comes via the Council Tax – a local property tax which accounts for only about 20 per cent of the funds spent by local authorities on service provision.

Most of the funds from the ODPM are allocated to local authorities via the Revenue Support Grant, which provides funding for the various service areas for which a local authority is responsible. For each service area (for example, education, social services) there are allocations (formerly known as 'standard spending assessments'), which represent what central government believes the authority should spend (see Audit Commission 1993; West *et al.* 2000a, 2000b). The system used by central government to allocate funds for education to local government is designed to compensate for extra costs incurred by authorities in different parts of the country and with different population characteristics. The allocation for education thus includes an additional element to take into account the additional costs incurred by local authorities as a result of the levels of disadvantage in the authority, the population density and additional costs associated with London and the South East of England (Department of the Environment 1990).

Local authorities do not have to spend at the level of this allocation, but research (West *et al.* 1999) has found that their expenditure on education is very closely related to, but on average slightly higher than, the government's allocation. In 2001–2, the Education Standard Spending Assessment per secondary school pupil ranged from £2,905 (Rutland) to £5,336 (Lambeth) (Education Funding Strategy Group 2001). Across England the average amount per secondary school pupil was £3,313 (this excludes the Isles of Scilly and Corporation of London, which have very few schools). The highest levels were for the inner London LEAs; here the levels of need are the highest of any region in the country, as measured by known eligibility for free school meals, at 42 per cent, compared with 16 per cent in England as a whole (DfES 2001c).

Local authorities decide their own education budgets and set these annually; funds are allocated to schools using formulae ('Fair Funding') whose parameters are set by government (see West *et al.* 2000a, 2000b, 2001). In short, all state-funded schools (community, voluntary and foundation) receive most of their funds via their local authorities, although the principal source of these funds is central government. It is important to note that most of the funds are allocated to schools according to pupil numbers weighted for their age. There is limited scope for LEAs to target funds on disadvantage (Mortimore and Whitty 2000; West *et al.* 2000a).

Are expenditure and results related?

An obvious question at this juncture is to ask whether there is any evidence to associate higher spending with higher test or examination results. This has been a controversial issue and has been examined by a number of researchers. Much of the research has been carried out in the USA, where there is much less redistribution than in England (Odden and Picus 1992), and has shown mixed results (see Hanushek 1998), and although a number of studies do suggest a positive association between resourcing levels and outcomes, others do not. Mayston notes:

> The apparent lack of any clear positive relationship between resourcing and educational attainment, however, runs counter to intuitive expectations and to many outside observers appears mysterious.
>
> (Mayston 1996: 128)

West *et al.* (2001) noted that the majority of studies in the UK have attempted to construct statistical models relating examination results to a range of predictor variables, with expenditure (or a proxy for expenditure, such as pupil–teacher ratio or class size) included as one of many other, frequently highly intercorrelated, variables – typically these include measures of socio-economic status, unemployment and poor housing. They noted that because of the high levels of association between such variables it is virtually impossible to detect the effect of any one of the variables using the approach adopted. Using a somewhat different approach West *et al.* found evidence that higher expenditure by LEAs (school-level data were not available) was associated with better examination results once poverty had been controlled for, lending support to the use of increased expenditure as a means of combating educational disadvantage.

It is also of interest to note that Mayston, in a report examining the relationship between school spending and pupil outcomes, argued that 'existing studies have produced estimates of the impact of expenditure on pupil attainment that are likely to be biased downwards' (2002: 4).

Using a very different approach, Blatchford *et al.* (2002) found a significant effect of class size – which is clearly related to expenditure – on children's educational progress in the reception year for both literacy and mathematics. However, the study found no clear evidence of an effect of class size on progress in Years 1 or 2, for either subject area. Their findings indicated – unsurprisingly perhaps – that as class sizes increased less time was available for teaching and for listening to children read individually.

Interestingly, a study by Bradley *et al.* found that the change in pupil/teacher ratios is negatively related to the change in performance at the five or more GCSE A* to C level: 'This result suggests that schools which allow their pupil/teacher ratios to increase can expect this to have a negative effect on their exam performance' (2000: 379). This finding again points towards a positive relationship between expenditure and results.

Notwithstanding the debate about whether or not additional resources do improve levels of attainment, the government would appear to support the view that resources should be targeted where needs are the greatest on the one hand, and on the other that additional funds can improve levels of attainment. We now outline in broad terms how resources have been targeted in recent years in an attempt to improve levels of attainment.

Targeted policies to raise achievement

Policy context

In this section we examine government policy addressed to the raising of attainment, specifically as it relates to England. It is important to acknowledge that many of the education reforms introduced since 1988 can be seen as attempts to raise attainment – ranging from the introduction of the national curriculum and national assessment and the introduction of school performance tables (see also Chapter 6) to the creation of the Office for Standards in Education (OFSTED) with its programme of regular independent school inspection.

It is noteworthy that since it was elected into office in 1997, the

Labour government has increasingly directed funds to support specific initiatives, designed in many cases to meet DfES 'targets' (see Appendix D). It has also focused on 'standards' and 'achievement' in particular. A number of policies and initiatives have been introduced. Some, like the national literacy and numeracy strategies, are designed for all primary schools, whilst others are more targeted on achievement and others are more focused on participation. For example, recent targets are aimed at ensuring that all pupils who are permanently excluded obtain an appropriate full-time education and at reducing unauthorised absence from schools by 10 per cent between 2002 and 2004 (DfES 2002m).

In addition to these *specific targets*, a number of new *targeted policies* have been introduced that are focused on disadvantaged areas and aimed at boosting achievement in those areas. In the case of many of these it is too early to say if there has been an impact on achievement. Nevertheless, it is important to acknowledge that policies have been introduced with the explicit aim of reducing 'underachievement'. As the Minister of State for School Standards noted soon after his appointment in 2002:

> The Government's strategy is to use a combination of general policies to raise standards across the board with targeted policies to raise achievement in some of our toughest areas ... Targeted policies are designed to help schools in challenging circumstances overcome special obstacles that stand in their way. These include the extra resources for Excellence in Cities and Excellence Clusters, the programme for schools in challenging circumstances.
> (David Miliband MP, Minister of State for School Standards, 8 July 2002 [DfES 2002e])

The targeted policies referred to are associated with additional funding that is channelled to schools and LEAs; virtually all of these are related to raising levels of achievement. The use of 'targeted' support is not new, but the Labour government is spending more on its own initiatives than did the previous Conservative government. In 1996–7, the last year of the Conservative administration, 4.4 per cent of current expenditure on schools and early years came direct from central government (and not via the Revenue Support Grant to local authorities). By 2000–1, this had increased to an estimated 13.6 per cent (calculated by authors from DfES 2001h).

The main way in which funds have been channelled to schools for targeted support has been through the Standards Fund. For the financial year 2002–3, there were a total of 60 grants under the Standards Fund (DfES 2002f, 2002g). Standards Fund expenditure is increased from £177 million in 1996–7 to an estimated £750 million in 2000–1 (DfES 2001h).

These grants were divided into six main categories, as shown in Figure 8.1.

Government initiatives targeting disadvantage

In this section we provide details of selected government initiatives designed to target disadvantage and raise attainment. These include Sure Start, an initiative for the early years, and a number of initiatives funded through the Standards Fund, namely, Excellence in Cities, Schools in Challenging Circumstances, Ethnic Minorities Achievement Grant, Study Support and the Pupil Retention Grant.

Early-years provision

Early-years provision has been shown to have beneficial outcomes for children. A systematic review of eight randomised controlled trials of out-of-home day care in the USA before the age of 5 years found positive outcomes (see Acheson 1998). Altogether, over 2,000 children were allocated randomly to a group that received day care and a group that did not. The follow up ranged from six months to twenty-seven years. Most of the studies targeted families from lower socio-economic groups and most included some home visiting and training for parents. Although the formal educational component varied, all were concerned with attaining cognitive concepts. The studies all found that IQ increased with participation in day care but this was not found to persist much beyond the end of the care. Interestingly, however, in terms of educational performance, scores tended to be higher in the groups that received day care. One of the studies (the Perry or Highscope Project) followed up individuals to the age of 27 and found that those from the day-care group were more likely to have positive social outcomes in terms of, for example, high-school graduation, fewer teenage pregnancies, fewer arrests and higher earnings.

School improvement

Grants in this category are to 'enable schools to raise their levels of achievement; and to enable LEAs to provide schools, especially those causing concern, with support and challenge' (p. 5).

Grants include 'schools facing challenging circumstances'.

Inclusion

Grants in this category are designed to 'remove barriers to progress, address special educational needs and promote social inclusion. In particular, to reduce exclusion, raise attendance, provide full-time education for children out of school and address key social needs' (p. 5).

Grants include: social-inclusion pupil support; teenage pregnancy; drug, alcohol and tobacco prevention; study support.

Standards and curriculum

Grants in this category are designed 'to raise standards of achievement across the curriculum' (p. 5).

Grants include: national literacy and numeracy strategies; ethnic minority achievement; playing for success.

Diversity and excellence

Grants in this category are designed to 'raise performance, achieve excellence and transform school education through a targeted programme of support' (p. 5).

Grants include: Excellence in Cities; specialist schools.

Teachers and support

This grant is designed 'to develop the skills and enhance the status of all teachers and headteachers' (p. 5).

Capital and infrastructure

This category is designed 'to help raise standards through effective investment in school buildings and infrastructure, including the capacity to use Information Communications Technology (ICT)' (p. 5).

Figure 8.1 Standards Fund categories and examples of grants 2002–3.

Source: DfES (2002f).

Small-scale studies relating to pre-school education have also been carried out in the UK. Research indicates that in comparison to no experience, all forms of pre-school experience have a positive impact (Sammons and Smees 1998). However, a crucial determinant in terms of educational attainment is the *quality* of provision – frequently small group size, high adult to child ratios, a balanced curriculum and trained staff.

Given the positive research evidence on the benefits of pre-school education and other early intervention, the expansion of such provision for those in poverty has become a focus of government policy. West and Sparkes (2002) report on a number of government initiatives, including the opening of new Early Excellence Centres to demonstrate good practice in education, childcare and integrated services and to disseminate good practice, and the Sure Start programme. Sure Start is a particularly innovative programme set up in 1999 and is considered to be the cornerstone of the government's drive to tackle child poverty and social exclusion (DfES 2002h). The aim of Sure Start is to work with parents-to-be, parents and children to promote the physical, intellectual and social development of babies and young children – particularly those who are disadvantaged.

Sure Start focuses on children up to the age of 4 years. It is a locally delivered cross-departmental government initiative and is designed to improve the health and well-being of children and families and children before and from birth by setting up local Sure Start programmes to improve services for families with children under the age of 4, and spreading good practice learned from local programmes to everyone involved in providing services for children (DfES 2002h).

The programmes are not identical as they are designed to meet local needs, but all bring a number of diverse and core services together and include: outreach and home visiting; support for families and parents; support for high-quality play, learning and childcare experiences for children; primary and community health care; support for children and parents with special needs. By April 2002, over 400 Sure Start programmes had been announced, of which over 200 had been approved and were delivering services (the remainder were in the planning stage). It is too early to report on the outcomes of this programme.

Excellence in Cities

Excellence in Cities (EiC) is a large-scale initiative that acknowledges the need to invest heavily in inner-city schools to improve levels of attainment. It was set up in 1999 and targets resources on areas of need. One of the reasons for focusing attention on inner-city schools is that in some of these schools that achievement is at its lowest. For example, the White Paper 'Schools achieving Success' (DfES 2001i) noted that there were 480 secondary schools in England (around 15 per cent of all secondary schools) in which 25 per cent or less of pupils achieved five or more high-grade (A* to C) GCSEs. Sixty-five per cent were in largely urban areas, and the levels of poverty, as measured by known eligibility for free school meals, were often above 35 per cent (compared with the national average for secondary schools of 16 per cent in 2001).

The Excellence in Cities programme originally focused on secondary schools in six large conurbations – inner London, Birmingham, Manchester, Liverpool, Leeds and Sheffield (Phase 1 authorities). The following year it was expanded to thirty-three new LEAs (Phase 2), including parts of outer London, Tyne and Wear, Teeside, Bristol, Leicester, Nottingham and Hull and other deprived metropolitan authorities in Merseyside and Greater Manchester, with expansion to a subset of primary schools in Phase 1 authorities (DfES 2002i). Further expansion to ten new authorities took place in 2001 (Phase 3). In 2002 there were fifty-eight LEAs involved in Excellence in Cities.

The three key facets of the strategy for secondary schools are:

- the Gifted and Talented programme, which supports the most able pupils, through activities within the school and extension activities outside school;
- Learning Mentors, who provide support to pupils who have particular obstacles to learning;
- Learning Support Units, which are aimed at tackling disruption in schools; pupils whose behaviour disrupts the learning of others can be removed from the classroom and given appropriate support.

In short, the three core strands of the Excellence in Cities policy are thus extending opportunities for 'Gifted and Talented' pupils, providing schools with access to a Learning Support Unit for pupils who would benefit from time away from the normal classroom and providing a Learning Mentor for pupils who are perceived to need one.

Other aspects of the Excellence in Cities policy include expanding and reformulating the specialist (see Chapter 6) and beacon schools programmes (see DfES and OFSTED 2002), developing City Learning Centres, which are school-based ICT centres designed to act as centres of excellence; and introducing Excellence in Cities Action Zones, which focus on low performance in small clusters of schools.

Some preliminary findings from the independent evaluation of the policy have been published (Stoney *et al.* 2002). It is also of interest to note that the policy has been extended to include a Primary Pilot for selected primary schools, and small clusters of schools in disadvantaged areas outside the main urban conurbations known as Excellence Clusters. Moreover, an early Labour government initiative that established statutory Education Action Zones (EAZ) is to be combined with the 'Excellence' initiatives (DfES 2001j). Statutory Education Action Zones were designed to encourage innovation and were supported by private-sector cash and 'in-kind' support. The government has stated its intention to continue to support ex-Zone schools following the end of each EAZ's five-year statutory term. The aim is for many of these to be integrated into Excellence in Cities, with an increase in the number of EiC Action Zones (designed to raise standards in one or more secondary schools and associated primary schools) and Excellence Clusters.

Schools in challenging circumstances

It is of relevance in the current context to refer to one small pilot project focusing on schools with low levels of pupil attainment. In September 2001, the Labour government started funding a small pilot project with eight well-managed secondary schools facing a combination of very high levels of deprivation and/or very high levels of pupil turnover and/or a very large proportion of pupils who speak English as a second language. The proposals hinge on schools finding new ways to use the skills of their teaching staff and other adults in order to improve the achievement of their pupils. The proposals include teachers planning together, observing each other, radically reducing class size and working with the community to integrate activities with community regeneration programmes (DfES 2001i).

Ethnic Minority Achievement Grant

Over the years, both Labour and Conservative governments have provided funds to address the achievement of pupils from minority ethnic groups. From the 1960s onwards money was allocated for this purpose under what was known as Section 11 funding, named after the part of the Local Government Act 1966 that sanctioned the funding. Section 11 enabled central Government to make grants to local authorities for the purpose of promoting race equality by the provision of special funding for black and minority ethnic communities (West *et al.* 1994). In 1999/2000 Section 11 was replaced by the Ethnic Minority Achievement Grant, which is primarily concerned with provision for minority ethnic pupils in schools and is designed specifically to meet the particular needs of pupils for whom English is an additional language (EAL); and to raise standards of achievement for those minority ethnic groups who are particularly at risk of underachieving (DfES 2002j).

According to the White Paper 'Schools Achieving Success' (DfES 2001i), the Ethnic Minority Achievement Grant (EMAG) will be targeted and evaluated to do more to reinforce national strategies through mainstream teaching. Amongst the commitments made by the government were:

- to make resources available through linking EMAG with programmes aimed at raising standards such as Excellence in Cities;
- to monitor achievement targets that LEAs set as a condition of receiving EMAG to ensure that they focus on closing the achievement gap;
- to monitor the progress of pupils from ethnic minority groups;
- to support teachers in helping pupils who are unable to speak English;
- to recruit more teachers from ethnic minority backgrounds.

(DfES 2001i: 24)

Study support

Unlike the other initiatives described, study support embraces a wide range of diverse programmes, many of them locally generated, often with business support (see, for example, Kleinman *et al.* 1998), and involves pupils in out-of-school learning. There are also many different types of study support. MacBeath *et al.* (2001), for example, include the following specific types: subject-focused study support (for example, mathematics, English); study skills; sport; aesthetic; peer education (for example helping with paired reading); drop-in (for example homework clubs); mentoring; and study centres.

A major evaluation of study support (MacBeath *et al.* 2001) involving over 8,000 pupils tracked from Years 7 and 9, found evidence that pupils who participated in study support did better than expected from baseline measures of academic attainment, attitudes to school and attendance at school. The research found that study support appeared to be particularly successful for those from minority ethnic communities. Boys and girls appeared to benefit to a similar extent. There appeared to be an independent effect of study support at GCSE as measured by the score on the best five GCSEs, on the number of GCSEs at grades A* to C and on mathematics and English GCSE results. It was found that GCSE attainment was more affected by 'subject-focused, drop-in provision and Easter revision courses' (ibid.: 7). However, it must be noted that the study compared those who participated in study support with those who did not and there could be differences between these two groups that may also help explain the differences observed. For example, the researchers noted that there was a lower likelihood of participation by those with low self-esteem. This is perhaps always likely to be a problem with study support activities.

Using a different approach, Sharp *et al.* (2002) examined the impact of a national initiative set up by the DfES in conjunction with the Football Association Premier League, the Nationwide League and their clubs and LEAs. This scheme, known as 'Playing for Success', involves establishing study support centres in professional football clubs. The centres use the 'medium and environment of football to support work in literacy, numeracy and ICT' (ibid.: 1) and focus on 'underachieving' pupils in Years 6 to 9; the initial numeracy and reading comprehension scores of participants were found to be well below average for their age. The evaluation used nationally standardised tests of numeracy and reading comprehension specifically designed for the evaluation to assess pupils' progress; it involved comparing pupils who had participated in the scheme with a control group who had not. It was found that on average the participants made significant progress in basic skills, and this was particularly significant in relation to numeracy and ICT. Interestingly, the beneficial effects were not affected by pupils' gender, deprivation, ethnicity, fluency in English or special educational needs.

Incentives to reduce exclusions and truancy

As we discussed in Chapter 5, truancy and exclusions are associated with poor educational outcomes. The Labour government has recognised the need to tackle these issues and has set itself the target of reducing school truancy by one-third and reducing permanent exclusions to 8,400 by 2002 (see DfEE and OFSTED 2001). This target was met in 1999/2000 (see Chapter 4).

In seeking to reduce school exclusions, the government used a novel 'incentive/disincentive' approach through its 'social inclusion: pupil support' grant (part of the DfES Standards Fund until 2003–4), which was allocated to LEAs by a formula based on pupil numbers weighted by free school meals entitlement. LEAs were required to devolve at least 77 per cent of this grant to schools as 'pupil retention grant'. This was designed to assist with reducing levels of exclusion and truancy and to promote the inclusion of children with behavioural difficulties in mainstream schools.

West and Pennell (2002) note that this was not an incentive-based system but a mixture of an incentive and disincentive system, with schools being allocated funds but then having money withdrawn if pupils were excluded. Under the Pupil Retention Grant (PRG), LEAs are required to develop a formula, agreed with schools, for distributing this grant between schools. Formula factors suggested by the DfEE (1999d) were 'pupil turnover, numbers of looked after children or in contact with Social Services, numbers of ethnic minority pupils, or incidence of youth crime'. LEAs and schools were able to agree procedures at a local level for using the PRG to support pupils once they had been permanently excluded, but if such agreement could not be reached, the school's allocation of PRG was reduced by £3,000 to

£6,000 per year for each pupil permanently excluded (DfES 2002f).

From the above discussion, it is clear that government money *is* being targeted on disadvantaged areas and on pupils at risk of social and school exclusion. Moreover, whilst the system that is used to target resources on disadvantage via the Revenue Support Grant is open to criticism for lacking transparency, the targeting is clearer in the case of these specific initiatives.

Conclusions

In terms of government policy, a wide range of approaches has been used to counter disadvantage and low levels of achievement. The national funding formula (formerly the Education Standard Spending System, now the Education Formula Spend) used to fund local education authorities provides additional resources that are intended to provide compensation for the additional cost of providing services in an area where there are high levels of disadvantage. In addition, through its Standards Fund and a range of other funding streams from other government departments, the government has developed policy initiatives designed to focus attention particularly on disadvantage.

These are varied and include targeting funds directly on LEAs and schools with high levels of disadvantage and developing initiatives to focus attention on particular groups of pupils with low levels of attainment and/or high levels of deprivation. There is evidence to suggest that some of these approaches could have a positive impact on achievement levels.

A point to which we return in Chapter 10 is the need for the government to ensure that accountability mechanisms are in place to focus attention on the achievement of *all pupils*. However, it can be argued that, in terms of achievement, the government's targets (see Appendix D) have primarily been aimed at raising the attainment of higher-performing pupils (see also Gillborn and Youdell (2000) for a discussion of the 'A-to-C economy').

Our case-study schools are notable in that their efforts to raise achievement have focused on all pupils. A greater drive by government at a national level to improve the attainment levels of all pupils is likely to be successful given the fact that schools as organisations have clearly responded to the 'five or more high-grade GCSE' target.

We would also argue that the policy in relation to providing incentives and disincentives to reduce the number of school exclusions was an interesting one, which may have played a part in reducing school exclusions. We would argue that greater financial incentives to admit and retain pupils who have low levels of achievement or are 'hard to teach' should be considered by the government. This is further explored in Chapter 10.

Chapter 9

Schools raising attainment
Case studies

Introduction

Earlier chapters have examined how students from different groups perform at school and how their levels of achievement vary. We have examined a range of factors that may help to explain some of the variation in performance, including those related to both home and school. We have also explored the findings from research on school effectiveness and school improvement, and highlighted the ways in which government policies may affect attainment.

Although some of the ways in which schools might attempt to raise achievement have been discussed generally in earlier chapters, we now want to focus very directly on individual schools and how they have successfully tackled underachievement among their students.

It is clear from the previous chapters that some common themes emerge when we examine underachievement in schools and as we have seen there are almost certainly a number of prerequisites that are needed before underachievement can be properly addressed. In particular, it is important to note that the school effectiveness research stresses a number of key features of 'effective' schools – such as leadership and good monitoring of performance – and this is apparent in the case studies that are presented in this chapter.

This chapter provides two case studies of schools and describes the strategies that they have adopted to raise the overall attainment of pupils. It is important to note that the strategies selected by schools will vary according to the characteristics of the student population. Moreover, as research evidence has not clearly identified strategies that have been successful in combating low levels of achievement, schools are more open to experiment with different approaches in order to establish which methods appear to be most successful with the students in their school. It is important to stress that in many cases, experimenting is what we are talking about – the research evidence is far from clear-cut about exactly what works and what does not.

The case study schools have been chosen to highlight the different ways in which attainment has in practice been raised. The schools are located in very different parts of the country – one, which we have called 'Beech School', is in a disadvantaged London LEA, whilst the other ('Maple High School') is in a shire LEA in the east of England. Although, as we shall see, the schools are different in key respects, their examination results at GCSE level have improved over the years. This cannot be attributed to major changes in the characteristics of the student body, as this has not changed significantly over the period in question.

Case study – Beech School: the role of the headteacher and school improvement

Introduction

Our first case study is a mixed comprehensive school for 11 to 18 year olds with approximately 1,700 students on roll. The majority of the students are drawn from two nearby large council estates. The percentage known to be eligible for free school meals is 36 per cent, which is well above the England average of 16 per cent for secondary schools (DfES 2001c). Most of the children are white, but a growing number do not have English as their first language. The percentage of students with a statement of special educational needs is 2.3 per cent and the percentage of those with non-statemented special educational needs is 20.1 per cent (DfES 2001k); this compares with 2.5 per cent and 20.7 per cent respectively in secondary schools in England (DfES 2001c).

A distinctive feature of the area in which the school is located is the very low number of adults who have had successful experience of higher education. The OFSTED report (1999b) notes that a significant number of students are from crowded households.

Examination results and inspection evidence

The school's GCSE results have improved markedly in recent years. Table 9.1 gives details of the percentage of students in the Year 11 cohort that achieved five or more high grade GCSEs between 1996 and 2001 for the school and for England.

In terms of the government's key indicator, the percentage of pupils gaining five or more high grade GCSEs (grades A* to C) has increased from 17 per cent in 1996 to 39 per cent in 2001 – an increase of twenty-two percentage points. This compares with a five percentage point increase nationally.

Table 9.2 gives details of the percentage of students in the Year 11 cohort who achieved no GCSEs between 1996 and 2001 for the school and for England.

As we can see, the percentage of pupils with no passes has

Table 9.1 Percentage of students achieving five or more GCSEs grades A* to C (Beech School)

Year	% of students at Beech School	% of students in England
1996	17	45
1997	22	45
1998	23	46
1999	36	48
2000	38	49
2001	39	50
Change 1996 to 2001	+22	+5

Source: DfES performance tables 1996–2001.

Table 9.2 Percentage of students achieving no GCSE passes (Beech School)

Year	% of students at Beech School	% of students in England
1996	18	8
1997	10	8
1998	8	7
1999	5	6
2000	0	6
2001	0	6
Change 1996 to 2001	−18	−2

Source: DfES performance tables 1996–2001.

decreased from 18 per cent to 0 per cent over the same time period compared with a two percentage point decrease nationally from 8 per cent to 6 per cent.

The school's examination results showed further improvements in 2002, with 46 per cent of pupils obtaining five or more high grade GCSEs and, once again, all pupils gaining at least one GCSE pass (at A* to G). Moreover, virtually all of the pupils (98 per cent) obtained five or more GCSE passes at A* to G.

It is important to note that the school is a community school and so the local education authority controls its admissions. This means that the improvements in examination results cannot be attributed in a significant way to changes in its intake; in fact, it is noteworthy that because of its popularity, pupils can only get into the school from within a very small radius of the school from the local council estates, where households are often overcrowded.

The school was last inspected in 1999 (OFSTED 1999b). At that time the inspectors reported that immediately following the previous inspection, the school had fallen into decline. However, the report goes on to say:

> A new headteacher, appointed midway between the two inspections has transformed the school. Standards are now rising, behaviour is very good, teaching has become a strength and an excellent ethos has been established.
>
> (OFSTED 1999b: 7)

Changes that took place

The question arises of how these changes took place. A study carried out by Haydn (2001) addressed this issue. He interviewed twenty-three teachers at the school and the headteacher. The interviews with teachers focused on their explanations for the improvements that they all agreed had taken place. Haydn found that the factor that was mentioned most frequently as assisting teachers to teach was the establishment of a controlled and co-operative working atmosphere; this was mentioned by twenty-one of the twenty-three interviewees.

Haydn also noted that another factor that staff felt had been crucial when the headteacher was appointed (having previously been the head of the school's successful history department) was that pupils were required to adhere to strict codes of conduct or they would risk being excluded. Haydn reported that staff praised the headteacher for his willingness to deal with difficult pupils and to fully support staff.

The headteacher indicated that pastoral care and support of teachers had been the most urgent issue to address in enabling the school to make such good progress. This is what he said:

> Much of the publicity about education is predicated on the idea that there is a lot of inadequate performance – this is particularly damaging when a school has got a poor reputation – teachers have got to be looked after and supported, through actions, not just words ... If staff are giving many, many hours of time within and outside school working with pupils, and for pupils, fully committed to doing their best for the pupils in their care, they have got to feel valued and appreciated.
>
> (Quoted in Haydn 2001: 426)

The headteacher also regarded restoring control to the school as important and particularly valued the support of the local education authority in the early months of his headship. During this time exclusions from school were in the region of 100 to 200 per month, but were felt to be vital in order to restore the confidence of both teachers and parents (see Haydn 2001). It is significant that since 1998 there have been no permanent exclusions. Recent developments in the school have focused on developing behaviour-management systems that are continually strengthening the original system. The headteacher noted that these have been designed to develop 'an ethos where people feel protected'.

The headteacher indicated that the support of the school governors was an important element in achieving success. He also stressed the importance of focusing on the improvements in the percentage of pupils achieving at least one GCSE at grades A* to G – as shown in Table 9.1, all pupils achieved at least one pass in both 2000 and 2001. The headteacher also pointed out that 'by getting those from the lower end of the ability range on board there has been an extremely positive effect on the whole school'.

Haydn (2001) noted that although target setting, which is advocated in the school improvement literature, was part of the school's strategy for improvement, it was not a key feature for teachers' explanations for the progress that the school had made. Three points emerged that did seem to be pinpointed by staff: 'supporting teachers in establishing the right to learn'; 'joy in work'; and 'a culture of collaboration', as shown in Figure 9.1.

Given our earlier discussion about the role of school effectiveness, Haydn noted that the factors highlighted above are not fully acknowledged either in school improvement literature or in DfES material. A final point made by Haydn was that the potential for improvement from *within* the school may have been underestimated.

• 'Supporting teacher in establishing the right to learn'

'One of the key elements underpinning the success of [Beech School] has been the success in creating a working climate where teachers can enjoy teaching, and pupils who want to learn can do so in a relaxed and co-operative learning environment.'

(Haydn 2001: 429)

• 'Joy in work'

'One of the most striking features of the conversations with teachers at [Beech School] was the extent to which they enjoyed their work, and found their classroom teaching, and work within the school fulfilling and rewarding. Those arguing for "naming and shaming", "keeping up the pressure" and the public identification of failing, coasting, non-target meeting schools and teachers should keep in mind that no-one is trying to do it badly, and that many teachers in inner-city schools are performing heroically in very difficult circumstances.'

(Ibid.: 431)

• 'A culture of collaboration'

'Perhaps the most striking thing about my visits to the school was the extent to which the head of history, who was to become the headteacher, was able to get people to achieve remarkable success by getting them to work together. The more successful departments had not been used as a stick to beat the others with.'

(Ibid.: 432)

Figure 9.1 Factors accounting for improvement.

Source: Haydn 2001.

Case study – Maple High School: raising attainment – a focus on boys

Introduction

Our second case study is a mixed community comprehensive school for 11 to 18 year olds with 1,500 students on roll. It serves a market town and a very spread-out rural community and, as is the case with Beech School, the improvements cannot be attributed to significant changes in its intake. The headteacher joined the school in 1996. The information provided below is taken from the school's most recent OFSTED report (1997) and from the DfES performance tables. The account of the school's initiatives to raise pupil attainment was provided by the headteacher of Maple High School and updated with her.

The social and economic characteristics of the area the school serves are mixed, but overall are in line with the national average (OFSTED 1997). Attendance is above the national average. Almost all the children are white and come from homes in which the first language is English. The percentage of pupils known to be eligible for free school meals was around 10 per cent in 1997, which was below the national average. In 2001, 1.8 per cent of the students had statements of special educational need and 11.5 per cent had non-statemented special educational needs (2001k). In September 2002, the school became one of the first mathematics and computing specialist schools.

School examination results

Maple High School's GCSE results have improved in recent years. Table 9.3 gives details of the percentage of students in the Year 11 cohort who achieved five or more high grade GCSEs between 1996 and 2001 for the school and for England.

In terms of the government's key indicator, the percentage of pupils gaining five or more high grade GCSEs (grades A* to C) has increased from 42 per cent in 1996 to 67 per cent in 2001 – an increase of twenty-five percentage points. This compares with a five percentage point increase nationally.

Table 9.4 gives details of the percentage of students in the Year 11 cohort who achieved no GCSEs between 1996 and 2001 for the school and for England.

Table 9.3 Percentage of students achieving five or more GCSEs grades A* to C

Year	% of students at Maple High School	% of students in England
1996	42	45
1997	53	45
1998	59	46
1999	64	48
2000	64	49
2001	67	50
Change 1996 to 2001	+25	+5

Source: DfES performance tables 1996–2001.

Table 9.4 Percentage of students achieving no GCSE passes (Maple High School)

Year	% of students at Maple High School	% of students in England
1996	2	8
1997	1	8
1998	3	7
1999	1	6
2000	1	6
2001	0	6
Change 1996 to 2001	–2	–2

Source: DfES performance tables 1996–2001.

As we can see, the percentage of pupils with no passes de-creased from 2 per cent to 0 per cent over this period compared with a two percentage point decrease nationally from 8 per cent to 6 per cent.

It is important to note that the school is a community school and so the local education authority controls its admissions. This means that the improvements in examination results cannot be attributed to changes in its intake.

Raising attainment in Maple High School

The headteacher made a report about raising attainment at her school, a strategy that was adopted when she arrived at the school in 1996 (see Hargadon 2001); this has been updated to reflect the situation at the end of the academic year 2001/2.

> It is very important to stress that we have not aimed as a school to focus on the achievement of boys – we have, however, focused a great deal on promoting attainment, especially at key stage 4. It has been inevitable, because most of our underachievement has been by boys, that they have particularly benefited from this work.
>
> (Headteacher of Maple High School)

The headteacher believes that there are key reasons for underachievement by boys. These are shown in Figure 9.2.

In the light of these various factors, the school set up a range of strategies to promote attainment. This started with Year 11 'in order to have an immediate effect'. However, this now starts much earlier, in Year 7, as noted by the headteacher:

> As the results have steadily improved, we have found the impact of the changes have led to a change in culture and so the positive approach to learning is rubbing off in all aspects of the school and appears to be having a very positive effect.
>
> (Headteacher of Maple High School)

The headteacher noted that a range of strategies has been implemented in order to promote a more positive school culture and ethos, as shown in Figure 9.3.

The school has detailed academic information – from Key Stage 2 – on each student and uses this throughout the school to check if students are performing at the level that the school feels they are

---

- Peer pressure on boys to 'muck around' and not work hard.
- Boys overestimating how well they are going to do in examinations.
- Boys being less keen than girls on coursework.
- Boys not being as tolerant as girls of 'mediocre teaching'.
- Boys not taking responsibility for their own learning.

Figure 9.2 Key reasons for the underachievement of boys.

Source: Headteacher of Maple High School (in Hargadon 2001).

- Good quality display throughout the school including areas to celebrate success.
- A good and consistent praise and rewards system.
- Improvement of central areas in the school including the library.
- Effective use of media, including TV, to praise the school.
- A fortnightly newsletter which tells everyone in the school community all the exciting things taking place and celebrates our successes.
- Huge celebration assemblies at the end of each term.
- Reminding the students of how great the school is and encouraging them to achieve at the highest level.
- Setting of internal exams and linking assessment to each student's potential.
- Regular feedback to parents which focuses on achievement against potential attainment.
- Giving students responsibility so that they feel involved through school council, student members of working parties and supporting younger students.

Figure 9.3 Range of strategies introduced to promote positive ethos.

Source: Headteacher of Maple High School (in Hargadon 2001).

capable of. Both qualitative and quantitative information are used so that staff are aware from the earliest stage if a student is under-achieving:

> Where there is underachievement we have target setting, monitoring and special six-week achievement schemes throughout the school to target those students . . . It involves a meeting with parents and students at the start (with ex-students who have been on the scheme) and a follow-up meeting . . . individually with senior teacher, year co-ordinator and the tutor as well as the parent/s to celebrate their achievements . . . At the end there is a small prize for those who have done well . . . In very successful cases it is the turning point for students who then go on to achieve at their potential level. We give students, and their parents, regular information about their level of attainment so they constantly know at what level they are achieving and can't overestimate it.
>
> (Headteacher of Maple High School)

Another strategy used by the school is to attempt to appoint effective teachers. The school works with teachers:

> to promote effective discipline and the senior management team offer support in classes where discipline can be poor so that there is always a positive working atmosphere. We believe, and research backs it up, that students prefer well-managed lessons where they have no choice but to stay on task. Boys in particular feel that if there is the opportunity to muck around they have to take it in order not to be seen to be a 'boff'.
>
> (Ibid.)

Target setting is another strategy that Maple High School has used:

> Target setting in years 10 and 12 is linked to data on records and followed up throughout GCSE and post-16 years. For both year groups we hold a morning session where we set the whole concept of target setting and having goals within a very positive context. Older students talk about their involvement in strategies which promote success. Students are given information about their potential and use these to look at their predicted grades.
>
> (Ibid.)

Specific support for Year 11 students, prior to taking their public examinations, is also provided; one such strategy is mentoring of students:

> There are several measures particularly designed to support year 11. There is voluntary mentoring of over 100 students in year 11 by staff with fortnightly meetings. Staff are strongly encouraged to get involved in this, taking on one or two students ... There are target sheets for each meeting and a copy goes to the co-ordinator of the scheme. In addition we run a COMPACT scheme using outside mentors from businesses to support some 15 students. These students also have targets for punctuality, school work, attendance, community work and work placements.
>
> (Ibid.)

Another strategy that the school has used is study support:

> One of our most effective strategies is to offer two-day study residentials to any of year 11 who wish to attend . . . We now organise four of these and target different grade ranges with each one. We hold the one for the weakest group closest to the exams. We rent out a local youth hostel or scouts centre and focus on five core subject areas and study skills. The location is close to school so that staff can come and go to run their sessions. This year well over 70 per cent of the group participated, and for the first time we had more boys than girls on the trip for the weakest. It is optional, and has proved to have a noticeable effect on these students when you compare their predicted grades against final attainment at GCSE. From March onwards there are revision clubs in every subject in school at lunchtime or after school and we run, and pay for, an additional late night bus to enable students to participate in these.
>
> (Ibid.)

In terms of results, the five or more GCSE A* to C rate in the school increased as shown in Table 9.3. The boys' results increased from 40 per cent in 1996 to 56 per cent in 1999. The gap between the boys and girls narrowed from twenty-two percentage points in 1995 to eleven percentage points in 2001.

This account of school improvement indicates a wide-reaching, whole school, multifaceted approach.

Conclusions

Our two case study schools have both shown remarkable improvements in achievement at the end of compulsory education. The schools are located in different parts of the country and have differing pupil profiles. The headteachers adopted quite different approaches in order to raise achievement levels, but there are some interesting similarities. One of these is that in both cases the focus has been on all pupils in the school – not solely on those who are likely to obtain five or more high grade GCSEs. The fact that both schools have been successful in ensuring that all pupils obtain qualifications is testimony to the importance of this focus – and in contrast to the picture nationally, where there is still a significant minority who fail to achieve any qualifications at the end of Year 11. In Chapter 10 we address some of these issues again when we outline implications for policy and practice of the research reviewed and case studies reported in this book.

Chapter 10

Discussion and policy implications

Introduction

In this final chapter we discuss the key themes that have emerged from our examination of underachievement in schools. We also examine the likely impact of government policies on underachievement and provide an analysis of further issues that need to be considered by the government. The final section concludes by outlining implications for policy and practice for policy makers and practitioners.

The concept of underachievement

We started this book by examining the concept of underachievement. We noted that the concept is complex and has a number of different meanings. It is a multifaceted concept but if defined too narrowly it is of little value in terms of policy or practice. We chose to use the concept to differentiate groups of pupils who are relatively low attaining compared with others. Whilst in any population of pupils some will perform less well than others, we noted that there are links between achievement and a variety of different forms of disadvantage and other factors including social class, gender and ethnic background. Our focus has been on academic achievement, but we have also highlighted other outcomes – such as destinations post-16 and entering higher education. It is clear from our discussion that some of the issues that are associated with low levels of achievement are long-standing and hard to change.

Social class, poverty and education

Our findings in relation to social class revealed clear differences between different social groups: pupils who are from lower socio-economic groups (particularly those from unskilled manual backgrounds) and who are from low-income families achieve less well on average in a range of tests, examinations and assessments than those who are from higher socio-economic groups and who are from families on higher incomes. The data also indicate that students from families where the parents have higher levels of education on average gain better results. The differences between social classes are found at all stages of the education process and extend to participation in education post-16.

We noted, however, that it was important not to assume a causal link between social class or poverty and lower performance. The research revealed that teacher expectations appear to be lower for children from working-class backgrounds and teachers may be more likely to label children from certain social backgrounds as disruptive; school policies and practices may also be part of the problem.

In terms of progress made by students from lower socio-economic groups and from low-income families, the evidence suggests that schools have less impact in terms of progress in subjects where parental involvement is likely to be greater – such as reading and writing. This suggests that parental involvement is an important factor. What is less clear, at this stage, is what sort of involvement is important and what kinds of involvement should be further encouraged. Activities such as reading with children and visits to the library have been highlighted in research. These findings have important implications for policy makers and schools as they reinforce the notion that parental involvement of a very clearly defined type may have an impact on attainment and progress.

Whilst there is evidence to suggest that young people from lower socio-economic groups have made larger proportionate increases in attainment since the early 1990s, achievement levels are still markedly poorer than for those from higher socio-economic groups. This suggests that further changes are needed to counter the pervasive impact of social class on achievement, which is apparent from the earliest of stages.

Gender and achievement

The analysis revealed shifting gender differences over time and a consequent change in the focus of concern. In the 1970s, a major concern was the limited opportunities available to girls in certain subjects (predominately the hard sciences). More recently the focus of attention has switched to boys, who are now seen as performing less well than girls generally and particularly in the secondary sector. However, reviews of the apparent 'underperformance' of boys point out that this phenomenon is not new but that previously it had been concealed from the public by the adjustment of 11-plus test results in order to obtain equal numbers of boys and girls in grammar schools. This practice continued in parts of the UK up until the 1980s.

Looking at more recent evidence on the performance of boys and girls, it appears that at the primary stage the findings are not altogether consistent but it is probably reasonable to say that girls' performance is superior for English. The differences are much less obvious for mathematics and science.

At the end of compulsory education, analyses of GCSE results show a superior performance of girls, with the gender gap increasing over time. A range of hypotheses have been put forward for the higher relative achievement of girls than boys, including earlier maturation, different modes of assessment, and so on. One that has not been well developed as yet is the possibility that girls are aware that they are likely to encounter discrimination in the labour market once they leave school and one way of countering this is for them to maximise their achievement levels at school to try to improve their position relative to boys in the workforce. Indeed, if this is the case there is evidence that the strategy may pay off, with the value added to women's earnings by higher qualifications, notably postgraduate qualifications, being greater than for men's. This results in a reduction of the 'gender gap' in earnings between the sexes from just under forty percentage points for those with no higher-education qualifications to just over ten percentage points for those with higher degrees (Blundell *et al.* 1997).

A number of proposals have been put forward to address the so-called 'underachievement' of boys. However, the research evidence about successful ways of tackling this issue in schools is limited. Nevertheless, a number of recommendations have been made, based on inspection evidence and views of teachers and pupils (see also our case studies in Chapter 9).

Ethnicity and achievement

The research and data that we examined reveal a complex picture of the educational performance of different ethnic groups in England. Although the evidence is not clear cut, it is apparent that pupils from certain ethnic groups perform well in tests and examinations, whilst others do not. A major problem is the limited data that are currently available on the achievement of young people from different ethnic groups. In particular there are no national data sets available, in marked contrast, for example, to the United States, and so it is necessary to rely on a wide range of studies, many small-scale, which may be specific to the particular populations under investigation. This is particularly likely to be the case with the inner London studies given the high levels of disadvantage in this part of the country, coupled with the high percentage of children from minority ethnic groups who live in London.

It is not clear what accounts for the differences between ethnic groups, but it does appear on the basis of available research that there are complex interactions between a range of factors, notably social class, gender, peer and teacher influence, cultural background, neighbourhood and the differential effectiveness of schools. Despite the lack of clarity, among the variety of reasons for the relatively low achievement levels, social deprivation on the one hand and the policies and practices within schools, including unintentional racism, on the other are probably the most significant. In addition, lack of fluency in English is likely to explain the underachievement of at least some ethnic groups.

In terms of the strategies that schools can use to raise attainment levels, there are suggestions that mentoring may be of value. In addition, there appear to be a number of key areas in raising ethnic minority achievement that have been identified by LEAs and OFSTED as important. But clearly more investigation is needed to evaluate the particular approaches that schools have initiated.

More encouragingly there is evidence to suggest that achievement levels of young people from some ethnic groups have improved over time – in terms of both the actual and proportionate increases – but for other groups of pupils there remains considerable cause for concern.

Other factors and achievement

The evidence that we presented revealed that there was a multitude of other factors associated with low levels of achievement (for example, family problems, poor attendance, poor behaviour, pupil mobility, health problems, and so on). Many of these are not readily amenable to school policies or practices, although in a number of cases there are ways in which school policy might mitigate the impact of disadvantage. This is the case, for example, with pupil mobility. In other cases, it would appear that government policy might be able to influence practice. This is likely to be the case with the reductions in school exclusions that have taken place in recent years given that a high priority was given to this issue along with financial incentives and disincentives.

It is important to note that the *concentration* of pupils facing a range of challenges in their lives is a particular difficulty facing some schools and is clearly beyond their control – this is the case with schools that are located in areas where levels of deprivation are particularly high. In these cases, schools are likely to have to cope with a range of difficulties not encountered in more prosperous areas.

What is very clear from our discussion is that there are many different factors associated with low levels of attainment. Moreover, although we have looked at each of these separately, we have only touched upon the complexities of the interactions between them. It is important to recognise that the different factors that we have explored rarely act independently of others.

School structures

We examined school structures and the associations that exist between school structures and achievement. The market reforms in England have provided opportunities for certain categories of schools to 'select in' certain types of pupils and 'select out' others. As we discussed, at a national level there have been changes in levels of segregation between schools, which seem to be related to the overall economic situation. However, at a local level there is evidence of increased segregation in some LEAs, which appears to be associated with some of the market-oriented reforms that have been introduced. Interestingly, there is some evidence of competition having had a positive impact on results within a local area as schools try to improve their performance to match competitor schools.

The evidence more generally points to the need to adopt measures to reduce pupil selection by secondary schools if the aim is to increase equity. Whilst there may be some advantages for high-ability children being educated in grammar schools, the damaging effects of those not selected for grammar schools, in our view, outweigh any advantages of selection. These effects are not only educational. There are likely to be psychological effects for those not selected:

> Teachers in secondary schools say that many pupils arrive with a sense of failure. In consequence the schools ... work to enhance self-esteem and self-confidence of their pupils. By contrast grammar teachers say that their pupils arrive with a sense of success and most pupils are motivated to work towards the high academic standards expected in their schools.
>
> (Department of Education, Northern Ireland 2000: 3)

The same arguments apply in relation to partial selection by either overt or covert means. Where schools are able to select in this way, other schools in the locality are at a distinct disadvantage, having been 'creamed' of higher ability pupils.

In our view it is important that policy makers take account of the impact of school structures, both positive and negative, on pupils, teachers, parents, schools and communities. This ties in with what we consider to be important arguments relating in particular to *social cohesion*; it is only by enabling children from different social backgrounds to mix with each other and to learn with each other that a socially cohesive society can be created and sustained. In our view, a socially cohesive society is most likely to be fostered in a system whereby schools are mixed in terms of both social background and ability. On the basis of international research evidence we might hypothesise that with a less segregated system the *range* of skill levels noted in the UK might be reduced.

This view may of course conflict with the market-oriented approach that we now have in schools in England and with parental 'choice' as the key factor. Whilst parental choice is undoubtedly here to stay – policy makers are unlikely to return to a situation where the consumer has less of a role – there are ways around this problem. First of all, legislation can be enacted and enforced to ensure that schools are not allowed to select overtly or covertly. And, second, the incentive structures could be changed so that schools with disadvantaged intakes are adequately resourced given the additional difficulties they encounter; funding formulae used by LEAs could also be more weighted towards meeting social and educational needs than at present.

There are of course other structural issues that need to be considered. In particular, pupils' motivation needs to be sustained and this may require further policy changes to encourage higher attendance levels to ensure that achievement is maximised. Consideration also needs to be given to the 'tiering' of national tests and GCSE examinations in order to avoid particular groups of pupils being unfairly disadvantaged in terms of the level of test or examination for which they are entered. The bigger issue of the nature of the curriculum is not one that we have tackled in this book, but consideration needs to be given to ensuring that young people when they leave school are proficient in literacy, numeracy and ICT skills. This is an area that we would argue still needs to be fully addressed at the secondary level in particular.

School effectiveness research

Gorard has argued that one impact of school effectiveness research has been the apparent marginalisation of the role of 'context factors' in relation to school achievement, noting that:

> The key predictors of examination success derive from the background characteristics of the student, and this is true *regardless* of the type of school attended. To put it another, perhaps more helpful, way – the inequalities in society outweigh the differences between schools.
>
> (Gorard 2000: 571)

On the basis of the research we have examined, we would agree with the importance attributed to social background. Nevertheless, school effectiveness research has confirmed that schools do differ in terms of the extent to which they are associated with pupils' progress and it is vital that this is fully acknowledged.

However, in the light of the criticisms of school effectiveness research, we would argue that there is a need to take into account a range of additional individual pupil – and indeed family – characteristics as well as school factors when attempting to assess the impact of schools on attainment or progress. These could include individual motivation and home-related activities (such as the level of parental assistance and the use of private tutors). By focusing on pupils and their families, as part of a school within a locality with other schools, and in a community with particular characteristics, improved models could be produced that could take account of many of the problems that have been identified.

Why is it important to focus on schools?

We consider that all possible strategies should be explored in the effort to raise pupils' attainment and that the focus should be on what *schools* can do now to help overcome the effects of disadvantage. This is because a societal programme to alleviate the underlying problems, for example child poverty, cannot be achieved in the short or even the medium term. Rather, these are long-term goals; and the processes by which, for example, a reduction in poverty might improve achievement levels – assuming that the link is causal – are not clear. In the meantime, teachers, policy makers and politicians who are concerned about social exclusion need to focus on what can be done in the here and now – not on what might happen in the future assuming that the political will is still there.

At the same time it is important to be aware of how disadvantage can impinge on schools. If children come to school hungry and tired, they will not be able to learn effectively; if children are surrounded by adults who are out of work or in unskilled jobs, they are less likely to see the relevance of education in terms of their own future lives.

If teachers have to spend a lot of time dealing with the 'outside school' problems faced by their pupils (for example, accommodation, parental absence, and so on) it is clear that they will not be able to spend the necessary time on preparation and teaching work.

Similarly, school leadership may be affected if the headteacher and members of the senior management team are required to make sure that children are safe and secure. In these circumstances it is likely that a considerable amount of time will be spent liaising with statutory services (for example, social services, the health service and the police). The same will apply in dealing with school-based problems such as poor attendance, exclusions and high levels of school mobility – for example, one study found that the time taken by school *teaching* staff to permanently exclude a pupil is in the region of 60 hours – which could otherwise be spent on teaching and teaching-related activities (Sparkes and West 2000).

Government policy

Targeting

In terms of government policy, a wide range of approaches has been used to target disadvantage and low levels of achievement. The funding mechanism used by the government targets resources on deprived areas. In addition, through its Standards Fund, the government has developed a variety of policy initiatives designed to focus attention particularly on disadvantage.

These are varied and include targeting funds directly at LEAs and schools with high levels of disadvantage, and developing initiatives to focus attention on particular groups of pupils with low levels of attainment and/or high levels of deprivation. There is evidence to suggest that some of these approaches are likely to have a positive impact on achievement levels, but whether they will be enough to reduce achievement gaps is a different matter.

We would argue, however, that more needs to be done by the government to recognise the extra burden and responsibility placed on staff in some schools (headteachers, other members of the senior management, teachers) caused by the concentration in their schools of pupils facing multiple problems. Further ways of helping these schools need to be considered, first by identifying their needs and, second, by providing additional resources to meet these needs. For example, the cost of just the one exclusion described by Sparkes and West (2000) was estimated to be over £1,700.

Structures

Government policy has involved targeting resources on disadvantaged areas. However, perhaps because of this and also because of political sensitivities, the issue of school structures has not been addressed in a systematic way. One of the outcomes of the quasi-market in schools is that schools continue to be in competition with one another. Although beneficial effects on achievement have been identified, schools, particularly in some localities, may have become more polarised and research certainly indicates that there is not a level playing field as far as school admissions are concerned, with opportunities for cream skimming in abundance.

One specific example – in this case, mobile pupils – serves to illustrate how this competition might impact on both schools and disadvantaged pupils. Dobson notes on the basis of empirical work carried out in a sample of primary schools:

> High mobility can affect aggregate school performance in tests where there is a net loss of high achieving pupils and where low-achievers are not in school long enough to be brought up to 'expected' levels.
>
> (Dobson *et al.* 2000: 116)

> More fundamentally, the emphasis on inter-school comparisons and targets is reported to be making schools less willing to take in lower achieving pupils at non-standard times ... If indeed schools are now more reluctant to take in such pupils, social exclusion is built into the education system at an early age.
>
> (Ibid.: 118)

Case studies

Our two case study schools have both shown remarkable improvements in achievement at the end of compulsory education. The schools are located in different parts of the country and have differing pupil profiles. The headteachers adopted different approaches in order to raise achievement levels, but there are some interesting similarities. In both cases the focus has been on all pupils in the school – not solely on those who are likely to obtain five or more high-grade GCSEs. The fact that both schools have been successful in ensuring that all pupils obtain qualifications is testimony to this focus – and in contrast to the picture nationally where there is still a significant minority who fail to achieve any qualifications at the end of Year 11. A wide range of strategies has been adopted that target different groups of pupils in different ways with a view to raising attainment.

Implications for policy and practice

A number of implications arise from the research that we have analysed and the case studies that we have presented. Those for government, local education authorities and schools are presented below.

Government should:

- ensure that where accountability mechanisms are in place these serve to reinforce the achievement of *all* pupils;
- ensure that all schools abide by the Code of Practice on School Admissions and that the criteria used in the event of oversubscription are clear, fair and objective and do not enable creaming of certain categories of pupils;
- ensure that interviewing, which provides scope for selection, is prohibited;
- provide greater financial incentives to schools to admit and retain pupils who have low levels of achievement, pupils with a history of truancy or school exclusion, or mobile pupils;
- publish data obtained from schools on known eligibility for free school meals, ethnic composition and gender along with data already available relating to other school characteristics;
- change the emphasis in the debate about school standards away from the current focus on the numbers of 16 year olds achieving five or more GCSEs at grades A* to C – at present 50 per cent achieve this target, the remaining 50 per cent do not; and schools need to be provided with incentives to ensure that all young people are given opportunities to maximise their achievements and not focus on those that are likely to enhance their league table position by reaching the five Cs threshold;
- prescribe minimum levels of competence for literacy, numeracy and ICT to raise expectations of teachers and students alike – these should be such that the vast majority of 16 year olds reach certain 'minimum levels of competence', and they should be reported in performance tables alongside examination results to ensure that there are incentives for schools to focus attention on maximising competence in these areas for all pupils, even the lower achievers; these qualifications should be compulsory for all pupils – they would not need to be examined separately, but could draw on students' school work.

Schools should:

- develop whole-school policies to address low levels of achievement;
- set their own targets as determined by the school's *own* priorities to ensure that the needs of all pupils are being met; however, all schools should be expected to ensure that all pupils leave school with the equivalent of at least one GCSE at grades A* to G;
- learn from the 'better' departments within a school – in almost all schools, some departments are likely to be more effective than others; the strategies used may be transferable to other departments (Sammons *et al.* 1997b);
- Undertake regular monitoring of attainment and progress for different groups of pupils – girls, boys, those from different ethnic minority groups, and those eligible for free school meals – which should be used by schools as part of their own self-evaluations of performance to ensure that they are delivering a high quality education to all pupils;
- monitor and evaluate the impact of any new policies introduced – for example, setting practices, single-sex teaching groups – to ensure that they are benefiting all groups of pupils;
- make use of the various types of study support to enhance achievement – there is some evidence that mentoring and other forms of study support have been successful in raising levels of attainment;
- experiment with a wide range of strategies such as those described in the two case studies to see what works in particular school settings;
- use all community and business resources available to maximise the resources available to the school and its pupils; by doing so, pupil motivation may be increased;
- seek to improve pupils' motivation by means of adapting the curriculum offered.

LEAs also have an important role to play. It is recommended that they:

- work with schools and support them in their efforts to raise achievement of all pupils;

- systematically collect and analyse school-based data, including attainment data and pupil background information, and other relevant information and feed it back to schools in a timely and 'user-friendly' format;
- provide opportunities for schools to work co-operatively with one another to share best practice and learn from each other;
- assist schools in setting challenging targets that focus on all pupils, not just specific groups;
- facilitate the evaluation of school-based initiatives designed to reduce achievement gaps between different groups of pupils;
- accepting that the scope is limited, review their funding formulae to maximise the funding of schools with the most disadvantaged intakes;
- maximise resources and share expertise by taking part in collaborative arrangements with other LEAs, higher education providers, employers, and so on.

In conclusion, underachievement of certain groups of pupils continues to be a cause for concern in the UK, for both policy makers and practitioners. In this book we have attempted to provide up-to-date information about the ways in which different factors are associated with attainment and some possible ways forward. Despite the continuing concern with underachievement, we still do not have conclusive answers and, given the complexity of the issue, we should not be overly optimistic about solutions being readily found. However, as our case-study schools show, achievement levels of all pupils can be raised and this should be the aim of education policy if young people's lives are to be enhanced and their contribution to society maximised.

Appendices

Appendix A

The school system in the UK

England and Wales

Compulsory schooling in England and Wales is from 5 to 16 years. Primary education comprises Key Stage 1 (age 5 to 7) and Key Stage 2 (age 7 to 11). Secondary education caters for pupils aged 11 to 16 or 18. Secondary education comprises Key Stages 3 (age 11 to 14), 4 (age 14 to 16) and 5 (age 16 to 18).

Over nine out of ten state secondary schools are classified as comprehensive. The remainder (all in England) are grammar schools (academically selective) and secondary modern schools (for pupils who are not selected for grammar school).

The national curriculum (which requires certain subjects to be studied) relates to 'Key Stages'. Teachers carry out continuous assessment of pupils' progress and towards the end of Key Stages 1 (age 7 years), 2 (age 11 years) and 3 (age 14 years) teachers assess pupils in each national curriculum subject. Pupils are assessed by means of national curriculum test tasks in English, mathematics and science. At the end of compulsory secondary education (Year 11, age 16) pupils are generally entered for external examinations (General Certificate of Secondary Education (GCSE)) in individual subjects. Courses leading to pre-vocational examinations are also offered (such as General National Vocational Qualifications and GCSEs in vocational subjects). Pupils who wish to go on to university typically study for General Certificate of Education Advanced (GCE A) levels. These are generally taken at the age of 18. In the first year of the post-16 curriculum (Year 12) pupils typically study for around four GCE Advanced

Subsidiary (AS) qualifications. They then study around three of these subjects at a higher level in the second year, which leads to a full GCE Advanced Level (or A2) per subject. Before 2001, there were Advanced Supplementary qualifications. There are also Vocational A levels (Advanced Vocational Certificate of Education (VCE)) qualifications that may be taken.

Northern Ireland

In Northern Ireland compulsory education lasts from age 4 to 16. The majority of children between the ages of 4 and 11 are educated in primary schools. Key Stage 1 covers 4 to 8 years, and Key Stage 2 covers ages 8 to 11. Key Stages 3, 4 and 5 cover the same ages as in England and Wales.

For all children of compulsory school age (other than those in independent schools) there is a common curriculum known as the Northern Ireland Curriculum. At secondary level in Northern Ireland, there are grammar schools (academically selective) and secondary schools (non-selective). Grammar schools provide a range of courses for pupils aged 11 to 18 years, whilst secondary schools provide a similar range of courses for 11 to 16 year olds (although some offer post-16 opportunities). At the end of the compulsory school phase most pupils take the General Certificate of Secondary Education (GCSE) examinations, whilst at the end of upper secondary education GCE AS and A levels are offered, as are vocational A levels.

Scotland

Compulsory education in Scotland begins at the age of 5 and lasts until the age of 16. Primary education covers seven years (age 5 to 12). Virtually all pupils in state secondary schools attend comprehensive schools.

There is no official 'national curriculum' as such, rather 'national guidelines' that provide a framework for teaching between the ages of 5 and 14. In the final two years of compulsory education, the Scottish Certificate of Education examinations at Standard Grade form the basis of the curriculum.

During the period between the ages of 5 and 14 years, pupils are assessed according to the '5 to 14 national guidelines'. Classroom assessment is supported by the use of national tests in reading, writing and mathematics. At the end of compulsory education (age 16), Scottish Certificate of Education examinations at Standard Grade are taken by pupils. Standard Grade is awarded at three levels in most subjects: credit (the highest), general and foundation. In the post-compulsory sector, a range of new qualifications were introduced in 2000 to replace the Scottish Certificate of Education Higher Grade (to which reference has been made in this book). These qualifications are at the following levels: Access; Intermediate 1; Intermediate 2; Higher; and, from 2001, Advanced Higher. Entry to higher education is generally determined by Highers and Advanced Highers.

Appendix B

Programme for International Student Assessment

The Programme for International Student Assessment (PISA) is a collaborative study first administered in 2000 in thirty-two countries, twenty-eight of them members of the Organisation for Economic Co-operation and Development (OECD). A standardised methodology was used to give internationally comparable results.

The main purpose of PISA is to assess the ability of 15 year olds to apply knowledge and skills in three broad areas (or domains) of literacy: reading, mathematics and science. Unlike previous international tests, it looks at young people's ability to use their knowledge and skills to deal with real-life situations rather than examining how well they have mastered a specific school curriculum (OECD 2001; Office for National Statistics 2001).

PISA's three domains of literacy are:

- reading: the ability to understand, use and reflect on written texts to participate effectively in life;
- mathematical: the ability to formulate and solve mathematical problems in situations encountered in life;
- scientific: the capacity to acquire and use scientific knowledge and to draw evidence-based conclusions.

In 2000, the main focus was on the domain of reading literacy; the focus in 2003 and 2006 is on mathematical and scientific literacy respectively.

PISA was administered in England and Northern Ireland by the Office for National Statistics. A separate study was carried out in

Scotland, which contributed to the UK figures. Wales did not participate in PISA 2000. In England, pupils in each sampled school took a written assessment lasting about two hours, administered by the school under test conditions. In 2000, all pupils were assessed in reading literacy; in addition, a random sub-sample of pupils was assessed in mathematical and scientific literacy (DfES 2001m).

In addition to the written assessment, pupils answered a questionnaire giving details about themselves. Headteachers of the sampled schools answered a questionnaire about their school (DfES 2001k). It should be noted that the information relating to school resources and such like was derived from this questionnaire. Details of how the three domains are defined and of proficiency levels are provided elsewhere (OECD 2001; DfES 2001m).

Appendix C

The Youth Cohort Study

The Youth Cohort Study is a series of longitudinal surveys of young people in England and Wales, which focuses on their education, training and labour-market experience, their qualifications and a variety of other issues.

In the YCS a sample of an academic year group (or cohort) is contacted in the spring following the completion of compulsory education (age 16 years); the young people are contacted again one or two years later (DfES 2001b). So far, nine cohorts of young people have been surveyed.

The YCS 2001 report (DfES 2001b), which we refer to throughout this book, relates to young people surveyed for the first time in spring 2000 (the ninth cohort) who had completed Year 11 the previous academic year (and also makes comparisons with earlier cohorts). The survey was conducted amongst a representative sample of 25,000 young people in England and Wales, who became eligible to leave school in the 1998/9 academic year.

The response rate was 55 per cent for the 2000 survey. The data were collected by postal self-completion questionnaires sent in spring 2000. The data were weighted to correct as far as possible for any bias arising from non-response. With this weighting, the overall results on attainment and participation correspond well with the official estimates. The YCS is thus an invaluable source of information relating to attainment and participation in the context of various socio-demographic and other variables. The results, as with any survey, are subject to sampling error and biases resulting from non-response and response error. It is important to note the YCS has slightly different definitions and coverage to the official estimate (DfES 2001b).

Appendix D

National targets for English, mathematics, science and ICT: England

By 2004:
- 85 per cent of 11 year olds will reach the 'expected' level (level 4) in the Key Stage 2 English and mathematics tests;
- 35 per cent of 11 years olds will reach level 5 or above in the Key Stage 2 English and mathematics tests;
- all LEAs should have at least 78 per cent of their 11 year olds at level 4 or above in English and mathematics;
- each LEA was required to set individual targets for English and mathematics for 2004.

The first national targets for 14 year olds were announced in 2001:
- by 2004, 75 per cent will receive level 5 or above in English, mathematics and ICT and 70 per cent in science;
- by 2004, no LEA will achieve less than 65 per cent at level 5 or above in English and mathematics, and 60 per cent in science;
- by 2004, reduce to 15 per cent the proportion of 14 year olds who do not achieve at least one level 5 at Key Stage 3 in English, mathematics or science.

There are now further targets:
- by 2006, the number of schools in which fewer than 65 per cent of pupils achieve level 4 or above will be significantly reduced;
- by 2007, 85 per cent will receive level 5 or above in English, mathematics and ICT and 80 per cent in science;
- by 2007, the number of schools where fewer than 60 per cent of 14 year olds achieve level 5 or above will be significantly reduced;
- by 2007, 90 per cent of pupils will reach level 4 in English and mathematics by age 12;
- between 2002 and 2006, the proportion of those aged 16 who get qualifications equivalent to 5 GCSEs at Grade A* to C will rise by two percentage points each year on average and in all schools at least 20 per cent of pupils will achieve this standard by 2004 rising to 25 per cent by 2006.

Figure D.1 National targets for English, mathematics, science and ICT.

Source: DfES 2002a, 2002m.

Notes

1 What is underachievment?

1 It is important to note that much of this research makes reference to 'levels of qualifications'. Level 1 qualifications are GCSE passes at grades D to G or a Foundation General National Vocational Qualification (GNVQ). A level 2 qualification, for example, is five or more GCSE passes at grades A* to C, a National Vocational Qualification level 2 or an Intermediate GNVQ. A level 3 qualification is either 2 GCE Advanced levels, an NVQ level 3 or an Advanced GNVQ (or equivalent). Level 4 is degree level or a higher vocational level qualification.

2 The predecessors of GCSEs grades A* to C were General Certificate of Education Ordinary (GCE O) level grades A to C and Certificate of Secondary Education (CSE) grade 1 up to 1986/7.

3 It is also important to note that comparisons over time of GCE Advanced (A) levels need to be treated with caution, as a grading scheme was in operation until 1987 that set out the distribution of grades, which in broad terms resulted in approximately 10 per cent of the entry gaining a grade A and 10 per cent failing. Grades from 1988 were not awarded on this basis and currently grades A, C and E are determined on the basis of examiner judgement with the remaining grades determined arithmetically (see QCA 2002).

4 In 1987/8, the method involved a survey of school leavers of any age, from all schools *except* special schools. Between 1989/9 and 1990/1, a survey of school examinations was carried out, based on 15 year old pupils in all schools *except* special schools. From 1991/2001, data have been taken from the official database on school performance tables, and are based on all schools *including* special schools. From 1996/7 percentages include GNVQ equivalencies (DfES 2001a).

5 GCSE point score: A to G count as 7 to 1 points respectively; A* counts as 8; GCSE short courses grades A to G count as 3.5 to 0.5 respectively; A* counts as 4. GNVQ: grades Distinction, Merit and Pass count as 7.5, 6 and 5 points respectively at Intermediate level, and 4, 3 and 1.5 points at Foundation level; these points need to be multiplied by 2 for GNVQ Part One and by 4 for GNVQ Full.

2 Social background and achievement

1 In this study, Payne (2000) defined low achievers as those in the bottom third of the national distribution of GCSE results (in England and Wales).

2 The Age Participation Index is defined as the number of home-domiciled young (aged less than 21) initial entrants to full-time and sandwich undergraduate courses of higher education expressed as a proportion of the average number of 18 and 19 year olds in the population in Great Britain (DfES and OFSTED 2002). The figures cited for 2001/2 are provisional figures. The actual percentage for 1999/2000 was 32 per cent.

3 The baseline assessment involved two elements: a checklist completed by the teacher including an assessment of motor skills, social and emotional development and attainment in English, mathematics and science; and a standardised assessment of early literacy skills (the Linguistic Awareness for Reading Readiness test of emergent literacy) (see Strand 1997 for details).

3 Gender and achievement

1 Such data should also be available nationally from 2003 as they are now being collected by the DfES annually.

2 At grades A to C.

3 Interestingly, in terms of entries there has been comparatively little change in recent years of the percentage of 15 year old pupils who entered five or more GCSEs; thus, in 1994/5, 87.5 per cent of 15 year old boys in schools were entered for five or more GCSEs compared with 91.1 per cent of girls (DfEE 1998). In 2000/1 (DfES 2002b) the percentages were 89 per cent and 92.6 per cent respectively.

4 In the following subjects, among others, more 15-year-old girls than boys in schools attempted GCSE examinations: English literature (86 per cent of girls versus 78 per cent of boys); history (33 per cent versus 32 per cent); French (57 per cent versus 50 per cent); German (23 per cent versus 20 per cent); Spanish (9 per cent versus 6 per cent); art and design (34 per cent versus 26 per cent); drama (19 per cent versus 11 per cent); religious education (20 per cent versus 13 per cent); music (8 per cent versus 6 per cent); home economics (10 per cent versus 1 per cent); humanities (4 per cent versus 3 per cent). More boys than girls attempted GCSE examinations in the following subjects: physics (7 per cent versus 5 per cent); chemistry (7 per cent versus 5 per cent); information technology (19 per cent versus 14 per cent); business studies (17 per cent versus 14 per cent); geography (40 per cent versus 33 per cent); and physical education (22 per cent versus 13 per cent).

5 GCE A/AS/VCE/AGNVQ point scores are derived as follows: an A level or VCE A level pass and an AS or VCE AS level pass are classified as grade E or above. Each grade at AS examination is counted as half that grade at A level. The double award VCE has different scores as does the Advanced GNVQ. Scores are calculated thus: A level – A is

10, B is 8, and so on, with E being worth 2; AS level – A is 5, B is 4, and so on, with E being worth 1; Advanced GNVQ 12 unit – distinction is 18, merit is 12 and pass is 6; Advanced GNVQ 6 unit – distinction is 9, merit is 6, pass is 3. VCE double award – AA is 20, AB is 18, BB is 16, BC is 14, CC is 12, CD is 10, DD is 8, DE is 6, EE is 4 (DfES 2002b).

4 Ethnic background and achievement

1 However, data on pupils' ethnic background is now being collected by the DfES.
2 In the 1992 YCS survey, White females outperformed males in terms of the attainment of 5 or more GCSE grades A* to C (41 versus 34 per cent) as did Other Asian females (51 versus 43 per cent) and Pakistani females (30 versus 23 per cent). However, the same proportion of Black males and females reached this level (23 per cent) and more Indian males than females reached this level (39 versus 36 per cent).
3 The DfES (2002n) pooled data for sweep 1 of cohorts 9 and 10. The figures for non-manual and manual groups were: White: 65 per cent and 39 per cent; Black: 46 per cent and 33 per cent; Indian: 75 per cent and 52 per cent; Pakistani/Bangladeshi: 53 per cent and 34 per cent; and Chinese/Other Asian: 78 per cent and 65 per cent.
4 Voluntary-aided schools are their own admission authorities and so unlike community schools are responsible for their own admissions. The significance of this is discussed in Chapter 6.

6 School structures and achievement

1 Specialist schools are state schools that follow the national curriculum but specialise in one of several specified subject areas: technology; languages; sports; art (visual, performing or media); business and enterprise; engineering; science; or mathematics and computing (DfES 2002k). Specialist school status is acquired through a bidding process, and schools wishing to specialise in this way are at the time of writing (November 2002) required to raise about £50,000 of sponsorship towards the cost of a capital project to improve their facilities for the specialist area(s). Once specialist status is conferred schools are eligible to receive additional capital and current grants from central government to complement business sponsorship (see West *et al.* 2000d). In September 2002, there were 992 such schools, accounting for 34 per cent of secondary-school pupils (DfES 2002k).
2 However, former grant-maintained schools still received additional 'transitional funding'.
3 City academies are designed to replace schools that are failing and build on the experience of city technology colleges and specialist schools. They are publicly funded independent schools with private- and voluntary-sector sponsorship and management. The amount of funding required is around 20 per cent of initial capital costs or up to about £2 million. As with both specialist schools and city technology

colleges, city academies have a specialist focus in at least one area of the curriculum and as with specialist schools the aim is for them to share expertise and resources with other schools in the area. They are not academically selective, although as with specialist schools they will be able to select up to 10 per cent of their intake on the basis of pupils' aptitude in the school's specialist area (see West and Pennell 2002).

References

Acheson, D. (1998) *Independent Inquiry into Inequalities in Health Report – Part 2*, London: The Stationery Office. http://www.archive. official-documents.co.uk/document/doh/ih/part2b.htm (2 September 2002).

Allen, A. (1998) 'What are ethnic minorities looking for?', in T. Modood and T. Acland (eds) *Race and Higher Education*, London: Policy Studies Institute.

Arnot, M., Gray, J., James, M., Rudduck, J. with Duveen, G. (1998) *Recent Research on Gender and Educational Performance*, London: OFSTED.

Audit Commission (1993) *Passing the Bucks: The impact of Standard Spending Assessments on economy, efficiency and effectiveness*, Vol. 1, London: Her Majesty's Stationery Office.

Audit Commission (1996) *Trading Places: The supply and allocation of school places*, London: The Audit Commission.

Batho, G. (1989) *Political Issues in Education*, London: Cassell Educational Limited.

Bee, H. (1994) *Lifespan Development*, New York: HarperCollins.

Bellamy, A. (2002) *Changes in Inequality in GCSE Achievement*, personal communication.

Blackburn, R. M. and Jarman, J. (1993) 'Changing inequalities in access to British universities', *Oxford Review of Education* 19(2): 197–215.

Blair, M. and Bourne, J. with Coffin, C., Creese, A. and Kenner, C. (1998) *Making the Difference: Teaching and learning strategies in successful multi-ethnic schools*, Research Brief No. 59, London: DfEE.

Blatchford, P., Martin, V., Moriarty, V., Bassett, P. and Goldstein, H. (2002) *Pupil Adult Ratio Differences and Educational Progress Over Reception and Key Stage 1*, Research Report No. 335, London: DfES.

Blundell, R., Dearden, L., Goodman, A. and Reed, H. (1997) *Higher Education, Employment and Earnings in Britain*, London: Institute for Fiscal Studies.

Boaler, J. (1997) 'Setting, social class and survival of the quickest', *British Educational Research Journal* 25(5): 575–95.

Borland, M. (1998) *Education for Children in Residential and Foster Care*, Research in Education, 63, Edinburgh: The Scottish Council for Research in Education. http://www.scre.ac.uk (3 September 2002).

Bourdieu, P. (1986) 'The forms of capital', reproduced in A. H. Halsey, H. Lauder, P. Brown and A. Stuart Wells (eds) *Education: Culture, economy, society*, Oxford: Oxford University Press.

Bradley, S., Crouchley, R., Millington, J. and Taylor, J. (2000) 'Testing for quasi-market forces in secondary education', *Oxford Bulletin of Economics and Statistics* 62(3): 357–90.

Bramley, G. (1989) 'A model of educational outcomes at local authority level, with implications for local expenditure needs', *Environment and Planning C: Government and Policy*, 7: 39–58.

Braswell, J. S. *et al.* (2001) *The Nation's Report Card: Mathematics 2000*, Washington DC: US Department of Education. http://www.nces. ed.gov/nationsreportcard/pubs/main2000/2001517.asp (2 September 2002).

Cabinet Office (2001) *Spotlight on Education of Children in Care*, 11 July, London: Cabinet Office. http://www.nds.coi.gov.uk/coi/coipress. nsf (2 September 2002).

Callaghan, J. (1976) 'The Ruskin College Speech', in J. Ahier, B. Cosin and M. Hales (eds) (1996) *Diversity and Change: Education, policy and selection*, London: Routledge.

Coe, R. and Fitz-Gibbon, C. (1998) 'School effectiveness research: criticisms and recommendations', *Oxford Review of Education* 24(4): 421–38.

Conlon, G. (2001) *The Incidence and Outcomes Associated with Late Learning in the United Kingdom*, Centre for the Economics of Education, London: London School of Economics.

Connor, H. and Dewson, S. with Tyers, C., Eccles, J., Regan, J. and Aston, J. (2001) *Social Class and Higher Education: Issues affecting decisions on participation by lower social class groups*, Research Report No. 267, London: Department for Education and Employment.

Crook, D., Power, S. and Whitty, G. (1999) *The Grammar School Question: A review of research on comprehensive and selective education*, London: Institute of Education, University of London.

Daly, P. (1996) 'The effects of single-sex and co-educational secondary schooling on girls' achievement', *Research Papers in Education* 11(3): 289–306.

Daugherty, R. (1995) *National Curriculum Assessment*, London: Falmer Press.

Department for Education and Employment (1995) *Statistics of Education: Public Examinations GCSE and GCE in England 1994*, London: DfEE.

Department for Education and Employment (1996a) *GCSE and GCE A/AS Examination Results 1994/95*, London: DfEE.

Department for Education and Employment (1996b) *Admissions to Maintained Schools*, Circular No. 6/96, London: DfEE.

Department for Education and Employment (1998) *GCSE/GNVQ and GCE A/AS Examination Results 1996/97*, London: DfEE.

Department for Education and Employment (1999a) *Schools Plus: Building learning communities*, London: DfEE.

Department for Education and Employment (1999b) *Minority Ethnic Pupils in Maintained Schools by LEA Area in England – January 1999*, London: DfEE. http://www.dfes.gov.uk/statistics/DB/SFR/s0029/sfr-1599.pdf (2 September 2002).

Department for Education and Employment (1999c) *Ethnic Minority Pupils and Pupils For Whom English is an Additional Language*, Statistical Bulletin 3/99, London: DfEE. http://www.dfes.gov.uk/statistics/DB/SBU/b0050/index.html (2 September 2002).

Department for Education and Employment (1999d) *The Standards Fund 2000/2001*, Circular 16/99, DfEE: London.

Department for Education and Employment (2001a) *Schools: Building on success*, London: The Stationery Office, Cm 5050.

Department for Education and Employment (2001b) *Blunkett Launches £35 Million Pilot of Pupil Learning Credits*, Press Release, 26 February 2001. http://www.dfes.gov.uk/pns/DisplayPN.cgi?pn_id=2001_0105 (2 September 2002).

Department for Education and Employment (2001c) *Statistics of Education: GCSE/GNVQ and GCE A/AS and Advanced GNVQ Examination Results 1999/2000 – England*, London: DfES. http://www.dfes.gov.uk/statistics/DB/SBU/b0266/sb06-2001.pdf (28 October 2002).

Department of Education and Employment and Office for Standards in Education (2001) *Departmental Report: The Government's expenditure plans for 2000–01 to 2001–02*, Cm 4602, London: DfEE.

Department of Education and Science (1988) *Statistics of Education School Leavers GCSE and GCE 1988*, London: DES.

Department of Education and Science (1990) *Statistics of Education School Examinations GCSE and GCE 1990*, London: DES.

Department for Education and Skills (2001a) *Statistics of Education: Public examinations GCSE/GNVQ and GCE/AGNVQ in England: 2000*, London: DfES. http://www.dfes.gov.uk/statistics/DB/VOL/v0279/vol02-2001.pdf (2 September 2002).

Department for Education and Skills (2001b) *Youth Cohort Study: The activities and experiences of 16 year olds: England and Wales 2000*, National Statistics First Release, SFR 02/2001, London: DfES. http://www.dfes.gov.uk/statistics/DB/SFR/s0230/sfr02-2001.pdf (2 September 2002).

Department for Education and Skills (2001c) *Statistics of Education: Schools in England 2001*, London: The Stationery Office. http://www. dfes.gov.uk/statistics/DB/VOL/v0288/vol04-2001.pdf (2 September 2002).

Department for Education and Skills (2001d) *Autumn Package of Pupil Performance Information, 2001*, London: DfES. http://www. standards.dfes.gov.uk/performance/pdf/GCSE-GNVQ_2001.pdf (2 September 2002).

Department for Education and Skills (2001e) *Summary of Research Evidence on Age of Starting School*, Research Brief, RBX No. 17–01, London: DfES. http://www.dfes.gov.uk/research/data/uploadfiles/ RBX17.pdf (2 September 2002).

Department for Education and Skills (2001f) *Statistics of Education: Pupil absence and truancy from schools in England, 2000/01*, Issue number 13/01, London: DfES. http://www.dfes.gov.uk/statistics/DB/ SBU/b0309/sb13-2001.pdf (2 September 2002).

Department for Education and Skills (2001g) *Permanent Exclusions From Schools, England, 1999/2000*, London: DfES. http://www.dfes.gov.uk/ statistics/DB/SFR/s0275/sfr32-2001.pdf (2 September 2002).

Department for Education and Skills (2001h) *Statistics of Education: Education and training expenditure since 1991–92*, London: DfES. http://www.dfes.gov.uk/statistics/DB/SBU/b0285/sb07-2001.pdf (2 September 2002).

Department for Education and Skills (2001i) *Schools Achieving Success*, White Paper, Cm 5230, London: The Stationery Office.

Department for Education and Skills (2001j) *Continued Support for Education Action Zone Schools – Timms*, Press Release, 14 November 2001, London: DfES. http://www.dfes.gov.uk/pns/DisplayPN.cgi?pn_ id=2001_0383 (2 September 2002).

Department for Education and Skills (2001k) *School Performance Tables 1996 to 2001*, London: DfES. http://www.dfes.gov.uk/cgi-bin/statistics/ search.pl?keyw=053&q2=Search (2 September 2002).

Department for Education and Skills (2001m) *Programme for International Student Assessment (PISA) 2000 Survey: Key Results*, London: DfES. http://www.dfes.gov.uk/research/data/uploadfiles/RB25-01.doc (2 September 2002).

Department for Education and Skills (2002a) *Statistics of Education: National curriculum assessments of 7, 11 and 14 year olds in England 2001*, London: DfES.

Department for Education and Skills (2002b) *Statistical Bulletin GCSE/GNVQ and GCE A/AS/VCE/Advanced GNVQ Examination Results 2000/01 – England*, London: DfES. http://www.dfes.gov.uk/ statistics/DB/SBU/b0334/ExamBull.pdf (2 September 2002).

Department for Education and Skills (2002c) *National Statistics Bulletin Statistics of Education: Pupil progress in secondary schools by school type in England: 2001*, London: DfES. http://www.dfes.gov.uk/statistics/DB/SBU/b0337/statspupilprogress.pdf (2 September 2002).

Department for Education and Skills (2002d) Data for January 1988 provided by DfES.

Department for Education and Skills (2002e) *Changing Lives*, speech by David Miliband MP, Minister of State for School Standards, 8 July. http://www.dfes.gov.uk/pns/DisplayPN.cgi?pn_id=2002_0140 (2 September 2002).

Department for Education and Skills (2002f) *Standards Fund 2002–2003*, London: DfES, SF Circular 2002–03. http://www.dfes.gov.uk/standardsfund/guidance.cfm (2 September 2002).

Department for Education and Skills (2002g) *Standards Fund 2002–2003*, London: DfES, SF Circular 2002–03 Annex B. http://www.dfes.gov.uk/standardsfund/guidance.cfm (2 September 2002).

Department for Education and Skills (2002h) *What is Sure Start?* London: DfES. http://www.surestart.gov.uk/aboutWhatis.cfm?section=2 (2 September 2002).

Department for Education and Skills (2002i) *Excellence in Cities Across the Phases*, London: DfES. http://www.standards.dfes.gov.uk/excellence/abouteic/?template=pub&articleid=4926 (2 September 2002).

Department for Education and Skills (2002j) *Ethnic Minority Achievement Grant*, London: DfES. http://www.dfee.gov.uk/ethnic/supment.htm (2 September 2002).

Department for Education and Skills (2002k) *New Investment in the Specialist Schools Programme Announced*, London, DfES. http://www.standards.dfes.gov.uk/specialistschools (2 September 2002).

Department for Education and Skills (2002m) *Education and Skills: Investment for reform*, London: DfES. http://www.dfes.gov.uk/2002 spendingreview (2 September 2002).

Department for Education and Skills (2002n) *Ethnic Gender Breakdown Time Series* and *Year 11 Attainment by Ethnic Group and Socioeconomic Group*, supplied by DfES (YCS team).

Department for Education and Skills and Office for Standards in Education (2002) *Departmental Annual Report*, London: DfES. http://www.dfes.gov.uk/deptreport2002/index.shtml

Department of Education, Northern Ireland (2000) *The effects of the Selective System of Secondary Education in Northern Ireland*, Research Briefing No. 4/2000, Bangor: DENI. http://www.deni.gov.uk/facts_figures/researchb/rb2000/rb2000_4.pdf (2 September 2002).

Department of the Environment (1990) *Standard Spending Assessments: Background and underlying methodology*, London: DoE.

Department of the Environment, Transport and the Regions (1998) *Chapter 2: Education SSA*, London: DETR. http://www.local.doe.gov.uk/finance/ssa/9900/subgroup/ch2.pdf (2 September 2002).

Dobson, J. M., Henthorne, K. and Lynas, Z. (2000) *Pupil Mobility in Schools Final Report*, London: University College London.

Donahue, P. L. *et al.* (2001) *The Nation's Report Card: Fourth-grade reading*, Washington, DC: US Department of Education. www.nces.ed.gov/nationsreportcard/pubs/main2000/2001499.asp (2 September 2002).

Education Funding Strategy Group (2001) *Education SSA: Current methodology and distribution*, EFSG 22, London: DfES. http://www.dfes.gov.uk/efsg (2 September 2002).

Egerton, M. and Halsey, A. H. (1993) 'Trends by social class and gender in access to higher education', *Oxford Review of Education* 19(2): 183–96.

Elwood, J. (1995) 'Undermining gender stereotypes: examination and coursework performance in the UK at 16', *Assessment in Education* 2(2): 283–303.

Epstein, D., Elwood, J., Hey, V. and Maw, J. (1998) *Failing Boys? Issues in gender and achievement*, Buckingham: Open University Press.

Fuller, E. J. and Johnson, J. F. (2001) 'Can state accountability systems drive improvements in school performance for children of colour and children from low income homes?', *Education and Urban Society* 33(3): 260–83.

Gaine, C. and George, R. (1999) *Gender, 'Race' and Class in Schooling: A new introduction*, London: Falmer Press.

Gallagher, A. M. (1997) *Educational Achievement and Gender: A review of research evidence on the apparent underachievement of boys*, Department of Education, Northern Ireland, Research Report No. 6, 1997.

Ganzach, Y. (2000) 'Parents' education, cognitive ability, educational expectations and educational attainment: Interactive effects', *British Journal of Educational Psychology* 70(3): 419–41.

Gewirtz, S., Ball, S. J. and Bowe, R. (1995) *Markets, Choice and Equity in Education*, Buckingham: Open University Press.

Gibson, A. and Asthana, S. (2000) 'What's in a number? Commentary on Gorard and Fitz's "Investigating the determinants of segregation between schools"', *Research Papers in Education* 15(2): 133–54.

Gillborn, D. and Gipps, C. (1996) *Recent Research on the Achievements of Ethnic Minority Pupils*, London: OFSTED.

Gillborn, D. (1998) 'Race and ethnicity in compulsory schooling', in T. Modood and T. Acland (eds) *Race and Higher Education*, London: Policy Studies Institute.

Gillborn, D. and Mirza, H. S. (2000) *Educational Inequality: Mapping race, class and gender: A synthesis of research evidence*, London: OFSTED. http://www.ofsted.gov.uk (2 September 2002).

Gillborn, D. and Youdell, D. (2000) *Rationing Education*, Buckingham: Open University Press.

Gillborn, D. (2002) *Education and Institutional Racism*. Inaugural lecture, London: Institute of Education, University of London.

Glennerster, H. (1998) 'Education: Reaping the harvest?', in H. Glennerster and J. Hills (eds) *The State of Welfare: The economics of social spending*, Oxford: Oxford University Press.

Goldstein, H. and Woodhouse, G. (2000) 'School effectiveness research and educational policy', *Oxford Review of Education* 26(3,4): 353–63.

Goldstein, H. (2001) 'Using pupil performance data for judging schools and teachers: scope and limitations', *British Educational Research Journal* 27(4): 433–42.

Gorard, S. and Fitz, J. (2000) 'Investigating the determinants of stratification between schools', *Research Papers in Education* 15(2): 115–32.

Gorard, S. (2000) 'Underachievement is still an ugly word: Reconsidering the relative effectiveness of schools in England and Wales', *Journal of Education Policy* 15(5): 559–73.

Gorard, S. and Taylor C. (2001) 'The composition of specialist schools in England: Track record and future prospect', *School Leadership and Management* 21(4): 365–81.

Gorard, S., Fitz, J. and Taylor, C. (2001a) 'School choice impacts: What do we know?', *Educational Researcher* 30(7): 18–23.

Gorard, S., Rees, G. and Salisbury, J. (2001b) 'Investigating the patterns of differential attainment of girls and boys at school', *British Educational Research Journal* 27(2): 125–39.

Gordon, P., Aldrich, R. and Dean, D. (1991) *Education and Policy in England in the Twentieth Century*, London: The Woburn Press.

Gore, T. and Smith, N. (2001) *Patterns of Educational Attainment in the British Coalfields*, Research Brief No. 314, London: DfES.

Greenhough, P. and Hughes, M. (1998) 'Parents' and teachers' interventions in children's reading', *British Educational Research Journal* 24(4): 383–98.

Gross, R. (2001) *Psychology: The science of mind and behaviour*, London: Hodder and Stoughton.

Hanushek, E. A. (1998) 'Conclusions and controversies about effectiveness of school resources', *FRBNY Economic Policy Review*, March: 11–25.

Hargadon, S. (2001) *Case Study of 'Maple High School'* fictitious name). http://www.standards.dfee.gov.uk (2 September 2002).

Hargreaves, D. (1997) 'School culture, school effectiveness and school improvement', reprinted in A. Harris, N. Bennett and M. Preedy (eds) *Organizational Effectiveness and Improvement in Education*, Buckingham: Open University Press.

Haydn, T. (2001) 'From a very peculiar department to a very successful school: Transference issues arising out of a study of an improving school', *School Leadership and Management* 21(4): 415–39.

Her Majesty's Inspectorate Audit Unit (1998) *Raising Standards – Setting Targets: Gender issues in raising attainment*, The Scottish Office. http://www.scotland.gov.uk/structure/hmi/pubrsst.htm (2 September 2002).

Higher Education Statistics Agency (2002) *Statistical Tables for 2000/01*. http://www.hesa.ac.uk (2 September 2002).

House of Commons (2002) *Hansard Written Answers for 8 July 2002 on Higher Education Statistics*. http://www.publications.parliament.uk/cgi-bin/dialogserverTSO

House of Commons Education and Employment Committee Eighth Report (1999) *Access for All? A survey of post-16 participation*, London: House of Commons. http://www.publications.parliament.uk/pa/cm199899/cmselect/cmeduemp/57/5702.htm (4 November 2002).

Inner London Education Authority (1990) *Differences in Examination Performance*, RS 1277/90, London: Inner London Education Authority (obtainable from Centre for Educational Research, London School of Economics).

Ireson, J. and Hallam, S. (1999) 'Raising standards: Is ability grouping the answer?', *Oxford Review of Education* 25(3): 343–58.

Jeffs, T. and Smith, M. K. (2001) *Social Exclusion, Joined-up Thinking and Individualization – New Labour's Connexions strategy*. http://www.infed.org/personaladvisers/connexions_strategy.htm (2 September 2002).

Johnston, L., MacDonald, R., Mason, P., Ridley, L. and Webster, C. (2000) *Snakes and Ladders: Young people, transition and social exclusion*, Bristol: The Policy Press.

Kiernan, K. (1997) *The Legacy of Parental Divorce: Social, economic and family experiences in adulthood*, Social Policy Research 131, York: Joseph Rowntree Foundation. http://www.jrf.org.uk/knowledge/findings/socialpolicy/sp131.asp (2 September 2002).

Kilpatrick, R., Barr, A. and Wylie, C. (1999) *The 1996/97 Northern Ireland Suspension and Expulsion study*, Research Report No. 13, Bangor: Department of Education Northern Ireland.

Klein, S. P., Hamilton, L. S., McCaffrey, D. F. and Stecher, B. M. (2000) 'What do test scores in Texas tell us?', *Education Policy Analysis Archives*, 8: 49. http://epaa.asu.edu/epaa/v8n49/ (2 September 2002).

Kleinman, M., West, A. and Sparkes, J. (1998) *Investing in Employability: The roles of business and government in the transition to work*. Commissioned by BT, London: LSE.

Le Grand, J. and Bartlett, W. (1993) (eds) *Quasi-Markets and Social Policy*, London: Macmillan.

London Borough of Hackney (2000) *Pupil Mobility in Hackney – Facts, Implications and Strategic Responses*, Report of the Director of Education, 19 June.

MacBeath, J. *et al.* (2001) *The Impact of Study Support*, London: DfES.

Mackinnon, D. and Statham, J. (1999) *Education in the UK: Facts and figures*, London: Hodder and Stoughton.

Maclure, S. (1992) *Education Re-formed*, London: Hodder and Stoughton.

McGrath, C. E., Watson, A. L. and Chassin, L. (1999) 'Academic achievement in adolescent children of alcoholics', *Journal of Studies on Alcohol*, 60: 18–26.

McPherson, A. and Willms, D. (1987) 'Equalisation and improvement: Some effects of comprehensive re-organisation in Scotland', *Sociology* 21: 509–39.

Malcolm, H., Thorpe, G. and Lowden, K. (1996) *Understanding Truancy: Links between attendance, truancy and performance*, Scottish Council for Research in Education, Research Reports Series 72.

Mantzicopoulos, P. Y. and Oh-Hwang, Y. (1998) 'The relationship of psychosocial maturity to parenting quality and intellectual ability for American and Korean adolescents', *Contemporary Educational Psychology*, 23: 195–206.

Mayston, D. J. (1996) 'Educational attainment and resource use: Mystery or econometric mystification?', *Education Economics* 4(2): 127–42.

Mayston, D. J. (2002) *Tackling the Endogeneity Problem When Estimating the Relationship Between School Spending and Pupil Outcomes*, Research Brief No. 328, London: DfES.

Modood, T. (1998) 'Ethnic minorities' drive for qualifications', in T. Modood and T. Acland (eds) *Race and Higher Education*, London: Policy Studies Institute.

Morris, M., Nelson, J., Stoney, S. M. with Benfield, P. (1999) *Disadvantaged Youth: A critical review of the literature on scope, strategies and solutions*, Research Report No. 169, London: DfEE.

Mortimore, P., Sammons, P., Stoll, L., Lewis, D. and Ecob, R. (1988) *School Matters: The junior years*, London: Paul Chapman.

Mortimore, P. and Whitty, G. (2000) *Can School Improvement Overcome the Effects of Disadvantage?*, London: Institute of Education.

Mujtaba, T. and Sammons, P. (1999) *Accounting for Variation in Pupil Attainment Across Key Stage 1 and Key Stage 2 in an Inner City LEA*. Paper presented at the British Educational Research Association Annual Conference, Brighton, September 1999.

Murphy, P. and Elwood, J. (1998) 'Gendered experiences, choices and achievement – exploring the links', *International Journal of Inclusive Education* 2(2): 95–118.

National Statistics (2002) *Social Trends, Number 32*, London: The Stationery Office. http://www.nationalstatistics.gov.uk/downloads/theme_social/Social_Trends32/Social_Trends32.pdf (2 September 2002).

National Statistics (2003) Ethnicity. http://www.statistics.gov.uk/cci/nugget.asp?ID=273 (also ID=263).

Newsom Report (1963) *Half Our Future: A report of the Central Advi-*

sory Council for Education (England), Ministry of Education, London: Her Majesty's Stationery Office.

Noden, P. (2001) 'School choice and polarisation', *New Economy* 8(4): 199–202.

Noden, P. (2002) 'Education markets and polarisation: Back to square one?', *Research Papers in Education* 17(4): 409–12.

Odden, A. R. and Picus, L. O. (1992) *School Finance*, New York: McGraw-Hill.

Office for National Statistics (2001) *International Student Assessment: Results for England*. http://www.statistics.gov.uk/pdfdir/isae1201.pdf (2 September 2002).

Office for Standards in Education (1997) *'Maple High School' [fictitious name] Section 10 Inspection Report*, London: OFSTED.

Office for Standards in Education (1999a) *Raising the Attainment of Minority Ethnic Pupils: School and LEA responses*, London: OFSTED.

Office for Standards in Education (1999b) *'Beech School' [fictitious name] Section 10 Inspection Report*, London: OFSTED.

Office for Standards in Education (2002) *Achievement of Black Caribbean Pupils: Good practice in secondary schools, HMI 448*, London: OFSTED.

O'Keeffe, D. J. (1994) *Truancy in English Secondary Schools: A report prepared for the DFE*, London: Her Majesty's Stationery Office.

Organisation for Economic Co-operation and Development (OECD) (2001) *Knowledge and Skills for Life, First results from the OECD Programme for International Student Assessment (PISA) 2000*, Paris: OECD.

Parsons, C., Hayden, C., Godfrey, R., Howlett, K. and Martin, T. (2001) *Outcomes in Secondary Education for Children Excluded from Primary School*, Research Brief No. 271, London: DfEE.

Pathak, S. (2000) *Race Research for the Future: Ethnicity in education, training and the labour market*, RTPO1, London: DfEE.

Payne, J. (2000) *Progress of Low Achievers After Age 16: An analysis of data from the England and Wales youth cohort study*, Research Report No. 185, London, DfEE.

Philips, A. (2002) *Look Who's Suffering, The Guardian* 2, 8–9, 26 August.

Plewis, I. (1991) 'Underachievement: A case of conceptual confusion', *British Educational Research Journal* 17(4): 377–85.

Powers, S., Gregory, S. and Thoutenhoofd, E. D. (2000) *The Educational Achievements of Deaf Children – a Review of the Literature*, Research Report No. 56, London: DfEE.

Powney, J., McPake, J., Hall, S. and Lyall, L. (1998) *Education of Minority Ethnic Groups in Scotland: A review of research*, Edinburgh: Scottish Council for Research in Education, and: http://www.scre.ac.uk/ summary (2 September 2002).

Qualifications and Curriculum Authority (2002) *The Story of the GCE Advanced Level*, London: QCA. http://www.qca.org.uk (2 September 2002).

Rampton, A. (1981) *West Indian Children in our Schools*, Cmnd 8273, London: HMSO.

Reynolds, D., Sammons, P., Stoll, L., Barber, M. and Hillman, J. (1997) 'School effectiveness and school improvement in the United Kingdom', in A. Harris, N. Bennett and M. Preedy (1997) *Organizational Effectiveness and Improvement in Education*, Buckingham: Open University Press.

Richardson, J. L., Radziszewska, B., Dent, C. W. and Flay, B. R. (1993) 'Relationship between after-school care of adolescents and substance use, risk taking, depressed mood, and academic achievement', *Pediatrics* 92(1): 32–8.

Robinson, P. (1997a) *The Myth of Parity of Esteem: Earnings and qualifications*, Centre for Economic Performance Discussion Paper 354, London: Centre for Economic Performance, London School of Economics.

Robinson, P. (1997b) *Literacy, Numeracy and Economic Performance*, Special Report, Centre for Economic Performance, London: London School of Economics.

Rodgers, B. and Pryor, J. (1998) *Divorce and Separation: The outcomes for children*, Joseph Rowntree Foundation, June 1998, Ref 6108. http://www.jrf.org.uk/knowledge/findings (2 September 2002).

Ruddock, G. (2000) *The International Mathematics and Science Study Repeat (TIMSS-R): First national report*, London: DfEE. http://www.dfes.gov.uk/research/data/uploadfiles/ACF2FF6.doc (2 September 2002).

Salisbury, J., Rees, G. and Gorard, S. (1999) 'Accounting for the differential attainment of boys and girls at school', *School Leadership and Management* 19(4): 403–26.

Sammons, P., Nuttall, D. and Cuttance, P. (1993) 'Differential school effectiveness: Results from a reanalysis of the Inner London Education Authority's Junior School Project data', *British Educational Research Journal* 19(4): 381–405.

Sammons, P. (1995) 'Gender, ethnic and socio-economic differences in attainment and progress: A longitudinal analysis of student achievement over 9 years', *British Educational Research Journal* 21(4): 465–85.

Sammons, P., West, A. and Hind, A. (1997a) 'Accounting for variations in pupil attainment at the end of key stage 1', *British Educational Research Journal* 23(4): 489–511.

Sammons, P., Thomas, S. and Mortimore, P. (1997b) *Forging Links: Effective schools and effective departments*, London: Paul Chapman.

Sammons, P. and Smees, R. (1998) 'Measuring pupil progress at key stage 1: Using baseline assessment to investigate value added', *School Leadership and Management* 18(3): 389–407.

Sammons, P. (1999) *School Effectiveness: Coming of age in the twenty-first century*, Lisse: Swets and Zeitlinger.

Sammons, P. *et al.* (1999) *Technical Paper 2: Characteristics of the EPPE project sample at entry to the study*, London: Institute of Education, University of London.

Schagen, I. and Schagen, S. (2001) *The Impact of Selection on Pupil Performance*. Paper presented at National Foundation for Educational Research Council of Members Meeting, 19 October 2001, Slough: NFER. http://195.194.2.100/research/outcome_popup.asp?theID=SEL (2 September 2002).

Sharp, C. *et al.* (2002) *Playing for Success: An evaluation of the third year*, Research Brief No. 337, London: DfES.

Shuttleworth, I. (1995) 'The relationship between social deprivation, as measured by individual free school meal eligibility, and educational attainment at GCSE in Northern Ireland: A preliminary investigation', *British Educational Research Journal* 21(4): 487–504.

Social Exclusion Unit (1998a) *Truancy and School Exclusion*, London: Social Exclusion Unit. http://www.socialexclusionunit.gov.uk/publications/reports/html/school_exclu/trhome.htm (2 September 2002).

Social Exclusion Unit (1998b) *Bringing Britain Together: A national strategy for neighbourhood renewal*, Cm 4045, London: Social Exclusion Unit. http://www.socialexclusionunit.gov.uk/publications/reports/html/bbt/nrhome.htm (2 September 2002).

Sparkes, J. (1999) *Schools, Education and Social Exclusion*, CASE paper 29, London: Centre for Analysis of Social Exclusion, LSE. http://sticerd.lse.ac.uk/dps/case/cp/CASEpaper29.pdf (2 September 2002).

Sparkes, J. and West, A. (2000) *Evaluation of the Learning for Life Programme*, Clare Market Papers 16, Centre for Educational Research, London: London School of Economics.

Steedman, J. (1985) 'Examination results in mixed and single-sex secondary schools', in D. Reynolds (ed.) *Studying School Effectiveness*, London: Falmer Press.

Stoney, S., West, A., Kendall, L. and Morris, M. (2002) *Evaluation of Excellence in Cities: Overview of Interim Findings*, London: DfES. http://www.standards.dfes.gov.uk/excellence/abouteic/?template=pub& articleid=5438 (2 September 2002).

Strand, S. (1997) 'Pupil progress during Key Stage 1: A value added analysis of school effects', *British Educational Research Journal* 23(4): 471–87.

Strand, S. (1999a) 'Ethnic group, sex and economic disadvantage: associations with pupils' educational progress from baseline to the end of key stage 1', *British Educational Research Journal* 25(2): 179–202.

Strand, S. (1999b) 'Baseline assessment results at age 4: Associations with pupil background factors', *Journal of Research in Reading* 22(1): 14–26.

Strand, S. (2002) 'Pupil mobility, attainment and progress during key stage 1: A study in cautious interpretation', *British Educational Research Journal* 28(1): 63–78.

Sukhnandan, L. (1999) *An Investigation into Gender Differences in Achievement. Phase 1: A review of recent research and LEA information on provision*, Slough: NFER.

Sukhnandan, L., Lee, B. and Kelleher, S. (2000) *An Investigation into Gender Differences in Achievement. Phase 2: School and classroom strategies*, Slough: NFER.

Swann, Lord (1985) *Education for All: Final report of the Committee of Inquiry into the Education of Children from Ethnic Minority Groups*. Cmnd 9453, London: HMSO.

Thomas, S. and Mortimore, P. (1996) 'Comparison of value-added models for secondary school effectiveness', *Research Papers in Education* 11(1): 5–33.

Thrupp, M. (1999) *Schools Making a Difference: Let's be realistic!*, Buckingham: Open University Press.

Tinklin, T., Croxford, L., Ducklin, A. and Frame, B. (2001) *Gender and Pupil Performance*, Interchange 70, Scottish Executive Education Department.

Tizard, B., Blatchford, P., Burke, J., Farquhar, C. and Plewis, I. (1988) *Young Children at School in the Inner City*, Hover: Lawrence Erlbaum Associates.

Troyna, B. (1991) 'Underachievers or underrated? The experience of pupils of South Asian origin in a secondary school', *British Educational Research Journal* 17(4): 361–76.

Walford, G. (1993) Selection for Secondary Schooling, in *Briefings for the Paul Hamlyn Foundation National Commission on Education*, London: Heinemann.

West, A. and Varlaam, A. (1990) 'Does it matter when children start school?', *Educational Research* 32(3): 210–17.

West, A., West, R. and Pennell, H. (1994) *A Better Cake: Towards a rational approach for financing education*, London: Secondary Heads Association.

West, A., Hailes, J. and Sammons, P. (1997) 'Children's attitudes to the national curriculum at Key Stage 1', *British Educational Research Journal* 23(5): 597–613.

West, A. and Pennell, H. (1997a) 'Educational reform and school choice in England and Wales', *Education Economics* 5(3): 285–305.

West, A. and Pennell, H. (1997b) 'Changing admissions policies and practices in inner London: Implications for policy and future research', in R. Glatter, P. Woods and C. Bagley (eds) *Choice and Diversity in Schooling: Perspectives and prospects*, London: Routledge.

West, A., Noden, P., Edge, A. and David, M. (1998a) 'Parental involvement in education in and out of school', *British Educational Research Journal* 24(4): 461–84.

West, A., Pennell, H. and Noden, P. (1998b) 'School admissions: Increasing equity, accountability and transparency', *British Journal of Educational Studies* 46(2): 188–200.

West, A., Edge, A. and Stokes, E. (1999) *Secondary Education Across Europe: Curricula and school examination systems*, Clare Market Papers 14, London: Centre for Educational Research, LSE. See also http://www.leeds.ac.uk/educol (2 September 2002).

West, A. and Hind, A. (2000) *Indicators for Vocational Education and Training: Exploitation of the European Community Household Panel (ECHP) survey*, Thessaloniki: European Centre for the Development of Vocational Training. http://www2.trainingvillage.gr/download/statistique/echp/index.html (2 September 2002).

West, A., Pennell, H., West, R. and Travers, T. (2000a) 'Financing school-based education in England: Principles and problems', in M. Coleman and L. Anderson (eds) *Managing Finance and Resources in Education*, London: Paul Chapman.

West, A., Pennell, H. and West, R. (2000b) 'New Labour and school-based education in England: Changing the system of funding?', *British Educational Research Journal* 26(4): 523–36.

West, A. and Pennell, H. (2000c) 'Publishing school examination results in England: Incentives and consequences', *Educational Studies* 26(4): 423–36.

West, A., Noden, P., Kleinman, M. and Whitehead, C. (2000d) *Examining the Impact of the Specialist Schools Programme*, Research Report No. 196, London: DfEE.

West, A. and Ingram, D. (2001) 'Making school admissions fairer? Quasi-regulation under New Labour', *Educational Management and Administration* 29(4): 459–73.

West, A., West, R., Pennell, H. and Travers, T. (2001) 'Financing school-based education in England: Poverty, examination results and expenditure', *Environment and Planning C: Government and Policy* 19(3): 461–71.

West, A. and Hind, A. (2003) *Secondary School Admissions in England: Exploring the extent of overt and covert selection*, London: Research and information on state education trust.

West, A. and Pennell, H. (2002) 'How new is New Labour? The quasi-market and English schools 1997 to 2001', *British Journal of Educational Studies* 50(2): 206–24.

West, A. and Sparkes, J. (2002) 'Examining the impact of nursery education vouchers and quasi-vouchers in England', in D. Dohmen and B. A. Cleuvers (Hrsg.) *Nachfrageorientierte Bildungsfinanzierung: Neue Trends für Kindertagesstätte, Schule und Hochschule*, Bielefeld: W. Bertelsmann.

White, P., Gorard, S., Fitz, J. and Taylor, C. (2001) 'Regional and local differences in admission arrangements for schools', *Oxford Review of Education* 27(3): 317–37.

Whitty, G., Edwards, T. and Gewirtz, S. (1993) *Specialisation and Choice in Urban Education: The City Technology College Experiment*, London: Routledge.

Wolford Symons, C., Cinelli, B., James, T. C. and Groff, P. (1997) 'Bridging student health risks and academic achievement through comprehensive school health programs', *Journal of School Health* 67(6): 220–27.

Yang, M. and Woodhouse, G. (2001) 'Progress from GCSE to A and AS level: Institutional and gender differences and trends over time', *British Educational Research Journal* 27(3): 245–67.

Index